Laughing Matters

Humour in the language classroom

Péter Medgyes

CAMBRIDGE
UNIVERSITY PRESS

PUBLISHED BY THE PRESS SYNDICATE OF THE UNIVERSITY OF CAMBRIDGE
The Pitt Building, Trumpington Street, Cambridge, United Kingdom

CAMBRIDGE UNIVERSITY PRESS
The Edinburgh Building, Cambridge CB2 2RU, UK
40 West 20th Street, New York, NY 10011–4211, USA
477 Williamstown Road, Port Melbourne, VIC 3207, Australia
Ruiz de Alarcón 13, 28014 Madrid, Spain
Dock House, The Waterfront, Cape Town 8001, South Africa

http://www.cambridge.org

First published 2002
Reprinted 2002

Printed in the United Kingdom at the University Press, Cambridge

Typeset in Sabon 10/12pt   System QuarkXPress™ [SE]

A catalogue record for this book is available from the British Library

Library of Congress Cataloging-in-Publication Data applied for

ISBN 0 521 79960 0 paperback

Contents

Contents

Contents

Thanks and acknowledgments

There are far more people I ought to thank than I can identify: hundreds of colleagues who attended my lectures and workshop sessions in many countries, as well as my own students at the Centre for English Teacher Training at Eotvos Lorand University in Budapest, Hungary.

I owe special thanks to the following persons for lending me 'funny stuff': Ildiko Arva, Laszlo Asboth, Aniko Bognar, George Bognar, Donard Britten, Istvan Diveky, Peter Doherty, Agnes Enyedi, Peter Fray, David A. Hill, Gyorgy Horlai, Ilona Hudak, Eva Illes, Anna Kellner, Laszlo Kellner, Linda Kellner, Zsolt Kiraly, Andras Kolozsi, Caroline Laidlaw, James Leavey, Katalin Lorincz, Pal Makadi, Gabi Matei, Katalin Miklosy, Adam Nadasdy, Mariann Nikolov, Rob Nolasco, Luke Prodromou, Judit Revesz, Keith Ricketts, Mario Rinvolucri, Christopher Ryan and Miklos Sebestyen.

My greatest supplier of humorous material was Ken Wilson. I wish I had been able to include even more of Gabor Salamon's bizarre ideas. Eva Gal did the tedious job of photocopying in good humour. Reka Medgyes was a caring critic of my pilot versions. And Valeria Arva gave me all the love and attention I desperately needed.

The first person I had mentioned the idea of *Laughing Matters* to was Penny Ur, as we were sitting next to each other on a never-ending bus ride in Recife, Brazil. She liked the idea then – I hope she still does. To be sure, her editorial guidance was much needed and heeded throughout the project.

The author and publishers are grateful to the authors, publishers and others who have given permission for the use of copyright material identified in the text. It has not been possible to identify the sources of all the material used and in such cases the publishers would welcome information from copyright owners.

pp. 18, 131 and *139* Cartoons from www.CartoonStock.com; *pp. 22, 76* and *77* IPF Könyvek; *p. 23* By kind permission of John Agard c/o Caroline Sheldon Literary Agency, 'Once Upon a Time' from *The Penguin Book of Utterly Brilliant Poetry* published by Penguin (1998); *p. 32* Game from *A-Z of Word Games* by Tony Augarde, OUP; *p. 53*

Acknowledgments

'Utter Connections' and *p. 208* 'Are you sure sir?' from *The Lighter Side of TEFL*, edited by Tom Kral (Washington, DC: US Information Agency, 1994), *p. 100* and *p. 25.*; *p. 59* 'Three Riddled Riddles' by Ian McMillan and Martyn Wiley; *pp. 66–70 Palindromes and Anagrams* by Howard W Bergerson, Dover Publications Inc. 1973; *p. 75 Further Fables For Our Time* Copyright ©1956 by James Thurber. Copyright © renewed 1984 by Rosemary A. Thurber. Reprinted by arrangement with Rosemary A. Thurber and The Barbara Hogenson Agency.; *p. 127* Originally published in book form in *Men Women and Dogs* ©1943 by James Thurber. Copyright© renewed 1971 by Helen Thurber, © 1981 by Helen Thurber and Rosemary A. Thurber. Reprinted by arrangement with Rosemary A. Thurber and The Barbara Hogenson Agency. All rights reserved.; *pp. 92*, 137 and *245* Cartoons reproduced with permission of Punch Ltd; *p. 93.* Epitaphs from *The Mammoth Book of Jokes* edited by Geoff Tibballs, Constable & Robinson Publishing Ltd., 2000; *p. 93* Epitaphs and Anecdotes from *Short and Sweet* Volume I by Alan Maley, Penguin Books, 1993; *pp. 101–103* and *105–106.* Limericks from *The Penguin Book of Limericks* edited by E. O. Parrott, Penguin Books. 1983; *pp. 108* and *109* 'Little Red Riding Hood and the Wolf' from Roald Dahl's *Revolting Rhymes* by Roald Dahl, copyright © 1982 by Roald Dahl. Used by permission of Alfred A Knopf Children's Books, a division of Random House, Inc. (USA); 'Little Red Riding Hood and the Wolf' from *Revolting Rhymes* by Roald Dahl published by Jonathan Cape. Used by permission of The Random House Group Limited; *p. 111* Extract from *Times Three* by Phyllis McGinley published by Secker & Warburg. Used by permission of The Random House Limited; 'Reflections at Dawn' from *Times Three* by Phyllis McGinley, copyright 1932–60 by Phyllis McGinley; Copyright 1938–42, 1944, 1945, 1958, 1959 by The Curtis Publishing Co. Used by permission of Viking Penguin, a division of Penguin Putnam Inc.; *pp. 126, 133, 139* and *246* Cartoons reproduced by permission of The Spectator Magazine; *p. 134* Kunsthistorisches Museum, Wien, for the reproduction of 'Children's Games' by Pieter Breugel; *p. 139* Cartoon reproduced by kind permission of The Oldie Magazine; *pp. 140* and *240* Cartoons from *More Snappy Answers to Stupid Questions* written and illustrated by Al Jaffee, edited by Albert Feldstein, New English Library, 1972; *p. 145* Titles from *The Book of the Amazing but True* by Steve Wright, Simon & Schuster, Copyright © Steve Wright, 1995; *p. 146* 'Stone Soup' adapted from *Using Folktales* by Eric K Taylor, CUP, 2000; *p. 148* Anecdote from *Short and Sweet* by Alan Maley, published by Penguin, 1993; *p. 154* From *Guinness Book of Humorous Anecdotes* by Nigel Rees, Guinness Publishing, 1993; *pp. 159–161* Stories adapted from *Urban Myths* by Phil Healey and Rick Glanville, Virgin Publishing, 1996; *p. 171 The Lost*

Continent © Bill Bryson. Extracted from *Notes From A Big Country*, published by Transworld Publishers, a division of the Random House Group Ltd. All rights reserved and HarperCollins: New York; *p. 176* Excerpt reprinted with permission of Simon & Schuster from *CATCH-22* by Joseph Heller. Copyright © 1955, 1961 by Joseph Heller. Copyright renewed © 1989 by Joseph Heller; *pp. 187–8* Sketch by David Nobbs, slightly adapted from *The Book of Comedy Sketches* edited by Frank Muir and S Brett, Elm Tree Books, 1982; *p. 193* Dialogue from *Criss Cross* by Melanie Ellis, Caroline Laidlaw and Péter Medgyes, Hueber Verlag; *p. 194 Behind the Fridge* Sketch by Peter Cook and Dudley Moore; *pp. 217* and *223* Quotes from 'They got it wrong' from *The Guinness Dictionary of Regrettable Quotations* edited by David Milsted published by Cassell, 1995; *pp. 218, 244* and *251* Excerpts reprinted with permission of Pocket Books, a Division of Simon & Schuster, Inc. from *Fractured English* and *Anguished English* by Richard Lederer. Copyright © 1996 by Richard Lederer; *pp. 222 Great British Inventions* by Mark Tanner; *pp. 224–5* Excerpts from *The Book of Heroic Failures* by Stephen Pile, Macdonald Futura Publishers Ltd, 1980; *p. 226 Idiot Letters* Reprinted by Permission of International Creative Management, Inc. Copyright © 1995 by Paul Rosa; *p. 235* Excerpt from *How to Handle Grown-ups* by Jim and Duncan Eldridge, Beaver Books; *p. 238 Please Mrs Butler* by Allan Ahlberg, Kestrel, 1983, Copyright © Allan Ahlberg, 1983 Reproduced by permission of Penguin Books Ltd.; *p. 247* Extract from *The Education of H*Y*M*A*N K*A*P*L*A*N* by Leon Rosten reprinted by permission of Constable & Robinson Ltd.

Introduction

Rationale

What is humour?

If you want to explain the meaning of a word or a concept, there are two possibilities. The easier option is to say: 'Come on, you know what I mean.' The more difficult one is to try to define it. Now, when a full-length book is devoted to a particular subject, such as humour, it's only fair that you go for the more difficult alternative.

Dictionaries offer several definitions of humour. For example:
  (i) Humour is something that makes a person laugh or smile.
 (ii) Humour is the ability to be amused by things.
(iii) Humour is the quality of being funny.

The trouble is that these definitions are:
  (i) only partially true – you don't always laugh or smile when you hear something humorous;
 (ii) wrong – humour is not an ability; or
(iii) circular – humour and fun are synonyms, so defining one with the other doesn't lead to better understanding.

It appears that grabbing the essence of humour is a daunting task, and I'm afraid I can't come up with a better definition than those quoted above. So I give up, accepting Wendy Cope's remark: 'If anyone needs me to define "funny" or "humorous", they have my sympathy.'

Nevertheless, humour is of vital importance for human beings to survive. Can you imagine a more dreary world than one devoid of fun? Luckily, our world is imbued with humour and a sense of humour is an inborn human capacity, like the ability to walk and talk. In my experience, even people who boldly claim to have a good sense of humour were born with this divine endowment ... In any case, *Laughing Matters* builds on the students' genuine sense of humour.

Humour and culture

I often come across variations of the same jokes, funny anecdotes or songs, spreading from country to country. And they work equally well everywhere, cutting across borders. Humour may be *universal*.

1

Other jokes, however, do not travel so well. What causes people in one culture to roar with laughter may be met with utter incomprehension in another. So, while some jokes have a universal appeal, others are *culture-bound*.

To compound the equation, humour is person-bound as well. Has it happened to you that you crack a joke, thinking that it is the funniest one ever? Then, after a moment of embarrassing silence, your friend innocently asks: 'Is that it?' Humour may be *idiosyncratic*.

Universal appeal, cultural differences and personal taste – these three aspects are not easy to reconcile. Anyone bold enough to write a book on humour walks a tight-rope. I hope I've been able to strike the right balance.

On the other hand, humour is possibly the best source of authentic cultural information about other peoples. It also helps build bridges between cultures and individuals: humour is an ideal form of promoting understanding and friendship. I like to think that those who have laughed together will never hurt each other.

Genres of humour

Humour comes in many guises; jokes, puns, cartoons and comedy sketches are humour *par excellence*, but poems, songs, proverbs and anecdotes may also produce a humorous effect.

There are certain genres of humour which may be enjoyed on your own, such as a funny film or book, while others typically call for company – for example, a joke is best when cracked in the company of partners. Humour can bond the participants; indeed, nothing can glue people together better than shared moments of fun. It is no wonder that at class reunions, for instance, former classmates take it in turns to amuse one another with funny stories from bygone years. I trust this book will also foster peer relations.

Humour and laughter

As I noted above, humour and laughter are not synonyms. Indeed, some of the best humour does not result in laughter, and may not even bring on a smile. In this book, too, you will find a lot of material which is meant to be entertaining and witty, with no intention of inducing laughter. In this sense, the book is more than what the title suggests.

Nevertheless, humour often stimulates laughter, which covers a wide range from a bellylaugh to a chuckle or a smile. We differ in terms of what we laugh at and how we laugh, but every one of us is always ready for a good laugh. *Laughing matters*.

Laughter saturates our lives. I remember reading somewhere that people are ten times more likely to laugh than to express any other form of strong emotion. Laughter may be accompanied by a whole range of physiological signs: quickening heart rate and breathing, slightly higher blood pressure, perspiration and faster brain activity.

However, the most visible changes can be recorded on our faces. Have you ever watched a face before, during and after laughing? You look at a tense or worn-out face before laughter. When a good joke is cracked, this face breaks into a hundred dimples and furrows. As the laughter abates, it gradually falls back into shape. But what a difference! The sad wrinkles are gone, only the happy ones stay on. And the owner of the face becomes reassured and reassuring.

They say that people who laugh a lot live longer. Perhaps. But one thing is certain: laughter improves the *quality* of life. And the quality of language learning.

Humour and jokes

For some people, humour is part and parcel of a joke with a punch line. Although this is an obviously false assumption, it is probably true that the joke is the most common form of humour.

A joke may be perceived as an intellectual challenge. Before the punch line, people with a high level of mental agility and ambiguity tolerance will set in motion their creative energies, and they may even hazard a guess. Then comes the punch line delivering the twist. If it is clever and concise, a laugh is guaranteed. The laughter will be at its loudest if the listener's reaction time is short. In other words, the effect of a joke greatly depends on the synergy between the joke, the joker and the 'jokee'.

Humour is a source of gratification for those who understand it. However, if someone continually misses the punch line, they become frustrated. 'He who laughs last laughs best', runs the adage, but in Cohen's paraphrase, 'He who laughs last is generally the last to get the joke'. Or the learner who is not very proficient in the language. *Laughing Matters* aims to develop the skill of understanding jokes in English.

Humour is a serious business

Our lives are pervaded with humour; some of our most serious moments may be full of wit, just as funny situations often have serious overtones. Similarly, I have noticed that people who pull a serious face sometimes look ridiculous and, conversely, some of the best comedians are very earnest people. In short, humour and seriousness are not mutually exclusive categories, but often permeate each other.

The same applies to the relationship between tragedy and comedy; these two vital aspects of human existence are inseparable concepts. Indeed, some of the funniest pieces of literature verge on the tragic, and vice versa. By the same token, picture the traditional image of the clown: one half of his face laughing, the other half crying. But it is children who embody this kind of ambivalence most naturally. There is little Jamie, for example. He bursts out crying, then switches to laughing, then cries again, and so on, until you get muddled up. Now, is he laughing or crying? Is this the end of the beginning or the beginning of the end?

Humour is often difficult to catch, but it is far more difficult to *produce* a book on humour – humorous texts and activities have to be both light-hearted as befits humour, and useful as befits learning. Although these two conditions are not always easy to meet, I have tried to reach a compromise. To be sure, this is meant to be a serious book: *Humour is no laughing matter!*

Humour and political correctness

Humour often shows its ugly face. Think of jokes, for example – most of them are pretty offensive, insulting an individual or a group of people: the poor, ethnic communities, the ugly, the 'intellectually challenged', women, the disabled, animal lovers, the elderly, and so on. And who does not belong to one or more of these categories? Furthermore, jokes have a tendency to violate taboos, such as death, murder, divorce, drinking, religion and sex.

Today, we live in an age of political correctness. What does P.C. mean? It means avoidance of forms of expression against the socially disadvantaged or discriminated against. Any fair-minded citizen is expected to support this 'freedom fight' and, as a result, nasty jokes are only whispered among close friends and read on special web pages these days.

I believe that sometimes we are oversensitive about this and unjustifiably veto funny jokes which the 'victims' would not be particularly hurt by; in fact they may often make the same jokes at their own expense. Nevertheless, I have rejected any specimen that might hurt or offend potential readers, because this book aims to appeal to a wide range of teachers and learners all over the world. This does not preclude you the teacher, however, from bringing to class less innocent stuff as well. You are the only one who can assess your students' level of tolerance – and your own! If you use such jokes, however, make sure your students are aware of the underlying message.

Humour in language teaching

Humour as such is 'unteachable'. If we try to explain a joke, it usually goes stale. What we can teach is the *language* of humour. After all, most humorous stuff is deeply embedded in language. We can use the language to make humour accessible for students and, conversely, use humour to make the language accessible. In my opinion, humour is one of the best vehicles for language teaching and its motivational value cannot be over-estimated!

And yet we do not often come across funny texts and activities in course materials. The reason why humour is in short supply is hard to understand, especially since the foreign-language class easily lends itself to humour; it is in fact an ideal arena to create a congenial atmosphere. Instead of investigating the causes of this neglect, let me supply a list of the main justifications for using humour in language teaching. Humour:

- is a good vehicle for providing authentic cultural information;
- builds bridges between cultures;
- practises language items in genuine contexts;
- brings students closer together;
- releases tension;
- develops creative thinking;
- provides memorable chunks of language;
- reinforces previously learnt items;
- generates a happy classroom;
- enhances motivation;
- enriches textbook-based courses;
- introduces a refreshing change from routine language-learning procedures.

Three caveats are due here. Firstly, all these features are not the pre-rogative of the 'fun lesson' – 'serious lessons' can also build cultural bridges, develop creativity, enhance motivation, and so on. Secondly, these items are not in any order of importance; it depends on the humorous text and the concomitant activity which aspects of the list above take precedence. Finally, and most importantly, these are *potential* benefits only and it is up to us teachers to fulfil this potential.

At this point, I'm reminded of Randolph Quirk, who warned that if you analyse humour for too long, your readers will never smile again. So I'd better turn to practical things.

Structure

General overview

Laughing Matters is a resource book with no pre-arranged order: you are invited to dip in at your convenience. After you've decided to embark on an activity, there is no point in wringing it dry – beware of overkill! The fundamental aims of the book are to spark off ideas, develop creativity and provide fun. Obviously, these aims can only be realised through language work, by introducing and practising English through the use of enjoyable texts and/or activities.

The book consists of ten sections. Section 1 supplies warm-up activities. Sections 2–9 are structured around different genres of humour: jokes and wisecracks, puns and puzzles, proverbs and quotations, poems and songs, pictures and images, stories and anecdotes, sketches and dialogues, and errors and failures. Section 10 is about children and schools, on the assumption that most learners are young people who study English at school. Each section opens with a short introduction, followed by 11–17 activities.

The book is meant to be teacher-friendly: you are spared the trouble of looking for texts and ideas to exploit them. However, this should not discourage you from finding better texts and coming up with better ideas. On the contrary, I'm convinced that the lesson stands a better chance of success if it is based on our collaborative efforts. And if you also manage to involve your students in this search, all the better!

Selecting the texts

My guiding principles of selection have been that the texts should be:

- humorous – after all this is a book on humour.
- short – most of the texts are no more than a few lines in length.
- meaningful – they can be understood with little background knowledge.
- authentic – the majority are real and unedited texts.
- useful – the language can be applied beyond the given context.
- varied – I've included a wide range of texts best suited for each genre.

The activities

Each activity is introduced by a one-sentence *Summary* to help you grasp the gist of the activity and decide whether it fits your teaching purposes. There are three rubrics for each activity: *Level*, *Time* and *Preparation*.

Level refers to the level of language difficulty, which does not necessarily overlap with the level of intellectual challenge.

Time allocation has been even more tentatively set than difficulty level. My estimates are largely based on my experience as a teacher, on the one hand, and my piloting the material with learners in several parts of the world, on the other.

Preparation, on the other hand, is usually straightforward and clearcut. The recurrent instruction 'Make copies (or a transparency) of Box ...' means that you should either have the facility available to make multiple copies or access to an overhead projector, in which case one transparency is enough. Either way, the point is that the text needs to be clearly visible to all students.

Each activity is structured around a sequence of 2–4 *steps*. The *boxes* supply photocopiable texts or models of language to be provided or elicited.

The majority of activities are supplemented by additional material: *Variations, Follow-ups* and/or *Extras. Variations*, as the word suggests, offer alternative ways of using the main activity, *Follow-ups* refer to opportunities for extension, quite often in the form of written homework, whereas *Extras* supply further texts and ideas for classroom use.

Enjoy!

Talk these days is often of the *learner-centred classroom*, with the message that the learning process should be centred on the learners' needs, wants and initiatives, a precondition for the students to be happy and content. I couldn't agree more. But let's not forget that only happy teachers can make happy students. The author of *Laughing Matters* would, above all, like to see *you* enjoy yourself as you're using this book to prepare and teach your class. If you have half as much fun as I had while writing the book, I have achieved this goal.

1 Funny starts

Everyone would probably agree that laughter improves the quality of life. We've got to laugh, haven't we? This section suggests ideas about how to introduce the topic of laughter with lots of light-hearted activities, including warmers, name games, number games and action games.

1.1 Wink first

Summary:	Students learn each other's names by attention-catching winks.
Level:	beginner – pre-intermediate
Time:	5–10 minutes
Preparation:	none

Procedure

1 Students stand in a big circle. Everybody lets their eyes wander over their classmates. When eyes meet, students wink at each other. They then go up to each other, shake hands and say:

    Student A (*Chandra*):   Hello, my name's Chandra.
    Student B (*Marek*):   Hi, I'm Marek.

Students all listen to the introductions and try to remember as many names as they can.

2 When everybody has introduced themselves to several partners, the game continues but, instead of introducing themselves, students greet each other:

    Student A (*Chandra*):   Hello, Marek.
    Student B (*Marek*):   Hi, Chandra.

1.2 **Funny names**

Summary:	Students adopt a funny word as their name.
Level:	beginner – pre-intermediate
Time:	5–10 minutes
Preparation:	none

Procedure

1 Each student writes down a couple of English words they find funny because of their sound or meaning, or both.
2 Everyone adopts as their name one of the funny words they have written down, and mills round, introducing themselves. For example:
   Student A: Hi! My name's Slurp.
   Student B: Hello! My name's Good-for-nothing.
   Students try to remember as many 'names' as they can.
3 Follow the same procedure as in *Step 1*, but this time everybody should greet their partners by their adopted names. For example, if Student C's choice is *cupboard* and Student D's is *tomato juice*, they greet each other like this:
   Student C: Hello, Tomato Juice.
   Student D: Hi, Cupboard.

Follow-ups

1 Students spend a little time thinking about why they find their 'name' funny. You may begin by demonstrating your own choice, like this:
   I love the word *pitta*. Do you know what it is? Well, pitta is a kind of bread. It's flat, and you can open it like a bag and put juicy stuff in it. Yum, yum. I also like this word because it sounds just like my first name: *pitta – Peter*.
   Now give students the chance to explain their preferences.
2 For homework, students could turn their description into a silly poem. In class, volunteers read out their poem for the whole class to enjoy. Here is a four-liner for my favourite word:
   'What is it you like to eat?
   Tell us, tell us, Peter!
   Soup or rice or cake or meat?'
   'Nothing more than pitta!'

1.3 Hi, Harry!

Summary:	This chain activity requires a great deal of concentration.
Level:	beginner – pre-intermediate
Time:	10–15 minutes
Preparation:	Bring to class small coloured sticky circles.

Procedure

1 Explain that this is a unique class, because everybody has the same first name: *Harry*. Students should get used to their new name by playing a silly game, which goes like this:

Student A:	Hi, Harry.
Student B:	Yes, Harry?
Student A (*pointing to Student C*):	Tell Harry.
Student B (*greeting Student C*):	Hi, Harry.
Student C:	Yes, Harry?
Student B (*pointing to Student D*):	Tell Harry.
Student C (*greeting Student D*):	Hi, Harry.
Student D:	Yes, Harry? etc.

2 If someone makes a mistake, their name will change to *One Spot* – thus called because the teacher will stick some kind of stigma on their forehead. So if, for example, Student D above says *Hi, Harry* (instead of *Yes, Harry?*), she/he gets a spot on her/his forehead, and the game will continue like this:

Student C:	Hi, One Spot.
Student D:	Yes, Harry?
Student C (*pointing to Student E*):	Tell Harry.
Student D (*greeting Student E*):	Hi, Harry.
Student E:	Yes, One Spot? etc.

3 Should someone make a second mistake, they get another spot, and so their name will become *Two Spot* (subsequently *Three Spot*, *Four Spot*), and so on until the whole class goes mad ...

1.4 Buzz

Summary:	This counting game is not as simple as it looks.
Level:	beginner – pre-intermediate
Time:	5–10 minutes
Preparation:	none

Procedure

1 Ask the class what makes a buzz-buzz sound. And a zubb-zubb sound (*buzz buzz* backwards)? Anyhow, the name of this game is 'Buzz'.
   Answers: a bee and a bee flying backwards.
2 Choose a taboo number, *five*, for example. Everybody stands up. The first student begins by saying *one*, the second *two*, the third *three*, the fourth *four*, but the fifth student, instead of *five*, says *buzz*. All multiples of five (10, 15, 20, 25 ...) say *buzz* as well. The counting proceeds as rapidly as possible. If someone should forget about buzzing when required, they sit down and drop out of the game. The last remaining student is the winner.

Variations

1 A more complicated variation of 'Buzz' is 'Buzz-Bizz'. The rules are the same as those for 'Buzz', except that there are two taboo numbers here. For example, *buzz* is substituted for *five* (and its multiples) and *bizz* for *three* (and its multiples plus all other numbers which contain a 3, such as 13). In addition, when it is the turn for someone to say, for example, *fifteen*, they should say *buzz-bizz*, as both *five* and *three* are involved.
2 Instead of saying *buzz*, students may do an agreed-upon action, such as clap their hands, tap on the desk, twiddle their thumbs, stamp their feet, etc.

1.5 Mr Roy's watch

Summary:	Apart from the fun, this game practises intonation.
Level:	beginner – pre-intermediate
Time:	10–15 minutes
Preparation:	none

Procedure

1 Read out this series of exchanges:

Teacher:	Mr Roy has lost his watch and number 8 has found it.
Number 8:	Who? Me, number 1?
Teacher:	Yes, you, number 8.
Number 8:	Not me, number 1.
Teacher:	Then who, number 8?

Number 8:	Number 11, number 1.
Number 11:	Who? Me, number 8?
Number 8:	Yes, you, number 11.
Number 11:	Not me, number 8.
Number 8:	Then who, number 11?
Number 11:	Number 5, number 8 ...

Check whether students have understood the rules of the game.

2 Read out the conversation again and get everyone to repeat it sentence by sentence. Pay special attention to correct intonation!

3 The class stand or sit in a circle. While keeping Number 1 for yourself, give each student a number from Number 2 upwards. Do a few dummy runs, so that everyone gets the hang of it. Then play the game 'in earnest'. It is sure to cause lots of slips – and laughter.

Variation

If you find that numbers are too impersonal, you may use the students' actual names or symbolic ones like names of colours, or fruits, or whatever else they would like to adopt for the period of the game.

1.6 O'Grady says

Summary:	Students perform actions – or refuse to do so.
Level:	beginner – pre-intermediate
Time:	10–15 minutes
Preparation:	none

Procedure

1 Explain that you will need a volunteer to come forward and issue a series of simple commands. The class will only obey if the commands are preceded by the clause *O'Grady says*, but will stay put if *O'Grady says* is not forthcoming. For example, if the command is *O'Grady says, 'Rub your nose'*, everybody rubs their nose, but if it is merely *Rub your nose*, nobody should lift a finger.

2 Before the game starts, everybody should jot down in their notebook ten simple commands which are easy to perform in the classroom. You may help those who get stuck with these commands. Depending on the language level of the class, here are two lists:

> *beginner*
> | cover your face | cross your arms | cross your legs |
> | fall asleep | lift your left hand | lift your right hand |
> | make a face | open your mouth | pull your ear |
> | pull your hair | put your head on the desk | say 'bow-wow' |
> | sing a song | sit down | stand up |
> | turn around | turn left | turn right |
>
> *pre-intermediate*
> | clap your hands | clear your throat | click your tongue |
> | clutch your fist | doodle in your notebook | give out a shout |
> | make a bow | roll your eyes | rub your nose |
> | scratch your chin | stamp your feet | stick out your tongue |
> | tap on the desk | touch your right elbow | twiddle your thumbs |
> | wink twice | yawn | |

3 A volunteer comes to the front of the class and reads out their list of commands, indiscriminately using and leaving out *O'Grady says*. When the first person has run out of commands, someone else takes over – and so on, until all the students have had their turn.

Variation

The volunteer performs the action even when omitting *O'Grady says*, in order to confuse classmates. In another version, she/he performs something other than what she/he is actually saying.

1.7 Five laughs

Summary:	Students describe different laughs.
Level:	beginner – pre-intermediate
Time:	10–15 minutes
Preparation:	Ask friends and colleagues to produce five or six laughs and record them on tape.

Procedure

1 Students listen to the five people laughing on the recording. Which of them make the class laugh? Which is the funniest?
2 Put these adjectives in a list on the board. Help students understand their meaning.

bitter	cruel	hearty	hysterical	ironical	loud
nervous	polite	scary	silly	soft	unnatural	

Students get into pairs and listen to the recording again. Stop after each laugh to give students enough time to choose and write down in their notebook the adjective which suits each laugh best.

3 Individual students offer their choice of adjectives laugh by laugh. Record votes for each objective on the board. In the end, summarise the results.

Variation

In more advanced classes, the list above may be supplemented with verbs such as:

cackle	chortle	chuckle	giggle	guffaw	snigger	titter

Can students describe any of the recorded laughs with the verbs of laughter on the board? Can they name situations where giggling, tittering, etc. would be appropriate?

Follow-up

Should you have a bold class, volunteers may be willing to produce a laugh for their classmates to examine. Before they act it out, they should make up their minds about the kind of laughter they want to produce. Having listened to the laugh, the others describe it with suitable adjectives. Does the 'laugher' agree with the judgments?

1.8 The laugh epidemic

Summary:	Students attempt to make each other laugh.
Level:	pre-intermediate – intermediate
Time:	10–15 minutes
Preparation:	none

Procedure

1 Students get into pairs. Explain that Partner A in each pair is very serious, determined not to laugh; Partner B is the 'funny guy'. Pairs stand up and face each other. Partner B has one minute to make Partner A laugh by grinning, gesturing, singing a silly song, telling

a joke, reciting a nonsense rhyme, imitating someone they both know – everything is permitted! Partner A tries to keep a straight face throughout, but if she/he breaks into laughter, Partner B gets a point. At this point they exchange roles.

2 After a few minutes, stop the activity and ask how many times Partner B managed to get Partner A to laugh. What tricks triggered the heartiest laughter?

3 After students have exchanged roles, they analyse the situation as in *Step 2.*

4 Volunteers entertain the whole class with the trick that worked best on their partner.

Variation

Everyone chooses to be either a 'serious guy' or a 'funny guy', and then behaves accordingly. Students stand up and begin to circulate. Any funny guy may stop any serious guy and do their best to make them laugh. When the serious guy eventually breaks into laughter, she/he has caught the laugh epidemic, as it were, and has also turned into a funny guy. Thus as the number of funny guys increases, so the number of serious guys diminishes. When there are only a few serious guys left in the class, they will be surrounded by several funny guys, all collaborating to pass on the disease. The activity ends when everybody has caught the laugh epidemic (or when you have run out of patience).

Acknowledgment

The main activity is based on an idea by Griffiths and Keohane in *Personalizing Language Learning* (Cambridge University Press).

1.9 Catch them laughing!

Summary:	Each student observes a classmate and then describes her/his laughing habits.
Level:	intermediate – post-intermediate
Time:	20–25 minutes (in class)
Preparation:	none

Procedure

1 Ask students these questions:
   • Do you laugh every day?
   • What kind of things in particular make you laugh?

- Who in the class is best at making others laugh?
- Who has the nicest/heartiest laugh?

2 Launch a 'laughing project'. Everyone observes a classmate of their choice for one month. What are her/his laughing habits? In what situations, how often and how does she/he usually laugh? When the month is up, each observer writes a short essay on their experience without supplying the name of the person under surveillance. Students then take it in turns to read out their essay, with the others trying to guess the person observed.

1.10 Laugh till you drop

Summary:	Students read a text on a bizarre laughing contest.
Level:	intermediate – post-intermediate
Time:	10–15 minutes
Preparation:	Make a copy of Box 1 and Box 2 for each student. (You could make a transparency of Box 1.)

Procedure

1 Students look at the woman in the picture and guess why she is laughing.

© Cambridge University Press 2002

2 The answer is provided in this extract. While students read the text, help with any unknown vocabulary.

BOX 2

Linda Lutz is laughing because she has just discovered she is the winner of the 'Laughing Contest', an annual competition in San Diego, California. Linda won two prizes simultaneously. One for the longest continuous laugh (she has been laughing for four hours and one minute) and the other for the most hilarious laugh. For her stunt, she received prizes and a free pass to the San Diego Zoo.

© Cambridge University Press 2002

3 Ask these questions:
- Did you guess right?
- How do you think Linda was able to laugh for more than four hours?
- Would you be able to beat her record?
- Could such a contest take place in your country too, or is it typically American? Why?

Acknowledgment

This is based on an activity from *When in Britain* by Nolasco and Medgyes (Oxford University Press).

1.11 Laughing quotes

Summary:	Students discuss witty sayings on laughter.
Level:	intermediate – post-intermediate
Time:	15–20 minutes
Preparation:	Make a copy of Box 3 for each student. Make a transparency or copy of Box 4.

Procedure

1 Distribute copies of Box 3. As students read the quotations, provide help with any unfamiliar words.

> **BOX 3**
> 1 The most wasted day is that in which we have not laughed. (French writer Sebastien Chamfort)
> 2 A good laugh is the best pesticide. (Russian-American writer Vladimir Nabokov)
> 3 The sound of laughter is the most civilised music in the world. (British writer Peter Ustinov)
> 4 Laughter is inner jogging. (American journalist Norman Cousins)
> 5 Laugh and the world laughs with you; weep and you weep alone. (American poet and writer Ella Wheeler Wilcox)
> 6 The human race has only one effective weapon, and that is laughter. (American writer Mark Twain)
> 7 People who laugh a lot live longer. (Anon.)
> 8 Laughter is the best medicine. (Anon.)
> 9 He who laughs last laughs best. (Anon.)
> 10 Smile is the shortest distance between two people. (Anon.)

© Cambridge University Press 2002

In groups, students discuss the meaning of each quote. They then choose the one with which they agree most.

2 Now show the class Box 4. Encourage students to make up a quotation which would suit the cartoon best.

Harley Schwadron Source: www.CartoonStock.com

© Cambridge University Press 2002

Who would fancy working in a company which specialises in humour research? Can they name a particular project they would like to launch?

18

Follow-ups

1 Encourage students to make up their own witticisms about humour
and laughter. You may like to offer these two examples:
    Humour is the yeast of life.
    Humour is no laughing matter.
2 Some students may have been inspired by the cartoon in Box 4. Can
they draw a cartoon to illustrate any of the quotes and sayings in this
activity?

1.12 A sense of humour

Summary: Students discuss the concept of a sense of humour.
Level: pre-intermediate – intermediate
Time: 10–15 minutes
Preparation: none

Procedure

1 Challenge students to define what a sense of humour is. Then tell
them this joke:

> Woman: The trouble with you, Brian, is that you have no sense
>   of humour.
> Man (*after thinking about it for a moment*):
>   Well, I don't think that's funny.

Ask why Brian needed time for his answer.
Suggested answer: Because he is slow and humourless.
2 Students discuss these issues in groups:
  • Do you know people with no sense of humour? What do you
    think of them?
  • How would you react if someone told you that you had no sense
    of humour? Would you accept this judgment?
  • Do you know anyone with a marvellous sense of humour? Can
    you describe this person?
  • Who have a better sense of humour: men or women?
  • Maltese-British writer Edward de Bono said: 'Humour is by far
    the most significant phenomenon in the human mind.' If you
    agree, explain why.
  • Is it important for a teacher to have a sense of humour? Why/not?

1.13 He who laughs last ...

Summary:	How good are students at getting the punch line?
Level:	pre-intermediate – intermediate
Time:	10–15 minutes
Preparation:	none

Procedure

1 Tell the class this well-known proverb: 'He who laughs last laughs best.' Is there an equivalent saying in the students' mother tongue?
2 The proverb was paraphrased by the American humorist Terry Cohen like this: 'He who laughs last is generally the last to get the joke.' Ask students:
   - In your mother tongue, are you quick or rather slow in getting punch lines?
   - What does your reaction time depend on?
   - If you miss the punch line, do you sometimes fake a laugh?
   - If yes, why? To save face or to please the joke-teller?
3 Test students' reaction time with this joke:

> I heard a new joke the other day. I wonder if I told it to you.
>   Is it funny?
> Yes.
>   Then you haven't.

Who was the quickest to get the punch line? And the slowest? Is there anyone who missed it altogether? Can somebody explain it to her/him?

Follow-up

Students in groups test each other's reaction time with one joke each. Who is the quickest member of the group to get the punch line? Challenge this person by asking them to explain the joke.

Extra

Provide funny paraphrases for the proverb 'He who laughs last laughs best.'

> He who laughs last has the last laugh.
> He who laughs last thinks slowest.
> He who laughs last is an Englishman.

After reading the paraphrases, students may like to add some of their own to the list.

1.14 Look into the mirror!

Summary:	This activity examines students' ability to laugh at themselves.
Level:	pre-intermediate – intermediate
Time:	10–15 minutes
Preparation:	none

Procedure

1 Put on the board these quotations and help with any unknown vocabulary:

> 1 Blessed are those who can laugh at themselves for they shall never cease to be amused. (Anon.)
> 2 You might as well laugh at yourself once in a while – everyone else does. (Anon.)
> 3 If you can't laugh at yourselves, make fun of other people. (Anon.)

Students discuss what connects these three quotations and what distinguishes them.

Suggested answer:
What connects them is the topic of self-irony. The first two quotes stress the importance and indeed the fun of being self-critical, whereas the third one stresses people's unwillingness to adopt a self-critical attitude. If the three were graded on a scale of wickedness, the first would be the least and the third the most wicked.

2 Ask students these questions:
 • Which do you find more fun: to laugh at your own follies or at other people's?
 • When was the last time that you laughed at yourself? Why was this?
 • Have you ever witnessed a famous person mock herself/himself in public? Did you think more or less of her/him afterwards?

Extras

1 Ethnic jokes can be offensive, but if we replace the country and the nationality with non-entities, they can be quite funny. Like the ones on the next page:

> 1 Friend: Have you heard the latest joke about the Udopian?
>   Peter: Be careful! I come from Udopia.
>   Friend: OK. I'll tell it slowly then.
> 2 Friend: Tell me, is it true that Marpians are lazy?
>   Peter: No, no! It's the Piltians who are lazy. We Marpians are stupid.

Ask which of the two jokes is better. Why? In the students' culture, who are more frequently the butt of jokes: their own fellow-citizens or rather people from other countries and cultures?

2 Read out the following two quotations by American comedians:
- No one ever went broke underestimating the taste of the American public. (H.L. Mencken)
- California is a fine place to live – if you happen to be an orange. (Fred Allen)

Ask students what, in their opinion, the implications of these quotes are.

Suggested answers:
Americans have awful taste and California is an awful place for human beings to live.

1.15 Smiles and jokes

Summary:	Two poems are compared to find features they have in common.
Level:	intermediate – post-intermediate
Time:	20–25 minutes
Preparation:	Make a copy of Box 5 and Box 6 for each pair of students.

Procedure

1 Divide the class into pairs. Give Partner A in each pair the poem 'Growing smiles' (Box 5) and Partner B 'Once upon a time' (Box 6).

BOX 5
Growing smiles

A smile is quite a funny thing,
It wrinkles up your face,
And when it's gone, you never find
Its secret hiding place.

But far more wonderful it is
To see what smiles can do;
You smile at one, he smiles at you,
And so one smile makes two.

He smiles at someone since you smiled,
And then that one smiles back;
And that one smiles, until in truth
You fail in keeping track.

Now since a smile can do great good
By cheering hearts of care,
Let's smile and smile, and not forget
That smiles go everywhere!
Anon.

BOX 6
Once upon a time

Once upon a time there lived
a small joke
in the middle of nowhere.

This small joke
was dying to share
itself with someone

but nobody came to hear
this small joke.

So this small joke told
itself to the birds

and the birds told this small joke to the trees
and the trees told this small joke to the rivers
and the rivers told this small joke to the mountains
and the mountains told this small joke to the stars

till the whole world
started to swell with laughter

and nobody believed
it all began
with a small joke

that lived in the middle of nowhere.

> Everybody kept saying
> it was me
> it was me.
> *John Agard*

Ask students to read their poem to their partner, so that they leave out the key word, *smile* and *joke* respectively, each time it occurs. They can use *bimp*, *bimps* and *bimped* instead. The listener in each pair tries to guess the word omitted.

2 Students in pairs show each other their poem and compare the two poets' messages. What distinguishes them but, more importantly, what do they have in common?

Suggested answer:
As far as their commonality is concerned, both smiles and jokes spread fast.

3 Say this proverb: 'Laugh and the world laughs with you; cry and you cry alone.' Ask the class if it is true. Is it also true that smiles, laughs and jokes are contagious, as it were? If someone smiles at them in the street, do they smile back? If someone begins to laugh, do they join in the laughter? If someone tells a good joke, do they pass it on to somebody else? Can they recall situations to exemplify the chain effect of smiles, laughs and jokes?

Acknowledgment

The poem by John Agard is from *The Penguin Book of Utterly Brilliant Poetry* (Penguin Books).

1.16 Funny news

Summary:	Students design a magazine page full of funny items.
Level:	intermediate – post-intermediate
Time:	20–25 minutes (in class)
Preparation:	Have some reusable adhesive or sticky tape ready.

Procedure

1 Ask students to browse through newspapers and magazines written in their mother tongue and cut out funny bits and pieces, including articles, headlines, jokes, cartoons, photographs, advertisements – anything is welcome as long as it is funny! Needless to say, humour

magazines are the best sources. Everyone designs a 'fun-page' from their cutouts, pasting the pieces on a sheet, the same size as an ordinary newspaper or magazine. Students should strive to make the layout look like a page in a real newspaper or magazine. In addition, they should prepare to summarise the content of the pieces in English.

2 Students bring their 'fun-page' to class. They get into pairs; in each pair Partner A plays the role of the 'editor' while Partner B plays the role of the 'foreigner'. As Partner B cannot read in L1, Partner A has to translate the gist of each piece, paying particular attention to the underlying humour. After a while, partners change roles.

3 Everybody displays their 'fun-page' on the wall and leaves it there for a couple of weeks for general entertainment.

Variation

In a multilingual class, the task is more authentic in that translation is really necessary for the partners to understand the content of the items on the 'fun-page'. On the other hand, L1 newspapers and magazines may not be so readily available.

Acknowledgment

For this activity, I was inspired by 'Happy News' in Sanderson's *Using Newspapers in the Classroom* (Cambridge University Press).

1.17 The Crazy Award

Summary:	A certificate is awarded to anyone who proves to be crazy enough.
Level:	pre-intermediate – intermediate
Time:	10–15 minutes
Preparation:	Make a copy of Box 7 for each student.

Procedure

1 Elicit from students synonyms and near-synonyms for *crazy*. Write them on the board and supplement the list with these if students ask for more:

absurd	bananas	bonkers	childish	daft	dumb
foolish	idiotic	loony	ludicrous	mad	nuts
ridiculous	round the bend		silly	stupid	witless

Point out that *bananas* and *round the bend* are often used with *go*, as *go bananas* and *go round the bend*.
2 Discuss with the class whether they agree that some of the most imaginative and creative people in the world have been a bit nutty. Can they give examples from their own experience?
3 Show students a copy of 'The Crazy Award' in Box 7.

BOX 7

THE CRAZY AWARD
I hereby certify that

IS BRAVE ENOUGH TO
say silly and bizarre things,
write mad, crazy things,
be totally and completely daft, and
enjoy every minute of it.

Signed

Dated

© Cambridge University Press 2002

Announce that this certificate may be awarded to anyone who has repeatedly proved herself/himself 'crazy'. For someone to be considered, two classmates have to put forward a written proposal explaining why the candidate is worthy of the award. If you accept the recommendation, sign and date the certificate, and hand it over in a mock ceremonial manner.

Acknowledgment

The idea of 'The Crazy Award' is inspired by 'The Licence' in Cranmer's *Motivating High Level Learners* (Longman).

2   Jokes and wisecracks

It is wrong to say that humour equals jokes, but it is probably true that jokes are the most common triggers of laughter. Nevertheless, course-books seldom contain jokes, perhaps because they 'don't travel well', as a materials writer explained to me. Although I admit that different cultures show significant differences in the kinds of jokes they prefer, I am yet to meet a culture which is short of jokes.

A piece of advice: All the jokes in this section are from sources in English, though many of them have their non-English equivalents as well. You the teacher are the only person who can tell which of the jokes 'travel well' in your culture and are likely to be enjoyed by your students. So take your pick!

2.1 Waiter, waiter!

Summary:	Students practise giving snappy answers in the restaurant.
Level:	pre-intermediate – intermediate
Time:	15–20 minutes
Preparation:	Make a copy of Box 8. (If there are more than 12 students in the class, you will need to have extra copies of the two-liners.) Cut up the jokes so that there is one line for each student.

Procedure

1 Restaurant jokes have innumerable variations. As a rule, the customer is served bad food, and when he complains, the waiter provides a snappy answer. For example:

> Waiter, call the manager. I can't eat this terrible food.
>   There's no point, sir. He won't eat it either.

Ask students to explain what makes this joke funny.

Suggested answer:
The waiter deliberately confuses two language functions: he takes a complaint for an invitation.

2 Distribute the pieces of paper. Help with any unknown words if necessary.

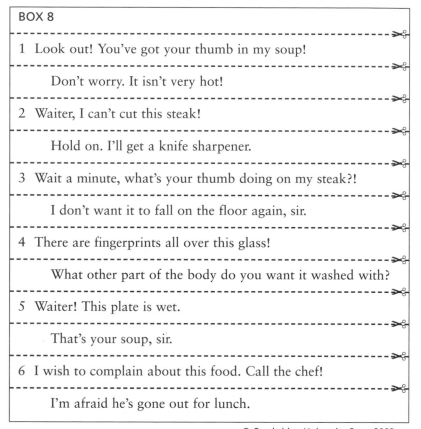

BOX 8

1 Look out! You've got your thumb in my soup!

   Don't worry. It isn't very hot!

2 Waiter, I can't cut this steak!

   Hold on. I'll get a knife sharpener.

3 Wait a minute, what's your thumb doing on my steak?!

   I don't want it to fall on the floor again, sir.

4 There are fingerprints all over this glass!

   What other part of the body do you want it washed with?

5 Waiter! This plate is wet.

   That's your soup, sir.

6 I wish to complain about this food. Call the chef!

   I'm afraid he's gone out for lunch.

3 Everybody stands up and looks for the person with the other line of their joke.
4 Give pairs a few minutes to memorise and rehearse their short dialogue. They should not only tell their joke, but also act it out. Which joke *and* performance do the class find the funniest?

Follow-up

Pairs take it in turns to tell their joke again. Make them explain the point of each joke.

2.2 There's a fly in my soup!

Summary:	This gap-filling activity is seasoned with flies in the soup.
Level:	pre-intermediate – intermediate
Time:	10–15 minutes
Preparation:	Make a copy of Box 9 for each student.

Procedure

1 'Fly jokes' are disgusting, yet very popular. Tell students this one for illustration:

> Waiter! There's a fly in my soup.
>   Would you prefer it to be served separately?

Now tell this one, but omit the last word. What is the missing word?

> Waiter! There's a fly in my soup.
>   If you throw it a pea, it'll play ... .

Answer: water-polo.

2 Explain that in the following jokes the cue sentence will always be: *Waiter! There's a fly in my soup.* Give each student a copy of the incomplete sentences in Box 9. Help with any unknown vocabulary.

BOX 9
1 If you leave it there, the ... will eat it.
2 I know, sir. It's ... soup.
3 I'm sorry, sir. The ... must have missed it.
4 It is the ... meat that attracts them, sir.
5 Don't make a fuss, sir. They'll all ... one.

© Cambridge University Press 2002

What is the missing word? Give students a few minutes to write their guesses on their handout.

3 In groups, students compare their guesses, discussing which of them appears to be the best for each sentence. Afterwards, you supply the original punch line.

Answer: 1 goldfish, 2 fly, 3 dog, 4 rotting, 5 want.

Follow-up

At home, each student should make up at least one fly joke. In class, they read out their joke with the key word missing. Can the others work it out?

2.3 Next please!

Summary:	Students state their preferences for doctor–patient jokes.
Level:	pre-intermediate – intermediate
Time:	10–15 minutes
Preparation:	none

Procedure

1 A common type of two-liner is the dialogue between the doctor and the patient. Since such jokes are obviously concerned with illnesses, they tend to be cruel. Like this one:

> Doctor! Doctor! Everybody keeps ignoring me.
>> Next, please!

Ask what makes this joke sadly funny.

Suggested answer:
The doctor, like everyone else, ignores him: he calls in the next patient without even bothering to ask him a question.

2 This is one of the blackest jokes I have ever heard!

> Is it serious, doctor?
>> I wouldn't start watching any new television serials.

Ask the class what other cruel pieces of advice might be given to this poor patient. Each sentence should start with 'I wouldn't ... .'

Suggested answer:
I wouldn't buy a calendar for next year, begin to learn a new language, buy a twin-pack shampoo, start reading 'War and Peace'.

3 Relatively speaking, these two jokes are innocent:

> 1 Doctor: When you get up in the morning, do you have a sore throat, a pain in the middle of your shoulders and feel terribly depressed?
> Patient: Yes, I do.
> Doctor: So do I. I wonder what it is.

> 2 Doctor: If you have any further questions, don't hesitate to ask.
>
> Patient: (*anxiously*) If the universe is expanding all the time, where does it all go?

Which of the jokes do students prefer? The cruel jokes in *Step 1* and *Step 2* or the mild ones in *Step 3*? Why?

Follow-up

In my experience, doctor–patient jokes are universal. Can students remember any in their mother tongue? Do these jokes lend themselves to translation? If students get stuck, please use any of these:

> 1 Patient: Are you positive I'll get well? I've heard doctors sometimes give wrong diagnoses – and treat patients for pneumonia who later die of typhoid fever.
>
> Doctor: Don't worry. When I treat a man for pneumonia, he dies of pneumonia.
>
> 2 Friend A: Every time I get drunk I see rabbits with red spots.
> Friend B: Have you seen your doctor?
> Friend A: No, just rabbits with red spots.
>
> 3 Doctor: I'm afraid I've bad news for you. You have only four minutes to live.
>
> Patient: Four minutes?! Is there really nothing you can do for me?
>
> Doctor: Well, I could just about boil you an egg.
>
> 4 Patient: Everyone hates me!
> Psychiatrist: Don't be ridiculous! Everyone hasn't met you yet.

2.4 Which do you want first?

Summary:	In good news / bad news jokes, you may choose between two awful alternatives.
Level:	pre-intermediate – intermediate
Time:	10–15 minutes
Preparation:	Make a copy of Box 10 for each student.

Procedure

1 'I have some good news and some bad news. Which do you want first?' Explain that many English jokes begin with these cues.
2 Give out copies of the two unfinished jokes in Box 10. One is a doctor–patient joke, the other is about galley slaves. Check that students know the meaning of *galley* and *slaves*.

BOX 10

1 After the operation, the doctor told his patient that he had good news and bad news. Which did he want first? The patient went for the bad news and the doc told him he had had to remove his right lung. 'Oh, what's the good news then?' the patient asked. '... .'

2 The captain is telling the galley slaves that he has some good news and some bad news. 'The good news is,' he begins, 'that you'll all be getting a glass of whisky tonight.' 'And what's the bad news?' asks a slave. '... .'

© Cambridge University Press 2002

3 After students have read the unfinished jokes, ask them what the good news in Joke 1 and the bad news in Joke 2 can be.

Original punch lines:
1 'Now there's enough room for your liver.'
2 'The captain wants to water-ski tomorrow.'

Are there any 'good news / bad news' jokes in their mother tongue? Ask volunteers to tell a few.

Extra

The following is a game aimed at building up a story which consists of alternately good and bad news. Students play in groups. The first player starts by reporting some good news. The next player then has to state a piece of bad news which contradicts the good news. And so on round the other members of the group, with each player adding some good or bad news in turn.

The example below is about an imaginary student, Josie.

Student A: Did you hear the good news? Josie's parents have bought a new house.

Student B: Yes, but the bad news is that the house is in very bad shape.

Student C: That's true, but the good news is that it has a wonderful view.

Student D: Don't forget the bad news, though. The house is 35 kilometres out of town. How will she come to school? etc.

Acknowledgment

The game in the *Extra* is from Augarde's *A to Z of Word Games* (Oxford University Press).

2.5 Entangled two-liners

Summary:	Students match corresponding sentences.
Level:	intermediate – post-intermediate
Time:	15–20 minutes
Preparation:	Make a copy of Box 11 for each pair of students.

Procedure

1 In English-speaking cultures, many jokes are based on waiter–customer and doctor–patient interactions (2.1, 2.2, 2.3). How about the students' culture? What other pairs of speakers are common in jokes? After preparing a list of typical interlocutors in groups, students share their suggestions with the whole class.

2 Here are a few more two-liners – but they have been split up. After you have distributed the handouts, help students with any unknown vocabulary. Then pairs should try to match the sentences in the two columns.

BOX 11

1 I'm sorry. Was I driving too fast?

2 You're late. You should have been here at nine o'clock.

3 I've had to walk five miles to deliver this letter to your farm.

4 I haven't had food for so long, I've forgotten what it tastes like.

5 I enjoyed your book a lot. Who wrote it for you?

6 I'm sorry to call you in the middle of the night.

7 If we get engaged to be married, will you give me a ring?

8 Guilty. Ten days or two hundred dollars.

☐ a Sure. What's your phone number?

☐ b You should have posted it!

☐ c I'm so glad you liked it. Who read it to you?

☐ d Either that, or flying too low.

☐ e That's all right. I had to get up anyway to answer the phone.

☐ f I'll take the two hundred, thanks.

☐ g Why, what happened?

☐ h Don't worry, it still tastes the same!

Answers: 1 d, 2 g, 3 b, 4 h, 5 c, 6 e, 7 a, 8 f.

3 In the eight dialogues on the previous page, who are the characters and what are the situations? Can students identify them?

Answers:
1/d = driver/police(wo)man – the driver was speeding
2/g = boss/employee – the employee was late
3/b = postman/farmer – twisted logic
4/h = beggar/passerby – the passerby is cynical
5/c = reader/writer – a snappy answer to a wicked question
6/e = friend/friend – the idiotic answer may be explained by sleepiness
7/a = woman/man – the pun is based on the double meaning of *ring*
8/f = judge/convict – the convict is being cheeky

Follow-up

Everyone should think of a joke like the ones in Box 11. Students take it in turns to tell their joke, while the others try to find out who the two characters are. Here are a few more two-liners to throw in if students get stuck:

1	Boss:	I called you in because I want to discuss the question of retirement.
	Worker:	But that's ridiculous. You're still a young man!
2	Wife:	If I left you for some man, would you be sorry?
	Husband:	Why would I be sorry for a man I don't know?
3	Judge:	Why did you shoot your husband with a bow and arrow?
	Woman:	I didn't want to wake up the kids.
4	Friend:	Do you think I'll lose my looks as I get older?
	Friend (?):	If you're lucky.
5	Reader:	Can you tell me where the Self-help section is?
	Librarian:	But doesn't that defeat the whole purpose?
6	Man:	My wife hasn't spoken to me for three days.
	Woman:	Perhaps she's trying to tell you something.
7	Friend:	Why are you leaving? It's only the interval.
	Friend:	But look, it says on the programme, 'Act Two – one month later'.

2.6 'Unfunny' dialogues

Summary:	Students turn trivial dialogues into jokes.
Level:	intermediate – post-intermediate
Time:	10–15 minutes
Preparation:	Make a copy of Box 12 for each group of students.

Procedure

1   Even the most vacuous dialogue may become a joke by having a twist added to it. Read out this dialogue:

> Boy: Can you see the screen all right?
> Girl: Yes.
> Boy: You're not sitting in a draught?
> Girl: No.
> Boy: Comfortable seat?
> Girl: Yes, fine.
> Boy: Good.

How could this dialogue be turned into a joke? What needs to be changed? Can anyone offer a witty punch line to replace 'Good'?
Original punch line: 'Mind changing places?'

2   Here are a few more dialogues waiting to be jazzed up. First help with any unknown words if necessary.

> **BOX 12**
> 1 Do you know the way to the post office?
>   No. I'm afraid I don't.
>   OK.
> 2 I made a million pounds' profit last year.
>   Honestly?
>   No kidding.
> 3 How did you break your arm?
>   Do you see that broken step?
>   Yes.
>   Well, I tripped over it.
> 4 A man walked into a pub where a pianist was playing, and said, 'Do you know your house is on fire?' 'Oh my goodness!' said the pianist.
> 5 Malcolm Brown next door blows his wife a kiss every morning as he leaves the house. I wish you'd do that!
>   I'm sorry, darling. I promise I will.

In groups, students try to delete the last 'unfunny' line and substitute a funny one. They should add a twist to at least a couple of the jokes.

3   Supply the original punch lines. Did anyone produce a similar punch line?

Answers:
1 Well, go down this road and take the first turning on the left.
2 Well, let's not go into that!
3 Well, I didn't.
4 'No,' said the pianist, 'but if you hum it, I'll try to follow you.'
5 But I hardly know the woman!

2.7 Expanding dialogues

Summary: Students develop a funny dialogue sentence by sentence.
Level: intermediate – post-intermediate
Time: 10–15 minutes
Preparation: none

Procedure

1 Read out this unfinished dialogue:

> Woman: What have you got in your sandwich?
> Man: Let's see. It looks like cheese again. It's cheese, cheese, cheese every day. It's driving me mad! Why does it always have to be cheese?
> Woman: Why don't you ask your wife to make you something different?
> Man: ...

Volunteers supply the finishing line, making sure that it is as flat as possible. For example:
> Man: Because she wouldn't listen.
> I simply don't dare.
> Hm, good idea!

2 Now students try to make up a funny line instead of the flat one. Listen to their suggestions, then supply the original:
> Man: I'm not married. I make my own.

3 Suppose the woman had no sense of humour, so her next sentence might be:
> Woman: You make your own sandwich? But then why don't you make, say, a ham sandwich for a change?

Realising that the woman did not get his joke, the man carries on with pretended innocence. What could his next sentence be? Students should offer ideas. For example:

Man: Good idea! I'll make a ham sandwich tomorrow then.
But I'm a vegetarian!
I don't know how to. Could you teach me?

Follow-ups

1 For homework, students expand the dialogue above. In class, they practise it in pairs, and then read out their version to the whole class. Whose is the most absurd dialogue?
2 If students have done other activities in this section, they should browse through them. After choosing a few jokes, they should replace the punch lines with genuinely flat ones. The more humourless they are, the better! For example, remind students of this restaurant joke:
Customer: There are fingerprints all over this glass!
Waiter: What other part of the body do you want it washed with?
Instead of this, the waiter's line may run like this:
Waiter: Oh, I'm awfully sorry. I'll bring you another glass right away.

2.8 Laugh in prison!

Summary:	This activity practises the skill of delivering jokes in an entertaining manner.
Level:	pre-intermediate – intermediate
Time:	10–15 minutes
Preparation:	Record three friends or colleagues telling the 'Sheep' joke.

Procedure

1 Before you read out the 'Prison' joke, mention that often the way we tell a joke is what makes it entertaining. Then pre-teach any new vocabulary, including such key words as *prison*, *convict*, *burst out laughing* and *cellmate*. Now read out the joke:

A convict spends his first night in prison. All of a sudden, another convict jumps to his feet and shouts, 'Sixty-three'. Hearing this, all the other prisoners burst out laughing.
   Later, another convict shouts, 'One hundred and eleven'. Hysterical laughter all round.

'What's going on?' says the new convict to his cellmate who is sitting next to him.

'Thing is we only have one joke book in the prison and everyone knows all the jokes off by heart. So we needn't tell the whole joke, you know. We just stand up and shout a number.'

A few days later, the new convict decides that it's time for him to try it out. So he stands up and shouts, 'Eighty-one'.

Silence.

Turning to his cellmate, he asks, 'What went wrong?'

'It was the way you said it, I guess.'

Ask what this joke illustrates.

Suggested answer:
It is not enough for a joke to be funny. It must be told in a funny way, too. Even the best jokes fall flat if the delivery is boring and, conversely, even the worst jokes may come off if told well.

2 Tell students this joke without trying to make it funny:

Doctor, doctor! I've just swallowed a whole sheep.
  How do you feel?
Quite baaa-d.

This wasn't a particularly good joke, was it? And yet it can make people laugh if told well.

3 Students listen to the three presentations, then choose the one which they think was the best delivery. Do they all agree? In their opinion, what attributes made their favourite funnier than the other two?

Suggested answer: intonation, pause, stress, speed, voice quality, acting talent.

Extra

Provide students with two pieces of data from the Guinness Book of Records.

1 Felipe Carbonell of Lima, Peru, told 345 jokes in one hour on 29 July, 1993.
2 Mike Hessman of Columbus, Ohio, USA, told 12,682 jokes in 24 hours on 16–17 November, 1992.

Could anyone in the class beat these records? Don't let them try in class ...

2.9 The rabbit and the butcher

Summary:	Students recreate a joke step by step.
Level:	beginner – pre-intermediate
Time:	15 –20 minutes
Preparation:	Make a copy of Box 13 for each student.

Procedure

1 Distribute the incomplete joke in Box 13.

> **BOX 13**
>
> A ..... (1) goes into a .....'s (2) shop and asks, 'Have you got any ..... (3)?'
>
> The ..... (4) says, 'We don't sell ..... (5) here. You need the .....'s (6) across the road.'
>
> The next day the ..... (7) comes into the shop and asks for some ..... (8) again. The ..... (9) tells him, 'Look, I told you yesterday, we don't sell ..... (10). You need the .....'s (11).'
>
> The ..... (12) comes in the next day and asks the ..... (13) again, 'Have you got any ..... (14)?'
>
> The ..... (15) goes mad. He says, 'Look, I'm sick of this. How many times do I have to tell you? I don't sell ..... (16). If you come in here again asking for ..... (17), I'm going to ..... (18) your ears to the floor.'
>
> The next day the ..... (19) comes in and asks the ..... (20), 'Have you got any ..... (21)?'
>
> '..... (22)? No.'
>
> 'Right,' the ..... (23) says, 'Have you got any ..... (24)?'

Put these words on the board. Do students know all of them?

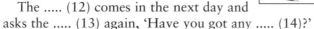

butcher	greengrocer	lettuce	nail(s)	rabbit

2 As students read the text, they try to fill in the gaps with one word each.

3 In pairs, students look at each other's solution and check for possible discrepancies.

Answers:
1 rabbit, 2 butcher, 3 lettuce, 4 butcher, 5 lettuce, 6 greengrocer, 7 rabbit,
8 lettuce, 9 butcher, 10 lettuce, 11 greengrocer, 12 rabbit, 13 butcher,
14 lettuce, 15 butcher, 16 lettuce, 17 lettuce, 18 nail, 19 rabbit, 20 butcher,
21 nails, 22 Nails, 23 rabbit, 24 lettuce.

Follow-ups

1 Everybody should learn this joke by heart at home and be prepared to tell it in as funny a way as possible. For example, they may alter their voice according to the character whose lines they are saying, exaggerate the butcher's anger, etc. In class, invite volunteers to recite the joke to the class.
2 Who considers themselves to be (relatively) good at telling jokes? Students may choose a mother-tongue joke, but only after they have translated it into English can they tell it to the class.

2.10 Snails and mushrooms

Summary:	It is not easy to tell a joke without getting mixed up.
Level:	pre-intermediate – intermediate
Time:	10–15 minutes
Preparation:	For the *Follow-up*, make a copy of Box 14 for each student.

Procedure

1 We all know people who are hopeless at telling jokes. Orsolya, a student of mine, told me this 'joke in a joke'. First tell the joke in the original:

> One day, the village pensioners decided to go and collect snails. On returning home in the evening, their baskets were full of snails, except for 90-year-old James Miller, whose basket was empty. Not a single snail in there! His granddaughter asked: 'But Grandpa, what happened?'
>
> 'Oh, don't even mention it,' said the old man. 'By the time I bent down to pick up a snail – Whoosh! – all of them had run away.'

Ask why the old man failed to collect any snails.
Answer: Because he was so slow that even snails had enough time to crawl away.

2 A lovely joke, isn't it? However, it is even funnier in the rendering of
Orsolya's father. He came home and told the joke to his family like this:

> One day, the village pensioners decided to go and collect
> *mushrooms* – and he kept saying *mushrooms* instead of *snails* as
> far as the punch line. When he realised that the joke would not
> work, he exclaimed, 'Gosh, I've messed it up!'

Ask if anybody can remember a situation in which they botched up a
joke. Did they manage to correct themselves? Were they embarrassed?
How did they try to save face? Did it work?

Follow-up

Here are two lovely jokes. Students should choose one and kill it in some
way. Afterwards, they should tell the joke in its ruined form to a partner.

BOX 14

1 A travel agent looks up from his desk to see an old lady and an
old gentleman as they're looking in the shop window at the
posters showing glamorous places around the world. The agent
has had a good week and takes pity on the poor couple. He calls
them into his shop and says: 'I know that on your pension you
could never hope to have a holiday, so I am sending you off on a
fabulous trip at my expense, and I won't take no for an answer.'
He takes them inside and asks his secretary to write two flight
tickets and book a room in a five-star hotel. They gladly accept,
and are off!

  About a month later the little old lady comes back to the shop.
'And how did you like your holiday?' the travel agent asks eagerly.

  'The flight was exciting and the room was lovely,' she says.
'I've come to thank you. But one thing puzzled me. Who was
that old guy I had to share the room with?'

2 Bill Gates dies and meets St Peter, who asks him: 'Where would
you like to go, Bill, Heaven or Hell?' Bill thinks for a moment
and says, 'Let me see both and then I'll decide.' First, Bill visits
Hell and – Wow! – it's full of beautiful women. Then he goes up
to Heaven, where all he can see is angels blowing their trumpets.
'How boring!'

  So he asks St Peter to send him to Hell. As soon as St Peter
opens the gate of Hell, Bill is grabbed by two devils and dragged
towards a pyre. 'But where are all the beautiful women?' Bill asks
in despair. And St Peter replies, 'Oh, they were just screen-savers.'

41

2.11 The interpreter

Summary:	Students are sensitised to the role of the audience.
Level:	pre-intermediate – intermediate
Time:	5–10 minutes
Preparation:	none

Procedure

1 Note that the success of a joke not only depends on its content and delivery, but also on the audience. A receptive audience gives the joke-teller the self-confidence needed to tell a joke in public. Before you read out the first part of this anecdote, deal with any unfamiliar vocabulary items; the key words are *deliver a lecture, interpreter, getting close* and *applaud*.

> Legend has it that a well-known American professor once delivered a lecture in Japan. His speech was 'translated' by the interpreter something like this:
> 'Professor is beginning speech with thing called joke. I am not certain why, but all professors believe it necessary to start speech with joke. [Pause] He is telling joke now, but frankly you would not understand it, so I won't translate it. He thinks I am telling you joke now. [Pause] Polite thing to do when he finished is to laugh. [Pause] He is getting close. [Pause] Now!'
> The audience not only laughed, but they stood up and applauded as well.

2 Before you finish the anecdote, ask the class these questions:
   • Why did this lecturer (and perhaps many others) begin their speech with a joke?
   (To establish good rapport with the audience.)
   • Why did the interpreter decide not to translate the professor's joke?
   (Because he assumed that the audience wouldn't understand it.)
   • What shows that he doesn't like the professor's joke?
   (The phrase 'with thing called joke'.)
   • Why did the audience pretend to like the 'joke' so much?
   (Merely out of politeness.)
   • How do you think the anecdote will end?

3 Here is the end of the story:

> After the speech, not realising why it had gone down so well, the professor thanked the interpreter with these words:
>
> 'I've been giving lectures in this country for several years, and you are the first translator who knows how to tell a good joke.'

3   Puns and puzzles

It is generally held that the most obvious feature of humour is ambiguity or double meaning. The simplest expression of this ambiguity is the pun. What is a pun? In its narrowest interpretation, it merely implies a sound or letter confusion. 'When I am dead I hope it may be said: "His sins were scarlet, but his books were read."' said Hilaire Belloc in his famous epigram. In a broader sense, jokes based on an amusing use of a word, phrase or sentence may also be called puns. Some people love puns and would agree with the American writer Christopher Morley, who once said: 'A pun is language on vacation.' Others hate puns (ugggh!), claiming that they are the lowest form of wit, to which Henry Erskine's quip was: 'Yes, they are, and therefore the foundation of all wit.'

However, this section covers more than puns. Offering examples of misunderstandings, riddles and puzzles, it delves into the world of language play at large. By the way, are you a punster in your mother tongue? Do you enjoy language play in English? Have you even created jokes based on double meaning, perhaps? Don't worry if you haven't – this section supplies a number of funny activities for your lessons. Let's be *pun pals*!

3.1 Twist your tongue!

Summary:	Tongue twisters are a good way of practising difficult sounds and clear articulation.
Level:	intermediate – post-intermediate
Time:	20–25 minutes
Preparation:	Make a copy of Box 15 for each small group of students.

Procedure

1 Ask if students remember tongue twisters in their mother tongue. Then put this short tongue twister on the board and practise it with the class in chorus, then individually:

> Red leather,
> Yellow leather.

2 Hand out a tongue twister to each group.

BOX 15

--->8

She sells sea-shells on the sea-shore,
The shells she sells are sea-shells, I'm sure,
For if she sells sea-shells on the sea-shore,
Then I'm sure she sells sea-shore shells.

--->8

Peter Piper picked a peck of pepper.
Did Peter Piper pick a peck of pepper?
If Peter Piper picked a peck of pepper,
Where's the peck of pepper
Peter Piper picked?

--->8

Whether the weather be fine,
Or whether the weather be not,
Whether the weather be cold,
Or whether the weather be hot,
We weather the weather
Whatever the weather
And whether we like it or not.

--->8

A tutor who tooted a flute
Tried to tutor two tooters to toot.
Said the two to the tutor:
Is it harder to toot, or
To tutor two tooters to toot?

--->8

There's no need to light a night-light
On a light night like tonight,
For a night-light's a slight light
On a night like tonight.

--->8

How much wood could a woodchuck chuck
If a woodchuck could chuck wood?
As much wood as a woodchuck would chuck
If a woodchuck could chuck wood.

After you have given the groups help with any unfamiliar words and pronunciation, urge them to rehearse their tongue twister in chorus until they can recite it fluently and by heart.

3 Here comes a playful dictation exercise. Groups take it in turns to recite their tongue twister in chorus. During recitation, all the listeners try to jot down in their notebook the tongue twister as they hear it. The chorus repeat their rhyme non-stop until the majority have managed to put it down and can gradually join the recitation.

4 Group members look at each other's notebook to check whether the tongue twisters have been correctly written down. If they get stuck, they should apply to the appropriate 'dictators' for assistance.

Extras

1 Put on the board this incomplete limerick and the six missing words under it:

> A ... and a ... in a ...
> Were imprisoned, so what could they do?
>   Said the ...: 'Let us ...!'
>   Said the ...: 'Let us ...!'
> So they ... through a ... in the ... .
>
> *flaw   flea   flee   flew   flue   fly*

After you have explained the meaning of any unknown words, students copy the limerick in their notebook, trying to fit the six words in the gaps.

Answers:
A flea and a fly in a flue
Were imprisoned, so what could they do?
   Said the fly: 'Let us flee!'
   Said the flea: 'Let us fly!'
So they flew through a flaw in the flue.

Insert the six words into the limerick on the board. After students have practised the tongue twister for a couple of minutes, begin to wipe off the six 'f' words. Meanwhile, students read the rhyme in chorus by supplying the vanishing words from memory. When all the 'f' words have disappeared, delete 'so what could they do', then 'said the', and so on, until nothing remains on the board – and yet the chorus carries on. Needless to say, this memory-jogging exercise can be applied to other tongue twisters as well.

2 Speaking of tongue twisters, I found this joke on the Internet:

> Two tourists were driving through Louisiana in the US. As they
> were approaching Natchitoches, they started arguing about the
> pronunciation of the town. They argued back and forth until
> they stopped for lunch. As they stood at the counter, one tourist
> asked the employee, 'Before we order, could you please settle an
> argument for us? Would you please pronounce where we are,
> very slowly?' The girl leaned over the counter and said,
> 'Burrrrrrrr, gerrrrrrr, Kiiiiiiiing.'

Read out this joke and ask who can explain the punch line.
Solution:
The girl did not realise that the two tourists were asking about the name of the
town and not about Burger King, the eating place.

3.2 Knock-knock!

Summary:	'Knock-knock' jokes may be childish, but adults enjoy them a lot too.
Level:	beginner – pre-intermediate
Time:	5–10 minutes
Preparation:	Make a copy of Box 16 for each pair of students. For the *Extra*, make a copy of Box 17.

Procedure

1 'Knock-knock' is a popular game which uses names as cues. (In the
80s it was so popular that the most widely sold British tabloid *The
Sun* launched a strip-cartoon series of 'Knock-knock' sketches.) All
knock-knocks are based on contorted pronunciation; the first two
utterances are always the same: 'Knock-knock. Who's there?' For
illustration, read out this one:

> Knock-knock.
>   Who's there?
> Ken.
>   Ken who?
> Ken you please open the door and let me in?

Explain that Ken's sentence should obviously have run like this: 'Can
you please open the door and let me in?'

2 Divide the class into pairs. Read out the knock-knocks in Box 16, but stop after each, so that everybody has time to identify the source of misunderstanding and supply the punch line correctly.

BOX 16
Knock-knock.
Who's there?

1 Luke.
     Luke who?
     Luke through the keyhole
     and you'll see who.

2 Cook.
     Cook who?
     Oh, I didn't know it was
     spring already.

3 Mary.
     Mary who?
     Mary Christmas and a
     Happy New Year.

4 Hatch.
     Hatch who?
     Bless you.

5 Sarah.
     Sarah who?
     Sarah doctor in
     the house?

6 Justin.
     Justin who?
     Justin old friend here to
     see you.

Answers: 1 Luke = Look, 2 Cook who? = Cuckoo, 3 Mary = Merry,
4 Hatch who? = Atishoo!, 5 Sarah = Is there a … ?, 6 Justin = Just an.

3 Give each student a copy of Box 16.

Extra

Incidentally, knock-knocks are no longer restricted to real names – anyone or anything may knock on the door. Make a copy of the 'Knock-knocks' in Box 17 and cut them up. Divide the class into pairs and give each pair one joke.

BOX 17	
Knock-knock. *Who's there?*	

Who.
  Who who?
Sorry, I don't speak to owls.
	Hawaii.
	  Hawaii who?
	Fine until you turned up.

Cows.
  Cows who?
Cows don't go *who*, they go *moo*.
	Boo.
	  Boo who?
	No need to cry!

Yah.
  Yah who?
Ride 'em, cowboy!
	Tank.
	  Tank who?
	My pleasure.

Police.
  Police who?
Police let me in, it's cold out here!
	Gopher.
	  Gopher who?
	Gopher a long walk and
	don't come back.

Jester.
  Jester who?
Jester a minute, I'll unlock the door.
	Eiffel.
	  Eiffel who?
	Eiffel down and hurt myself.

Hey, listen. I've got this great knock-knock joke for you! OK?
Knock-knock!
  Who's there?
Sorry! Sorry! I've completely forgotten the rest of the joke.
Sorry! Sorry! I've completely forgotten the rest of the joke *who*?

Pairs practise their joke until they can recite it to the whole class. After each recital, someone should explain the punch line.

3.3 Punny riddles

Summary: In its classic form, a pun is based on contorted
             sounds and letters.
Level: intermediate – post-intermediate
Time: 10–15 minutes
Preparation: Make a copy of Box 18a or Box 18b for each pair of
             students, depending on the level of the class.

Procedure

1 Ask the class whether they remember any mother-tongue puns from
   their childhood. Would they recite a few in English? Do they still find
   them funny? Give a few examples:
   • What flies and wobbles? (a jellycopter = helicopter)
   • What do you say to King Kong when he gets married?
     (Kong-gratulations = congratulations)
   • If your mum comes from Iceland and your dad comes from Cuba,
     then what are you? (An ice-cube = Iceland-Cuba)
2 Distribute copies of one of the boxes below. Explain that the drawings
   next to the riddles can help students answer the questions.

BOX 18a intermediate

1 What is the wettest
   animal?

2 What is black and white
   and red all over?

3 How did the sailor know
   there was a Man on the Moon?

4 What do you call a very
   small mother?

5 Why is six afraid of seven?

6 How do you count cows?

7 What do you give a hungry robber?

8 What do penguins ride?

9 How do you start a teddy
bear race?

BOX 18b post-intermediate

1 When a lemon asks for help,
what does it want?

2 Why couldn't the skeleton
go to the dance?

3 What do ducks watch on TV?

4 What do you call a sleeping bull?

5 Where do monsters get their
Christmas presents from?

6 What lives at the bottom of the sea, has
eight wheels and carries people around?

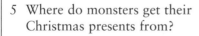

51

7 What's bad-tempered and goes with custard?

8 What happened to the cat who swallowed a ball of wool?

9 What did they give the man who invented door knockers?

© Cambridge University Press 2002

Students try to find the answers in pairs.

Answers:
Box 18a: 1 The rain deer = reindeer; 2 A newspaper = read;
3 He went to sea = see; 4 A minimum = a mini mum;
5 Because seven eight nine = ate; 6 With a cowculator = a calculator;
7 Beefburglars = beefburgers; 8 Ice-cycles = icicles/bicycles;
9 Ready, teddy, go! = steady.

Box 18b: 1 Lemonade = lemon aid; 2 He had no body to go with = nobody;
3 Duckumentaries = documentaries; 4 A bull-dozer = a bulldozer;
5 Santa Claws = Claus; 6 An octobus = an octopus;
7 Apple grumble = apple crumble; 8 She had mittens = kittens;
9 The No-bell Prize = Nobel Prize.

3 Volunteers supply the answers for the whole class.

3.4 Utter connections

Summary:	These authors and the titles are related through pronunciation.
Level:	intermediate – post-intermediate
Time:	15–20 minutes
Preparation:	Make a copy of Box 19 for each pair of students. Bring to class a large sheet of poster paper and some coloured pens.

Procedure

1 Box 19 contains book titles and authors. The task is to match the corresponding pairs; tell students that it will greatly help if they say aloud both the titles and the authors' names. Before the activity is launched, supply the meaning of any unknown vocabulary items.

BOX 19		
1 Getting Married	☐	a Max E. Mumm
2 Carpet Laying	☐	b Andrew Pictures
3 The Art of Smoking	☐	c Dinah Might
4 Bless You!	☐	d Lisa Lott
5 Do Your Best!	☐	e Nick O'Teene
6 Pebbles on the Beach	☐	f Walter Wall
7 The Long Goodbye	☐	g Justin Casey Sneeze
8 The Lady Artist	☐	h I. Malone
9 Nothing But the Truth	☐	i Sandy Shaw
10 Big Bang!	☐	j Ewan Me
11 Solitude	☐	k C.U. Later

© Cambridge University Press 2002

Students work in pairs. When most partners are ready, check the solutions.

Answers: 1j, 2f, 3e, 4g, 5a, 6i, 7k, 8b, 9d, 10c, 11h.

2 Students on their own invent funny author–title pairs like those in Box 19. While they are thinking, lay the poster paper on the floor. A few minutes later, invite volunteers to jot their ideas on the poster paper so that the authors and the corresponding titles are placed as far from each other as possible.

3 When the paper is full, ask everyone to come and connect the matching pairs with a line.

Extra

The answer to the following riddles is a pair of rhyming words (an adjective and a noun). Say the adjective–noun pairs and wait for an answer. For example:

What is an overweight rodent? (A fat rat)

What is		
1 a beautiful cat?	=	
2 an unusual seat?	=	
3 a comical rabbit?	=	
4 an angry boy?	=	
5 an irritated employer?	=	
6 a bashful insect?	=	

7 a large hog?	=
8 an uncontrollable boy or girl?	=
9 a joyful father?	=
10 a noisy group of people?	=

Once the correct rhyme has been provided, move on to the next item. For any that students can't identify, put the adjective–noun pair on the board and leave it there for the time being. When all the items have been dealt with, go back to the unresolved ones for a second check. Provide all the answers at the end.

Answers:
1 pretty kitty, 2 rare chair, 3 funny bunny, 4 mad lad, 5 cross boss, 6 shy fly, 7 big pig, 8 wild child, 9 glad dad, 10 loud crowd.

Can anyone devise similar adjective–noun pairs?

Acknowledgment

The extra is from *The Lighter Side of TEFL*, edited by Kral (United States Information Agency).

3.5 An intelligence test

Summary:	This Internet quiz tests students' level of intelligence.
Level:	intermediate – post-intermediate
Time:	10–15 minutes
Preparation:	none

Procedure

1 Write four questions on the board. First put up question 1 and wait until most students have written an answer in their notebook. Now listen to their suggestions; do not acknowledge or supply the correct answer until you have listened to several students. Then move on to question 2 – and so on, until all four questions have been dealt with in a similar fashion.

> 1 How do you put a giraffe into a refrigerator?
> 2 How do you put an elephant into a refrigerator?
> 3 The Lion King is hosting an animal conference. All the animals attend except one. Which animal does not attend?
> 4 There is a river you must cross, but it is inhabited by crocodiles. How do you manage it?

Answers:
1 Open the refrigerator door, put in the giraffe and close the door. (This question tests whether students tend to do simple things in an overly complicated way.)
2 Open the refrigerator, take out the giraffe, put in the elephant and close the door. (This tests foresight. Incidentally, the most frequent wrong answer is this: Open the refrigerator, put in the elephant and close the refrigerator.)
3 The elephant – it is in the refrigerator. (This tests memory and comprehensive thinking.)
4 Simply swim across the river. All the crocodiles are attending the animal conference! (This tests whether students can learn quickly from their mistakes.)

2 Ask who has answered all four questions correctly. Anyone with three correct answers? And with two? Tell the class jokingly that those who answered:

- four out of four questions correctly are intelligent adults; wealth and success await them.
- three have some catching up to do, but there is hope for them.
- two should go back to primary school.
- one should consider a career as a hamburger flipper in a fast food restaurant.
- zero should consider a career that does not require any higher mental functions at all – such as politics ...

However, before students lose heart, add that, according to statistics, around 90% of the adults tested got all four answers wrong. At the same time, many pre-schoolers gave several correct answers. This seems to disprove the theory that adults are cleverer than the average four-year-old!

Extras

1 You could ask another set of questions to give students one more opportunity. Ask them the following questions one by one. Stop after each question, so that everybody has time to think it over. You can help students by telling them that all the questions are linked to letters of the alphabet. Provide the answer before you move on to the next question.

1	What is found in the very centre of both America and Australia?
2	What's the difference between here and there?
3	What is the end of everything?
4	What part of London is in France?
5	Which is the loudest vowel?
6	What relatives are dependent on you?
7	Why is the letter T like an island?
8	Which is the shortest month?
9	What four letters frighten robbers?
10	When did only three vowels exist?

Answers:
1 the letter R, 2 the letter T, 3 the letter G, 4 the letter N, 5 the letter I because
it is always in the middle of noise, 6 your aUnts, Uncles, and coUsins because
they all need U, 7 because it is in water, 8 May, because it only has three
letters, 9 O I C U; 10 Before U and I were born.

2 More advanced groups may appreciate this short test. Write this sentence on the board in block capitals, and then ask everybody to read it once:

> FINISHED FILES ARE THE RESULT OF YEARS OF
> SCIENTIFIC STUDY COMBINED WITH THE EXPERIENCE
> OF YEARS.

Each student reads the sentence again and meanwhile counts out loud the letter 'F'. Quickly rub the sentence off the board and ask how many instances of 'F' they have counted.

Answer:
The letter 'F' appears six times in the sentence. People of average intelligence find three of them. If someone spotted four, they are above average. If they got five, they are way above the crowd. If anyone got six, they are a genius.

3.6 Coded messages

Summary:	When we write, we all have our own system of abbreviations – teenagers included.
Level:	pre-intermediate – intermediate
Time:	15–20 minutes
Preparation:	Make a copy of Box 20 for each student. For *Extra 2*, make a photocopy of Box 21 for each student.

Procedure

1 The following is an e-mail letter sent by Terry, an English teenager from London, to her friend, Jana in Prague. Give everybody a copy of the letter in Box 20 to read.

BOX 20

From: 'terry.gibbons'
        <terry.gibbons@tup.net>
To: janamitr@hotcake.rom
Subject: Hi from England!
Date: Wed, 13 Jan 2002 21:09:45

Hi Jana!

How R things in the Czech Republic? I hope U had an
EXCELLENT Xmas & New Year, & a great holiday. You've got
2 email me & tell me about all the cool things U bought!!

Thanx 4 the emails U sent me – sorry I've taken so long 2 reply,
but U would not believe the amount of work they've got me
doing at college. I've already done an exam which I think I did
pretty badly, but at least we get 2 retake it up to 4 times!

I take it that U heard about Muffin (he had cancer, according 2
the vet). It's a shame – now we are down 2 only 1 pet again! Oh
well, at least Eddie seems 2 be fit & well (& making as much
trouble as always!)

I haven't been going out that much recently – I went 2 a party on
New Year's Eve, & that's about the last time. It's my friend's
birthday on Saturday, though, so I think we're going 2 go out &
hit the town!!

I hope U R all able 2 come in Feb or March – I haven't seen U 4
ages! R U missing me?!!!?!

On the theme of my abbreviations guess what this means:
'NE1410IS?' Give up? R U sure? OK then, I'll tell U... ##### Oh
well, I thought it was funny.

OK then, enough of this merriment!! I had better go now, as I've
still got some homework 2 do, & I need a good night's sleep!

Email me back soon!

Loads & loads of love,
Terry

P.S. Eddie sends his luv & licks!!

2 While students are reading the letter, put these abbreviations on the board:

R =
U =
2 =
4 =
Thanx =
Xmas =
& =

After you have given help with any unfamiliar words, ask volunteers to restore the full forms on the board (but not yet the NE1410IS riddle).

Answers: R = are, U = you, 2 = to, 4 = for, Thanx = Thanks, Xmas = Christmas, & = and.

3 Now it is time to do the riddle. It is quite tricky, so students had better put their heads together in groups. Any guesses?

Answer: Anyone for tennis?

Follow-up

For homework, students answer Terry's letter on Jana's behalf. Encourage them to write a funny letter, using a similarly coded system. In class, everybody swaps their assignment with a partner. Were they both able to use the codes frequently and consistently?

Extras

1 Here is another riddle. The customer has just finished lunch. He gets up from his table and leaves a note for the waiter. This is what he has written:

1 0 0 4 1 8 0

Ask students about the meaning of this message; mention that saying the numbers aloud should help them guess. Do they remember how the numeral 0 may be pronounced?

Answer: I owe nothing for I ate nothing.

2 Those who fancy the absurd may enjoy the poem 'Three Riddled Riddles' by Martyn Wiley (1954–94) and Ian McMillan (1956–).

> **BOX 21**
>
> | i) | ii) | iii) |
> |---|---|---|
> | I have nine legs, | You see me at dawn | I taste like a grapefruit. |
> | I carry an umbrella. | with the clouds in my hair. | I swim like a chair. |
> | I live in a box | I run like a horse | I hang on the trees |
> | at the bottom of a ship. | and sing like a nightingale. | and people tap my face, |
> | At night | I collect stamps | rake my soil |
> | I play the trombone. | and coconuts. | and tell me jokes. |
> | What am I? | What am I? | What am I? |
> | | | |
> | Answer: | Answer: | Answer: |
> | I've forgotten. | I'm not sure. | I've really no idea. |

Acknowledgment

The poem in *Extra 2* is by Ian McMillan and Martyn Wiley. (See www.ian-mcmillan.co.uk)

3.7 The felt hat

Summary:	This funny rhyme introduces puns based on double meaning.
Level:	pre-intermediate – intermediate
Time:	5–10 minutes
Preparation:	none

Procedure

1 Before the lesson begins, put this rhyme on the board:

> Of all the felt I ever felt, I never felt a piece of felt which felt the same as that felt felt, when I first felt the felt of that felt hat.

Read the ryhme to the class, then explain that it is based on the two meanings of the word *felt*. Ask what these two meanings are.
Answer: a) the past tense of the verb *feel*; b) a thick soft material.

2 Students put down this rhyme in their notebook, then underline each occurrence of *felt*, using two different colour pens according to their meaning.
Answer: Of all the **felt** I ever <u>felt</u>, I never <u>felt</u> a piece of **felt** which <u>felt</u> the same as that **felt** <u>felt</u>, when I first <u>felt</u> the **felt** of that **felt** hat.

3 Divide the class into two teams. Explain that as you say the rhyme, the members of Team A have to stand up when they hear *felt* as a verb while the members of Team B stand up when they hear *felt* as a material. Now say the rhyme slowly, making sure that everybody has a bit of time to act as required.

Follow-up

Students may like the idea of creating silly rhymes like the ones above, exploiting the double meaning of words; they can do this as a homework assignment. In class, they take it in turns to read out their rhymes for the whole class to enjoy.

Extra

This rhyme goes along the same lines as the one above, except that it offers four roles: your Bob, our Bob, bob as the old British coin *shilling* and bob as a *punch*.

Your Bob owes our Bob a bob. If your Bob doesn't give our Bob the bob your Bob owes our Bob, our Bob will give your Bob a bob in the eye.

3.8 Fit for a pig

Summary:	These cheeky waiters pretend to misunderstand their customers.
Level:	intermediate – post-intermediate
Time:	10–15 minutes
Preparation:	Make a copy of Box 22 for each student.

Procedure

1 Give each student a copy of Box 22. As everyone reads the jokes, help with any unknown vocabulary, but don't clarify the ambiguities.

BOX 22
1 I can't find any chicken in the chicken soup!
   Well, you won't find any horse in the horseradish either!
2 Waiter, this food isn't fit for a pig!
   Hold on, I'll go and get some that is.
3 Do you serve crabs in this restaurant?
   We serve anyone, sir. Take a seat.

---

4 Waiter, I don't like all the flies in this dining room!
   Well, tell me which ones you don't like and I'll chase them
   out for you.
5 Excuse me, will my hamburger be long?
   No, sir, it'll be round.
6 Waiter, this soup tastes funny!
   Then, why aren't you laughing?

2 Divide the class into pairs. Read out the jokes one by one, with the
   pairs analysing the ambiguities and double meanings. Listen in and
   check whether their explanations are correct.

Answers:
1 One would not expect *horseradish* to contain horses, whereas chicken soup
  with no chicken in it is a letdown.
2 What the customer means is that not even a pig would eat such awful food.
  The cheeky waiter takes the customer to be a pig, who demands pig food.
3 The verb *serve* has two meanings: serve someone and serve something.
4 The customer is likely to have put the main sentence stress on *flies*, but the
  waiter pretends to have heard the word *all* stressed.
5 *Long* may refer to the duration of an activity (= take long) as well as to the
  shape of an object.
6 *Funny* has two meanings: strange and amusing.

3 Students try to translate the six dialogues in Box 22. After a few
   minutes, ask which ones are funny in their mother tongue, too. It is
   quite likely that most would not carry well into the students' mother
   tongue, as they are based on puns or *double entendre*.

Extra

It is usually the waiter who is snappy, but not always. In these two jokes,
the witty retort is made by the customer. Ask students to explain the two
jokes.

How did you find the steak, sir?
   Oh, I just moved the potato and there it was.
Waiter, do you have frog's legs?
   Yes, sir.
Good. Hop over the counter and get me a cheese sandwich.

Answers:
The first joke is based on the double meaning of *find*: *find* meaning *like* vs.
find in its literal sense.
In the second joke the waiter interprets the question literally (i.e. frog's legs as
a dish), which the customer turns into a metaphor (i.e. frog's legs meaning that
the waiter can leap like a frog).

3.9 Call me a taxi!

Summary: All the jokes here are based on the double meaning of words and phrases.
Level: pre-intermediate – intermediate
Time: 10–15 minutes
Preparation: Make a copy of Box 23 for each student.

Procedure

1 Before you distribute the handout, explain that in each dialogue ONE word is missing. For illustration, read out this classic without the last word and ask someone to complete it:

Call me a taxi, will you?

Certainly, sir. You're a ..... .

Answer: taxi.

Now give out the copies of Box 23 and provide help with any unknown vocabulary if necessary. Afterwards, everyone works on their own to find the missing word in the jokes.

BOX 23
1 Doctor! Doctor! I think I'm getting smaller.
   Well, you'll just have to learn to be a little ..... .
2 Have an accident?
   No thanks. I've just ..... one.
3 Do you believe in free speech?
   Of course I do.
   Good. Can I use your ..... ?
4 May I try on that dress in the ..... ?
   Well, we'd prefer it if you used the changing room.
5 Can you recommend anything for yellow teeth?
   How about a ..... tie?
6 Grandma and Grandpa are stuck at Victoria Station. There's been a bomb scare.
   Are they ..... ?
   No, bombs are really dangerous.

---

2 Provide the key and ask who has a different solution.
Answers: 1 patient, 2 had, 3 phone, 4 window, 5 brown, 6 safe.

3 Ask students who they think the characters in the jokes are. The taxi dialogue in the example probably involves a hotel guest and a bellboy. What about the rest?

Suggested answers:
1 doctor & patient, 2 two acquaintances, 3 two friends, 4 customer & shop assistant, 5 patient & dentist, 6 grandchildren.

Follow-up

Students practise these dialogues in pairs by placing themselves in the given situation. Remind them that intonation is the best vehicle for conveying emotions. After learning the dialogues by heart, pairs may volunteer to act them out.

3.10 And the winner is ...

Summary:	Ambiguous jokes are entered in a class competition.
Level:	pre-intermediate – intermediate
Time:	15–20 minutes
Preparation:	Make a copy of Box 24 for each student.

Procedure

1 Distribute the jokes in Box 24.

BOX 24

1 Return ticket, please!
     Where to?
   Back here, of course!
2 Keep that dog out of my house. It's full of fleas!
     Rex, keep out of that house. It's full of fleas!
3 I called you in because I want to discuss the question of retirement.
     But that's ridiculous. You're still a young man!
4 Excuse me, how do I get to the Albert Hall?
     Practise, my boy, practise!
5 They say you shouldn't say anything about the dead unless it's good.
     He's dead? Good!
6 Hello, is that Channel Airways? Can you tell me how long it takes to fly to Paris?
     Just a minute.
   Thank you very much.

---

7 Where do you live?
   Dimsby.
   I'm sorry.
   I said, 'Dimsby.'
   I heard what you said. I'm just sorry.
8 The police are looking for a man with one eye called Roger.
   What's the other eye called?
9 Did you wake up grumpy this morning?
   No, I let him sleep in.

While students read the jokes, provide help with any unfamiliar vocabulary. Write this chart on the board for students to copy in their notebook.

The most	Number of pun
funny	
morbid	
witty	
crazy	
cheeky	
silly	

2 Everybody chooses a joke for each of the adjectives, and writes its number in the appropriate column.
3 Students get into groups and discuss their choices. In the event of disagreement, the joke with the majority of votes will become the group's choice.
4 One spokesperson from each group comes to the board and jots down the number of the joke their group found the most funny, morbid, witty, etc. At the end, tot up the votes and announce the 'winner' for each category.

Follow-ups

1 If you have done 3.8 and 3.9 as well, you may wish to expand the list with the jokes in Box 22 and Box 23, so that they can also be included in the competition.
2 Jokes based on word-play and double meanings are notoriously difficult to translate into the mother tongue. Is it also difficult to do it the other way round? For homework, each student collects two or three

pun-like jokes in their mother tongue. In class, they share them in groups and decide which ones lend themselves easily to translation into English.

3.11 Oxymora

Summary: This activity is concerned with funny contradictions.
Level: pre-intermediate – post-intermediate
Time: 10–15 minutes
Preparation: For the *Extra*, make a copy of Box 25 for each student.

Procedure

1 Explain that an oxymoron is a phrase or sentence in which certain contradictory elements are used in conjunction; the self-contradiction often results in a poetic (e.g. bitter-sweet memories) or funny effect (e.g. I looked, and there he was, gone). (The Greek word *oxymoron* is itself an oxymoron, because its roots are of opposite meaning: *oxys* meaning *sharp* and *moron* meaning *foolish*.)

2 From the list below, choose the oxymora which suit the level of your class. Put those on the board one by one. Ask students about their meaning and the contradiction they contain.

> a plastic glass   civil war   a small fortune
> deafening silence   an industrial park   a sight unseen
> a working vacation   loyal opposition   an open secret
> old news   a fresh frozen pizza   a young fogey
> cruel kindness   light heavyweight   liquid gas
> accidentally on purpose

3 On the board, draw a vertical line with *very witty* at the top and *not at all witty* at the bottom. Students copy the line into their notebook and write each oxymoron on the line as they deem fit.

4 Students work in pairs and compare their charts.

Follow-up

Encourage students to recall further English oxymora. They may also like the idea of inventing some of their own: all they have to do is to play with apparently incompatible words. Can they also think of witty examples from their mother tongue?

Extra

Oxymora occur at sentence level too, as in the following examples. Hand out copies of these oxymora for everyone to enjoy:

BOX 25

1 If you don't receive this letter, please let me know.
2 I took so much medicine that I was sick a long time after I got well.
3 I'm oxymoronic even when I'm not.
4 I'm becoming more and more worried that there isn't enough anxiety in my life.
5 Always remember you're unique, just like everyone else.
6 I used to be indecisive; now I'm not so sure.
7 She gave life to a dead child.
8 The baby saw the light of day at night.
9 Where's the best place to go when you're dying?
   The living room.

3.12 Anagrams

Summary:	This activity focuses on anagrams – an ancient form of language play.
Level:	post-intermediate – advanced
Time:	10–15 minutes (in class)
Preparation:	none

Procedure

1 Explain that an anagram is the result of changes in the order of the letters of another word or phrase; it is particularly successful if the new coinage also relates to the original in meaning. Thus *silent* is an excellent anagram of *listen* not only because it consists of the same six letters, but also because the two words are conceptually related.
   (To illustrate the long-standing popularity of anagrams, history books record that Louis XIII of France appointed a Royal Anagrammatist. Incidentally, creating *anagrams* (= 8 letters) is great art, which in Latin reads as *ars magna* (= the same 8 letters!).)
2 Designing anagrams for names is a special form of art. Put this sentence on the board and ask what famous character lies hidden in it:

We all make his praise.

If nobody can guess, supply the person's initials: WS.

Answer: William Shakespeare. (By the way, Shakespeare used about 3,000 puns in his plays, often thrown into the most serious scenes.)

3 Turning names into anagrams is a great game. For homework, everyone should try to use the letters of their name to create one or several anagrams. Note that there are computer programs available to help the lazy. Short of such a program, students should try on their own. A smart student of mine, Andras Koltay, created nearly two dozen English and Hungarian anagrams out of his name. For illustration, you may decide to copy the best of his English products on the board. Provide help with the vocabulary if necessary:

Suggested answers:

Andras Koltay → Rat Lands Okay
Sad Royal Tank
Not a Lark's Day
Oakland Trays
Torn Yak Salad
A Yank Sold Tar

4 In class, everybody jots down the best anagram of their name on a piece of paper. Collect the pieces, then divide the class into pairs. Give each pair a piece of paper at random, and encourage them to guess the classmate's name behind the anagram. When a pair has successfully deciphered the name, give them another anagram. The activity finishes when you have run out of anagrams. The winner is the pair who have come up with the highest number of names.

Extra

If students like creating anagrams out of their names, you may set another piece of homework based on anagrams. Put these words and phrases on the board as cues. (Supply the second box for the more dedicated.) Everybody copies them and at home tries to find the suitable anagram behind each cue.

.....	→	the eyes (they see)
.....	→	it hears (this ear / hit ears)
.....	→	life's aim (families)
.....	→	ideals (ladies)
.....	→	enough? (one hug / huge no)
.....	→	real fun (funeral)
.....	→	twelve + one (eleven + two)
.....	→	wasn't here (the answer)

.....	→	serve a lot (elevators)
.....	→	Is pity love? (positively)
.....	→	devil in man (an evil mind)
.....	→	elegant man (a gentleman)
.....	→	careful first (traffic rules)
.....	→	models to sing (old-time songs)
.....	→	I'm not as active (vacation times)
.....	→	dirty room (dormitory)

In class, students in pairs check their solutions. At the end, provide the key.

Acknowledgment

I have used several examples from *Palindromes and Anagrams* by Bergerson (Dover Publications).

3.13 Palindromes

Summary: The focus of this activity is the palindrome – a sentence which reads the same way in both directions.
Level: intermediate – post-intermediate
Time: 10–15 minutes
Preparation: For *Extra 2*, make a copy of Box 26 for each student.

Procedure

1 Explain that a palindrome is a word that reads the same backwards and show how it works by listing a few palindromic words, such as *pop, dad, mum, nun, gag, wow, Bob, Anna, did* and *Madam*. Then put these short sentences on the board. (Underline the letter in the middle – if there is a middle letter).

Madam, I'm Adam.
Pull up if I pull up.
Too hot to hoot.

2 Put the first half of the palindromes below on the board for students to complete in their notebook. (Point out that any underlined letters are not repeated.) When you see that most students are ready, ask volunteers to come and write the missing parts on the board.

'Not New Yor<u>k</u>,' ..... (Roy went on.)
No, it is open o<u>n</u> ..... (one position.)
Must sell at ..... (tallest sum.)
He lived a<u>s</u> .....- (a devil, eh?)

3 For a change, the palindromes below have their opening half missing. After you have put them on the board, students do the same as in *Step 2*, but this time supplying the beginning of the palindromes.

(Was it a -)   ..... <u>r</u>at I saw?
(No, miss, i -)   ..... <u>t</u> is Simon.
(No lemon -)   ..... <u>s</u>, no melon.
(Step on -)   ..... no pets.

Extras

1 After Bob and Anna have taken an exam, they accuse each other of peeping. Can students turn this situation into a palindromic dialogue? Put the skeleton of the dialogue on the board:

Bob: '.....?'
Anna: '.....?'

If you find that too many students are at a loss, supply the key words *peep* and *did*.

Answer: Bob: 'Did Anna peep?' Anna: 'Did Bob?'

2 Ardent palidromists have written long poems which read the same backwards and forwards. In two special types of palindromes, it is the word and the line, respectively, which is taken as a unit. To illustrate such poems, here are a couple written by J.A. Lindon:

BOX 26

Ladies Long in the Tooth

Widows ate wives once?
That believe I well.
Shadows on Wives *pounce*,
Squat, where nearby crawl
    Others,
Eating, belching, eating ...
    Others
Crawl nearby where, squat,
Pounce wives on shadows ...
(Well, *I* believe that
Once wives ate widows!)

As I was passing...

As I was passing near the jail
I met a man, but hurried by.
His face was ghastly, grimly pale.
He had a gun. I wondered why
He had. A gun? I wondered ... why,
His face was *ghastly*! Grimly pale,
I met a man, but hurried by,
As I was passing near the jail.

Acknowledgment

I have used several examples from *Palindromes and Anagrams* by Bergerson (Dover Publications).

4   Proverbs and quotations

A proverb is a well-known statement that contains advice about life in general. A quotation is a sentence or a phrase from a book or speech others like to refer to. What the two have in common is wit, humour and brevity. Although few of them make you laugh wildly, you are bound to perceive their soft intellectual fabric. Personally, I am fond of both genres, because they have a universal appeal and, at the same time, are rich in cultural connotations.

On the other hand, I am aware that throwing in proverbs day in, day out may be too sophisticated whereas frequent references to the wisdom of the wise may be a sign of unoriginal thought. Winson Churchill was probably right in saying that 'For the uneducated people, it's really good to read collections of quotations.' You've been warned!

4.1 Mice and cats

Summary:	Folk tales and fables often end with a moral for people to learn from.
Level:	pre-intermediate – intermediate
Time:	10–15 minutes
Preparation:	For the *Variation*, make a copy of Box 27 for each student. For the *Extra*, make a copy of Box 28 for each student.

Procedure

1 Aesop's fables are popular all over the world. His fables often end with a moral in the form of a proverb. (Said to have been a slave on the Greek island of Samos, Aesop lived in the 6th century BC.) Read out the fable and check understanding. Read it out a second time if necessary.

> The mice wanted to protect themselves against the cat, but they
> didn't know how. So they decided to hold a meeting. Some mice
> said this, others said that. In the end, a young mouse spoke up
> boldly: 'Why don't we tie a bell to the cat's neck? This way we
> could all hear him coming round the corner, so we could hide.'
> 'Good idea! Hurray!' they all agreed. But then an old mouse
> said: 'All right, but who's going to tie the bell?' No one said a
> word.

2 Put up on the board six sayings which could well be the moral of this
fable. Explain any unfamiliar vocabulary items.

> 1 Actions speak louder than words.
> 2 Deeds, not words.
> 3 He who stares never dares.
> 4 Mice shall never be lions.
> 5 Easier said than done.
> 6 Belled kittens wear mittens.

The trouble with this list is that only three of the proverbs are real.
Which are real and which are fake? After students have worked on
their own, they discuss their guesses with a partner. Finally, check
with the whole class.
Answers: The real proverbs are 1, 2, and 5.

Variation

Should you have a more advanced group, you may prefer to do this
activity by showing the class the original Aesop fable, which is in fact a
rhyming verse. To make the task even more difficult, you could provide
a jumbled version of the poem.
    Make copies of the jumbled poem and give each student a copy. Their
job is to order the lines and reconstruct the original fable.

> **BOX 27**
>
>   line
> The mice held a meeting to decide   1
> That a bell should be tied
> How to protect themselves against the cat.
> Some said this and some said that,
> Till a young mouse spoke up boldly: 'I propose
> Unanimous applause. An old mouse rose
> To the cat's neck so he can be heard

Not one mouse volunteered a word.
And remarked: 'That's all very well,
But who's going to attach the bell?'
Coming round the corner, and we can hide.'

Once most students are ready, check the solution.

Answer: 1, 5, 2, 3, 4, 8, 6, 11, 9, 10, 7.

Extra

If the class like Aesop very much, let them read another fable simply for
pleasure.

BOX 28

The ant and the grasshopper

While a grasshopper was taking it easy in the shade one hot
summer's day, an ant struggled in the sun with a grain of rice that he
was carrying out to his nest. 'Hey, Mister Ant,' the grasshopper said.
'Why don't you take it easy, like me? You can work tomorrow.'

The ant paused. 'I'm saving up food now for the cold winter
ahead, and if you know what's good for you, you'll do the same,'
he said.

Three or four months later, winter came and it was very cold.
While the ant was snug in his nest, the starving grasshopper
shivered under a pile of dead leaves and wished that he'd paid
attention to the ant's advice.

What is the moral of the fable?

Answer: Never put off till tomorrow what you can do today.

4.2 Fake or real?

Summary:	This activity compares proverbs in English with those in the mother tongue.
Level:	pre-intermediate – intermediate
Time:	20–25 minutes (in class)
Preparation:	Have a pack of blank cards and some reusable adhesive or sticky tape ready. For the *Extra*, make a copy of Box 29 for each student.

Procedure

1 Proverbs tend to be truly international – many have their counterparts across languages. Does this apply to the students' culture, too? For homework, everybody collects five funny proverbs in their mother tongue. Using a bilingual dictionary, they look up their English equivalents. It is likely that while some of the proverbs have standard counterparts in English, others don't. While students jot down the 'real' ones as they find them in the dictionary, they translate the others to the best of their ability.

2 In class, give everyone five cards on which to copy the five proverbs they have selected. Students then take a bit of reusable adhesive or sticky tape, and attach their collection to the wall.

3 Everybody goes up to the wall with a black pencil. As they read the proverbs, they put a black cross next to any proverb which they think is fake, i.e. the translation of a proverb from the mother tongue which does not exist in English.

   Here are a couple of Hungarian proverbs which have no English counterparts and therefore have to be translated:
   Cheap meat has a thin broth (which means: Avoid cheap goods.)
   Don't wait for the roast pigeon to fly into your mouth (which means: Don't just sit back; get more proactive.)

4 Go through the proverbs marked with black crosses, and ask students who collected them whether they are really false. Start with the proverbs which have received the most crosses.

Extra

Hand out copies of this list of frequent English proverbs:

BOX 29

1 The early bird catches the worm.	7 One swallow doesn't make a summer.
2 He who pays the piper calls the tune.	8 Still waters run deep.
3 Don't count your chickens before they are hatched.	9 You scratch my back, and I'll scratch yours.
4 The proof of the pudding is in the eating.	10 Spare the rod and spoil the child.
5 Nothing ventured, nothing gained.	11 In for a penny, in for a pound.
6 A barking dog never bites.	12 You can't teach an old dog new tricks.

As a homework assignment invite students to (a) supply the mother-tongue counterpart of as many of the English proverbs as possible; and (b) translate those which don't seem to have an equivalent in the mother tongue.

In class, students compare their solutions in groups.

4.3 Anti-proverbs

Summary: Just one twist may turn a proverb into a witty sentence.
Level: post-intermediate – advanced
Time: 15–20 minutes
Preparation: Make a copy of Box 30 and Box 31 for each student.

Procedure

1 Write this proverb on the board:

> What's sauce for the goose is sauce for the gander.

Ask who can explain the meaning of this proverb. What is it in the students' mother tongue? Do adults often use it as a warning to children? In what situations, for example?

2 Students read the Thurber story in Box 30. Help them with any new words. (James Thurber (1894–1961) was not only a first-rate cartoonist, but certainly the most admired American humorist since Mark Twain. His works include stories, sketches, fables and essays, most of which appeared with his own illustrations in the *New Yorker* arts magazine.)

BOX 30

A little girl was given so many picture books on her seventh birthday that her father thought she should give one or two of her books to a little boy named Robert, who had dropped in by chance.

Now, taking books, or anything else, from a little girl is like taking candy from a baby, but the father of the little girl had his way and Robert got two of her books. 'After all, that leaves you with nine,' said the father.

A few weeks later, the father went to his library to look up a word in the Oxford English Dictionary, but couldn't find volume F–G. Then he discovered that three others were missing, too. He launched a search, and soon learned what had become of the four missing volumes.

'A man came to the door this morning,' said the daughter, 'and he didn't know how to get from here to Torrington. He was a nice man, much nicer than Robert, so I gave him four of your books. After all, there are thirteen volumes in the Oxford English Dictionary, and that leaves you nine.'

© Cambridge University Press 2002

75

After students have read the story, tell them that Thurber often finished his stories with a moral. Ask whether they think the proverb 'What's sauce for the goose is sauce for the gander' would suit the situation described. Although it might well do, Thurber changed the original proverb like this: 'What's sauce for the gosling is not sauce for the gander.' Does Thurber's change make sense? Discuss the meaning with the class.

3 A colleague of mine, Anna Litovkina, would call the type of proverbs Thurber created 'anti-proverbs'. Here are a few examples from her collection. Give everybody a copy of the list in Box 31. The real proverbs are in capital letters whereas the anti-proverbs are in small letters. Some vocabulary items may need explaining.

BOX 31

1　A BARKING DOG NEVER BITES.
　　A barking dog never bites, but a lot of dogs don't know this proverb.
2　WHEN IN DOUBT, LEAVE IT OUT.
　　When in doubt, say no. (a parent's advice)
3　THE BEST THINGS IN LIFE ARE FREE.
　　The best things in life are for a fee.
4　MARRIAGES ARE MADE IN HEAVEN.
　　Marriages are made in heaven knows what state of mind.
5　IGNORANCE IS BLISS.
　　If ignorance is bliss, why aren't more people happy?
6　AN APPLE A DAY KEEPS THE DOCTOR AWAY.
　　An onion a day keeps everybody away.
7　REVENGE IS SWEET.
　　Revenge is sweet, but not when you're the victim.
8　IF AT FIRST YOU DON'T SUCCEED, TRY AGAIN.
　　If at first you don't succeed, try reading the instructions.
9　A FRIEND IN NEED IS A FRIEND INDEED.
　　A friend in need is a friend to avoid.
10　A BIRD IN THE HAND IS WORTH TWO IN THE BUSH.
　　A bird in the hand is bad table manners.
　　A hair on the head is worth two in the brush.

Which of the anti-proverbs do students find the wittiest? Take a vote.

Follow-ups

1 Everybody should illustrate at least one of the anti-proverbs in Box 31 with a funny situation. They shouldn't write out their story in

full – notes will do fine. In groups, students take it in turns to tell each other their story, with the other members trying to identify the appropriate anti-proverb.

2 Students may enjoy creating anti-proverbs of their own or indeed nonsense proverbs which are not derivations of real ones. Another sample of anti-proverbs produced by Anna's class is based on 'The early bird catches the worm'.

> An early bird gets tired early.
> The early bird catches the cold.
> The early bird catches the worm. But the early worm feeds the bird!
> The early bird is a real nuisance when you want to sleep.
> The early bird suffers from insomnia.
> The early worm will be caught by a bird.

Acknowledgment

The story in Box 30 is a slightly adapted version of a Thurber fable from *Further Fables for Our Time* (Simon & Schuster). The anti-proverbs in Box 31 and *Follow-up 2* are from Litovkina's *A Proverb a Day Keeps Boredom Away* (Pécs-Szekszárd: IPF-Könyvek).

4.4 Hidden proverbs

Summary:	This activity demonstrates how concise proverbs usually are.
Level:	intermediate – post-intermediate
Time:	10–15 minutes
Preparation:	Make a copy of Box 32 for each student.

Procedure

1 All the sentences in Box 32 have been diluted. In other words, in each of them there is a proverb hidden among redundant words. The number in brackets refers to the number of words the proverb consists of. To give an example, write this sentence on the board:

> I have read no bad news in today's paper, which in itself is pretty good news. (5)

Laughing Matters

Now ask which proverb lies hidden in the sentence. Any guesses? Underline the words which make up the original proverb:

I have read <u>no</u> bad <u>news</u> in today's paper, which in itself <u>is</u> pretty <u>good</u> <u>news</u>.

2 Give everybody a copy of Box 32. Help with any unfamiliar vocabulary if necessary.

BOX 32

1 I suggest you think twice (or more) before you open your mouth to speak, or else you might get yourself in trouble. (5)
2 People often say that bedroom walls have eyes to see and ears to hear. (3)
3 It takes two people to dance tango, at least three to sing in a choir and at least four to make an orchestra. (5)
4 Girls will always be girls just as boys will be boys, so what's the difference? (4)
5 It's easy to come and easy to go when one has plenty of money. (4)
6 Men's love is said to be blind whereas women's love is deaf and dumb. (3)
7 It's much better if you arrive late than if you never arrive at all. (4)
8 Those who have cold hands usually – but not always – have a warm heart as well. (4)

© Cambridge University Press 2002

In pairs, students underline the words which they think made up the proverb. Afterwards, they share their suggestions with the whole class. Can they also explain the meaning of the proverbs or paraphrase them?

Answers:
1 Think twice before you speak.
2 Walls have ears.
3 It takes two to tango.
4 Boys will be boys.
5 Easy come, easy go.
6 Love is blind.
7 Better late than never.
8 Cold hands, warm heart.

Follow-up

In groups, students take it in turns to choose a proverb from Box 32 and make up a simple story to illustrate it. Are the situations clear enough for the others to guess the underlying proverb?

78

Extras

1 Give each student one proverb from the list below. Their homework assignment is to expand their proverb into a long sentence. In class, students take it in turns to write their sentence on the board, indicating in brackets the number of words the hidden proverb contains. The others make guesses.

Silence is golden.	Bad luck comes in threes.
Honesty is the best policy.	Haste makes waste.
Experience is the best teacher.	Look before you leap.
There's no place like home.	Charity begins at home.
Once bitten, twice shy.	If you snooze, you lose.
Many hands make light work.	Business is business.
All roads lead to Rome.	Money doesn't grow on trees.
Like father, like son.	Paddle your own canoe.
Nothing ventured, nothing gained.	Talk is cheap.
The past is past.	Still waters run deep.

2 The idea of hidden proverbs may be turned into a game. One person is sent out of the classroom, while the others choose a proverb. When the student returns to the classroom, she/he asks someone in the class a question. The person asked gives a one-sentence answer which must include the first word of the proverb. Now the student asks another question. In providing a simple answer, this second person must use the second word of the proverb – and so on, until all the constituent words of the proverb have been used. Can the student guess the proverb?

Acknowledgment

The idea in the second extra is from Augarde's *A to Z of Word Games* (Oxford University Press).

4.5 Quotes on books

Summary:	Quotation dictionaries abound in references to books, reading and writing.
Level:	intermediate – post-intermediate
Time:	10–15 minutes
Preparation:	Make a copy of Box 33 for each student.

Procedure

1 Distribute the quotations in Box 33. Help with any language difficulties.

BOX 33

1 There are three rules for writing a novel. Unfortunately, no one knows what they are. (Somerset Maugham)
2 I took a course in speed reading and was able to read War and Peace in twenty minutes – it's about Russia. (Woody Allen)
3 The man who doesn't read good books has no advantage over the man who can't read them. (Mark Twain)
4 All good books are alike in that they are truer than if they had really happened. (Ernest Hemingway)
5 Some books are undeservedly forgotten; none are undeservedly remembered. (W.H. Auden)
6 Education has produced a vast population able to read but unable to distinguish what is worth reading. (G.M. Trevelyan)
7 It took me fifteen years to discover I had no talent for writing, but I couldn't give it up because by that time I was too famous. (Robert Benchley)

After students have read the quotations, ask what they think is the common element in all seven of them.

Answer: They are all related to reading, writing and books.

2 Take a vote to find out which quote students like best. Those with the same favourite should join together to form a group. As they are discussing the meaning of their favourite quotation, they should give reasons why they think it is witty.

Follow-up

For homework, students may like to look up information about the author of their favourite quote. Back in class, those who have worked on the same source exchange information.

4.6 Pair us up!

Summary:	The aim of this game is to match cards.
Level:	post-intermediate – advanced
Time:	20–25 minutes
Preparation:	Make a copy of Box 34. (If there are more than 16 students in the class, you will need to have extra copies.) Cut up the quotations so that there is one for each student. Have some reusable adhesive or sticky tape at the ready.

Procedure

BOX 34
1 If something you say doesn't offend someone, then you're not saying anything. (Terence Trent D'Arby)
2 Old age isn't so bad when you consider the alternative. (Maurice Chevalier)
3 So little time and so little to do. (Oscar Levant)
4 I like life. It's something to do. (Ronnie Shakes)
5 The man who views the world at 50 the same as he did at 20 has wasted 30 years of his life. (Muhammed Ali)
6 Every time I paint a portrait I lose a friend. (J.S. Sargent)
7 Slang is a language that rolls up its sleeves, spits on its hands and goes to work. (Carl Sandburg)
8 How can I take an interest in my work if I don't like it? (artist Francis Bacon)
9 'Hello,' he lied. (Don Carpenter, quoting a salesman)
10 I found there was only one way to look thin – hang out with fat people. (Rodney Dangerfield)
11 I intend to live forever – so far, so good. (Anon.)
12 Let's not complicate our relationship by trying to communicate with each other. (Ashleigh Brilliant)
13 Imprisoned in every fat man a thin man is wildly signalling to be let out. (Cyril Connolly)
14 If you tell the truth, you don't have to remember anything. (Mark Twain)
15 England and America are two countries divided by a common language. (G.B. Shaw)
16 Drama is life with the dull bits left out. (Alfred Hitchcock)

1 Give each student a card to read. Explain that each card can be matched with one other which is broadly about the same theme. Get across the meaning of any unfamiliar words if requested. Students stand up and find the partner with the corresponding card. When the milling is over, each pair should justify why their two cards belong together.
   Answers:
   1 & 12 (communication), 2 & 5 (age), 3 & 16 (boredom), 4 & 11 (life),
   6 & 8 (art), 7 & 15 (language), 9 & 14 (lying), 10 & 13 (size).
2 Choose some space on the classroom walls for a display of quotations. Each pair goes up to this space and sticks their two cards next to each other.
3 Everybody walks around the classroom and reads all the quotations. If in doubt about the meaning of words or messages, they should contact the 'owners' of the quotations.

Follow-up

Challenge students to offer other arrangements of the cards. (For example: 7 and 8 may be considered to be related, because both of them are about work.)

4.7 Twisted quotes

Summary:	The humour of the quotations may stem from unexpected twists.
Level:	intermediate – post-intermediate
Time:	25–30 minutes
Preparation:	Make a copy of Box 35 for each student.

Procedure

1 Give everybody a copy of the quotes in Box 35. Help with any new vocabulary.

BOX 35
1 Stay with me; I want to be alone. (Joey Adams)
2 Oh, isn't life a terrible thing, thank God! (Dylan Thomas)
3 I'm not young enough to know everything. (Sir James Barrie)
4 A terrible thing happened again last night – nothing. (Phyllis Diller)
5 Excuse the mess but we live here. (Roseanne Sez)
---

6 My interest is in the future because I'm going to spend the rest of my life there. (C.F. Kettering)

7 The situation is hopeless but not serious. (O.J. Flanagan)

8 If my film makes one more person miserable, I've done my job. (Woody Allen)

9 Hard work pays off in the future – laziness pays off now. (Anon.)

10 Somebody is boring me; I think it's me. (Dylan Thomas)

Ask what all these quotes have in common.

Suggested answer: All end in a way contrary to expectation.

2 To illustrate the twists, ask the class what they find odd about the first quotation.

Suggested answer:

If someone says 'Stay with me', then they are likely to add '(because) I don't want to be alone'. After all, nobody would ask their partner to stay with them unless they enjoyed their company, would they?

Can students in pairs identify the twists in the other quotations as well? What would the sentences in Box 35 be like in normal situations? In pairs, students write down their suggestions.

Possible answers:

2 Oh, isn't life a wonderful thing, thank God!

3 I'm not old enough to know everything.

4 A terrible thing happened again last night – my house was broken into.

5 Excuse the mess but I haven't had time to tidy up.

6 My interest is in the future because there are so many interesting things awaiting me.

7 The situation is serious but not hopeless.

8 If my film makes one more person happy, I've done my job.

9 Hard work pays off in the future – laziness never pays off.

10 Somebody is boring me; I think it's my wife.

Variation

Change the order of steps. That is to say, give the 'normal' sentences as cues, leaving it up to the students to come up with witty paraphrases. Provide the first sentence as an example. Start with 'Stay with me; I don't want to be alone', hoping that somebody will suggest 'Stay with me; I want to be alone.' Needless to say, the task is much trickier this way!

4.8 Ham and eggs

Summary: This activity illustrates the absurd in quotations.
Level: pre-intermediate – intermediate
Time: 10–15 minutes
Preparation: none

Procedure

1 Put on the board this quote by the American poet Carl Sandburg:

> If we had a little ham, we could have some ham and eggs if we had some eggs.

What makes this sentence so odd? Students discuss the question in groups.

Possible answers:
It looks odd that a sentence begins with an 'if-clause', is followed by the main clause, only to finish with another 'if-clause'.

2 For homework, students create sentences on the basis of the strange pattern above. You may give a few examples as triggers:
   • If there were some boys in the class, it would be a mixed class if there were a few girls.
   • If it was morning, I would get up if I had gone to sleep last night.
   • If you played the piano, we could perform a sonata if I played the violin.

Extras

1 Write this on the board:

> There is one thing ... , namely that we can have nothing ... , therefore it is not ... that we can have nothing ... .

The same word is missing four times in this quotation by the English writer Samuel Butler. What is it?
Answer: certain.

2 Write this quote by the American comedian Ashleigh Brilliant on the board. Two adjectives with opposite meanings are missing. What are they?

> It's all very ... , or else it's all very ... , or perhaps neither, or both.

Answer: simple and complex.

4.9 Go to the polls

Summary: Students vote for the best quotation in each
             category.
Level: pre-intermediate – advanced
Time: 15–20 minutes
Preparation: Make a copy of Box 36a, Box 36b or Box 36c for each
             group of students, depending on the level of the
             class. Bring to class one sheet of poster paper, a few
             markers and some reusable adhesive or sticky tape.

Procedure

1 Distribute the quotes in Box 36a, Box 36b or Box 36c. You might like
   to add further quotations from Boxes 33 and 34. While students read
   the quotes and discuss their meaning in groups, help with any
   language difficulties.

BOX 36a pre-intermediate
1 No one is so ugly as their passport photo. (Arthur Bloch)
2 Work is much more fun than fun. (Noel Coward)
3 The future is much like the present, only longer. (Dan Quisen-
   berry)
4 I don't want to talk grammar. I want to talk like a lady. (G.B.
   Shaw)
5 I keep reading between the lies. (Goodman Ace)
6 I think you always feel braver in another language. (Anita
   Brookner)
7 Food is an important part of a balanced diet. (Fran Lebowitz)
8 Men and women, women and men. It will never work. (Erica
   Jong)

BOX 36b intermediate
1 Everything is funny as long as it's happening to someone else.
   (Will Rogers)
2 I am a believer in punctuality though it makes me very lonely.
   (E.V. Lucas)
3 I recently turned 60. Practically a third of my life is over.
   (Woody Allen)
4 My only hobby is laziness, which naturally rules out all the
   others. (Gianni Nazzano)

---

5 Seeing is deceiving; it's eating that's believing. (James Thurber)
6 Why do you call it rush hour when nothing moves? (Robin Williams)
7 At fifty, everyone has the face he deserves. (George Orwell)
8 Success always occurs in private and failure in full view. (Anon.)

BOX 36c advanced
1 The first half of our life is ruined by our parents and the second half by our children. (Clarence Darrow)
2 Marriage is a wonderful invention; but then again, so is a bicycle repair kit. (Billy Connolly)
3 Fate tried to conceal him by naming him Smith. (O.W. Holmes)
4 It's a sobering fact that when Mozart was my age, he had been dead for two years. (Tom Lehrer)
5 It's never too late to become the person you might have been. (T.S. Eliot)
6 One of the symptoms of approaching nervous breakdown is the belief that one's work is terribly important. (Bertrand Russell)
7 A genius! For thirty-seven years I've practised fourteen hours a day and now they call me a genius! (violinist Pablo Sarasate)
8 Unless you move, the place where you are is the place you will always be. (Ashleigh Brilliant)

2 Write the title 'Quotations' on the poster paper, then write these category labels one below the other, leaving some space between the lines:

The most
  witty
  wise
  happy
  cynical
  sad
  weird

Stick the poster on the wall. Now students have to choose one quotation for each of the categories above; the same quote may be chosen for several categories. Everybody stands up and writes the number of their choice next to the appropriate category on the poster.

3 When everyone has written up the number of their favourite quote, six students come to the poster, each taking responsibility for one category. They check which number has occurred most frequently for the six categories and read out the winning quotation for each.

Follow-up

The verdict may be queried! Anyone who has reservations about any of the winning quotes may argue against them and suggest others instead. Those in support of the winners should forward counter-arguments. The debate ends when the opponents' views are reconciled.

4.10 Graffiti artists at work

Summary:	Students create graffiti art.
Level:	pre-intermediate – intermediate
Time:	20–25 minutes
Preparation:	Make a copy of Box 37 for each student. Have a large sheet of poster paper, several coloured markers and some reusable adhesive or sticky tape available.

Procedure

1 Ask students what graffiti is and whether they appreciate this form of 'low culture'. Why/not? (Graffiti are words and pictures written or drawn on walls, posters, buildings, trains, etc. They are often rude, funny, or political. In many countries, graffiti artists are punished if caught defacing public places.)
2 Give each student a copy of Box 37. Help with any unfamiliar vocabulary.

BOX 37

1 We are the people our parents warned us about
2 The decision is maybe and that's final
3 Owing to lack of interest tomorrow has been cancelled
4 Gone for breakfast – if I'm not here by 12.30 gone for lunch as well
5 I used to be conceited but now I'm absolutely perfect
6 I used to use clichés all the time but now I avoid them like the plague
7 I've told you for the fifty-thousandth time – stop exaggerating
8 I muddled get my words sometimes up

---

9 Down with gravity
10 Down with the lift
11 Where do words go when you rub them out?
12 Where does the white go when the snow melts?
13 I like writing on walls – this is a door, you fool
14 Please don't write on walls – you want maybe we should type?
15 When God gave brains I thought he said trains so I asked for a small slow one

After reading the graffiti in Box 37, students choose the one they like best. Those who have chosen the same piece of graffiti should form a group.

3 In groups, students make a sketch of their favourite graffiti in the style of a graffiti artist. Their sketch should not be bigger than the size of a notebook.

4 After students have finished drawing, place the large poster paper in the middle of the floor. Everybody should come and stick their sketch on the poster paper to make a collage. Display the poster.

Follow-ups

1 The collage from *Step 4* should stay on the wall for a week or two. Meanwhile, students ask other teachers and students from other classes to look at the poster and say what they think of it. They systematically collect the interview data. When enough data have been collected, students report the different opinions back to the class.

2 Graffiti has become part of present-day urban culture. It is quite likely that your students also see anonymous scrawls in public places – and in English, too! Another rich source of graffiti humour is the Internet. How about collecting humorous pieces (but only decent ones)? Give everybody the chance to quote the funniest ones to the whole class.

4.11 Urban philosophers

Summary:	Deep down we are all philosophers, aren't we? …
Level:	pre-intermediate – intermediate
Time:	10–15 minutes
Preparation:	Make a copy for each student (or a transparency) of Box 38. Have a large sheet of poster paper and a few markers available.

Procedure

1 Distribute copies of Box 38.

BOX 38

Students now identify the characteristic feature these graffiti have in common.

Suggested answer: They all have a philosophical message to convey.

2 Write this graffiti in the middle of the poster paper, then read it out in a mock-serious, philosophical tone:

> Home is where television is

Students now change the order of the five words in the piece of graffiti. Alternatively, they may omit one or two words, but are not allowed to add new ones. They create sentences and draw them on the poster around the original in the style of graffiti artists.

Possible answers:
Where is television? Where is home? Is home television? Home is television. Is television home? Television is home. Where television is is home. Television is where home is. etc.

3 A few of the resulting sentences in *Step 2* sound so odd as to take on meaning only if they are pronounced in an affected manner. Students take it in turns to read out the sentences as 'philosophers'.

Follow-up

Some students may be keen to produce 'philosophical' graffiti at home. In class, they read them out. The more bombastic the graffiti sounds, the better!

4.12 Deadly quotations

Summary:	All collections of quotations are full of witty sayings on death. (But bear in mind that death may be a sensitive subject to some of your students.)
Level:	pre-intermediate – intermediate
Time:	10–15 minutes
Preparation:	Make a copy of Box 39 for each student. For the *Extra*, make a copy of Box 40 for each student.

Procedure

1   Many people say that there is nothing funny about death: 'Death is the last thing that makes people laugh'. Nonsense! If this were true, there would not be so many humorous quotations about passing away. Be that as it may, the quotes in Box 39 offer a sample of my favourites. After you have given a copy to each student, explain the meaning of the two key words: *funeral* and *obituary*.

BOX 39

1   Don't send funny greetings cards on birthdays or at Christmas. Save them for funerals when their cheery effect is needed. (P.J. O'Rourke)

2   Tragedy is when I cut my finger. Comedy is when you fall down an open hole in the street and die. (Mel Brooks)

3   Die, my dear doctor? That's the last thing I shall do. (Lord Palmerston)

4   Either they go, or I do. (Oscar Wilde, of his new bedroom curtains, as he lay dying)

5   If you live to the age of 100, you have made it because very few people die past the age of 100. (George Burns)

6   I always wait for 'The Times' each morning. I look at the obituary column, and if I'm not in it, I go to work. (A.E. Matthews)

7   Whenever a friend succeeds, a little something in me dies. (Gore Vidal)

---

8 It's not that I'm afraid to die. I just don't want to be there
when it happens. (Woody Allen)
9 If you don't go to people's funerals, they won't come to
yours. (Anon.)
10 He died a natural death. He was hit by a car. (Anon.)
11 Jog and die healthier. (Graffiti)
12 For those who think life's a joke, consider the punch line.
(Graffiti)
13 Death is nature's way of telling you to slow down. (Graffiti)

2 After students have browsed through the quotations, in groups they
discuss their meaning. They then choose three quotes which they find
the wittiest, and put them in order of priority.
3 Draw three columns on the board and write *Gold*, *Silver* and *Bronze*
at the top of each column. One spokesperson from each group comes
to the board and writes the number of their favourite quote in the
appropriate column. Award 3 points for a vote in the Gold, 2 in the
Silver, and 1 in the Bronze column. Add up the scores and announce
the results. Encourage students to applaud or boo, according to
whether or not the final scores have met with their approval.

Extra

Here are a few more jokes for students to work with. Which of the jokes
do students like the best? And the least? Why?

BOX 40
1 Granny, have you lived here all your life?
   Not yet, son, not yet.
2 Do you love me?
   Of course I do. I'd die for you.
   You always say that but you never do it.
3 Henrik Ibsen spent the last six years of his life, unable to write,
   staring out of his window in Christiania.
   One day when a nurse announced that he was feeling better,
   the grumpy old writer said: 'On the contrary!' – and died.
4 Two old ladies met in the park. After inquiring about each other's
   health, the topic of conversation turned to their respective husbands.
   'Oh,' said one. 'Harry died last week. He went out to the
   garden to dig up a cabbage for dinner, had a heart attack and
   dropped dead in the middle of the vegetable patch.'
   'Oh, my,' said the other. 'What did you do?'
   'I opened a can of peas instead.'

4.13 Epitaphs

Summary:	Oddly enough, epitaphs may be a source of fun as well.
Level:	intermediate – post-intermediate
Time:	25–30 minutes
Preparation:	Make an enlarged copy (or transparency) of Box 41 and a copy of Box 42 for each student.

Procedure

1 Teach the meaning of *tombstone* and *epitaph* with this cartoon:

BOX 41

ROWLAND BOWK
BORN 1932
STILL ALIVE

© Cambridge University Press 2002

Some people like walking in cemeteries and reading epitaphs on tombstones. Is there anyone in the class who enjoys this occupation? Isn't it a bit morbid? In fact, there are collections of witty epitaphs to show that humour and tragedy get on with each other quite well.

2 Distribute copies of the epitaphs in Box 42. Help with any unfamiliar vocabulary as students are reading the epitaphs.

BOX 42

1 Excuse my dust. *(Dorothy Parker's proposed epitaph)*
2 I told you I was sick!
3 By and by
   God caught his eye. *(epitaph for a waiter)*
4 Rest in Peas. *(on the tombstone of a farmer whose dying wish was to be buried in his vegetable garden)*
5 Life is a jest, and all things show it;
   I thought so once, now I know it.
6 He died in peace
   His wife died first.
7 Born 1903 – Died 1942
   Looked up the elevator shaft to see if
   the car was on the way down. It was.
8 Grim Death took me without a warning,
   I was well at night
   And dead at nine in the morning.
9 Sir John Strange
   Here lies an honest lawyer,
   And that is Strange.
10 Here lies Johnny Yeast
   Pardon me
   For not rising.
11 Here lies the body of Jonathan Blake
   Stepped on the gas pedal
   Instead of the brake.
12 Here lies Ezekiel Aikle
   Age 102
   The good die young.

3 Once students have grasped the witty messages, they select one epitaph. Challenge them to develop it into a short story written, oddly enough, by the deceased person. For example, 'I told you I was sick!' could begin like this:

> I was called the hypochondriac in the family. Whenever I sneezed – which happened very frequently – my wife would always say: 'Listen, children! Dad's sick again!' When I said it was no laughing matter, my wife said with pretend strictness, 'Into bed with you!', with the children chuckling ...

4 Volunteers take it in turns to read out their story. As soon as someone has recognised which epitaph a story is based on, they shout out their guess. The volunteer then continues with her/his story to the end.

Follow-up

Write these superlatives on the board:

Number of epitaph

The funniest
The saddest
The cruellest
The most cynical
The most moving

Challenge everybody to choose one epitaph for each category and get ready to justify their choices in groups.

Extra

Tell this joke and check whether students have understood it.

I heard of a funeral director with a sense of humour. He signs all his correspondence: 'Yours eventually'.

Answer:
'Yours sincerely' would be the normal ending, whereas 'Yours eventually' refers to the finality of life.

4.14 The House of Wisdom

Summary:	Students decorate the classroom wall with proverbs, quotations and graffiti.
Level:	beginner – pre-intermediate
Time:	1–2 minutes (each time)
Preparation:	Have some reusable adhesive or sticky tape ready at all times.

Procedure

1 If students are fond of the wisdom inherent in proverbs, quotes, graffiti and epitaphs, they may like to expand their collection with new items throughout the school year. Explain that anybody at any time may bring in a wise saying and stick it on the wall. Note, however, that each item must be prepared in an artistic fashion – no ugly scrap with a scribble is allowed for display!

2 At the beginning of the lesson, anyone may draw attention to the new saying – except for the artist or whoever caught the artist in the act of mounting her/his exhibit. The artist is then asked to read out the sentence she/he has chosen. Those who like this saying should give her/him a big hand.

Follow-up

This is a funny memory-jogging exercise. When a good number of sayings have already gone up on the walls, someone may shout out the beginning (or the end) of a sentence for a classmate to finish. Obviously, the person who created that particular saying is not allowed to supply the solution.

5 Poems and songs

Why did you include a section on poems and songs, I hear you ask. The answer is simple: In my experience, we all love poems and songs. In our mother tongue, yes, but do we like poems and songs in English, too? Do we know English well enough to appreciate and enjoy them? Well, it depends. Children's rhymes are easy to catch and, once caught, they will stick in our minds for good. The same goes for pop songs. Adult poems are a bit trickier, but if they are well presented, they can give a great deal of satisfaction. I believe poems and songs steeped in humour are particularly suitable for teaching English. But this equally applies to all the other sections in this book too, doesn't it? To paraphrase the Latin saying, *Amor omnia vincit.* (Love conquers all.) *Humour omnia vincit...* I'm sorry. I hope that the poems and songs in this unit will be funnier than this joke.

5.1 Jabberwocky

Summary:	Lewis Carroll's famous poem leads students into the realm of nonsense.
Level:	pre-intermediate – intermediate
Time:	5–10 minutes
Preparation:	For *Follow-up 1*, make a copy of Box 43 for each student.

Procedure

1 Tell the class that they are going to listen to a famous poem from the 19th century, written by Lewis Carroll. (Lewis Carroll (1832–1898), born Charles Lutwidge Dodgson, was a mathematician at Oxford University. His most famous books are 'Alice's Adventures in Wonderland' and 'Through the Looking-Glass', enjoyed by both children and adults throughout the world.) Warn students that the poem is full of words that they do not know. Don't reveal yet that most of the words are in fact meaningless! The task merely consists of guessing what the poem is all about. Now read out the poem.

BOX 43

'Twas brillig, and the slithy toves
Did gyre and gimble in the wabe:
All mimsy were the borogoves,
And the mome raths outgrabe.

'Beware the Jabberwock, my son!
The jaws that bite, the claws that catch!
Beware the Jubjub bird, and shun
The frumious Bandersnatch!'

He took his vorpal sword in hand:
Long time the manxome foe he sought
So rested he by the Tumtum tree,
And stood awhile in thought.

And, as in uffish thought he stood,
The Jabberwock, with eyes of flame,
Came whiffling through the tulgey wood,
And burbled as it came!

One, two! One, two! And through and through
The vorpal blade went snicker-snack!
He left it dead, and with its head
He went galumphing back.

'And has thou slain the Jabberwock?
Come to my arms, my beamish boy!
O frabjous day! Callooh! Callay!'
He chortled in his joy.

'Twas brillig, and the slithy toves
Did gyre and gimble in the wabe:
All mimsy were the borogoves,
And the mome raths outgrabe.

2 Students make guesses, justifying their choice by referring to the general tone of the poem, certain words, acting, or anything else.
3 Admit that this is a nonsense poem – there may well have been students who have discovered this already!

Variation

If you happen to teach a more advanced group, the list in the box on the next page may help students describe their impressions in *Step 2*. Put the adjectives on the board:

admiring   angry   comic   cynical   despairing   indifferent
ironic   jubilant   militant   respectful

Follow-ups

1 Hand out copies of Box 43 and give students time to read the poem.
2 The class may like to find out which are the nonsense words in the poem. After they have made their guesses, provide the solution.
   Answers:
   The nonsense words are:
   Verse 1 – brillig, slithy, toves, gyre, gimble, wabe, mimsy, borogoves, mome, raths, outgrabe.
   Verse 2 – Jabberwock, Jubjub, frumious, Bandersnatch.
   Verse 3 – vorpal, manxome, Tumtum.
   Verse 4 – uffish, whiffling, tulgey.
   Verse 5 – snicker-snack.
   Verse 6 – beamish, frabjous, Callooh!, Callay!

3 Encourage students to make guesses about the meaning of the 11 nonsense words in Verse 1: *brillig, slithy, toves, gyre, gimble, wabe, mimsy, borogoves, mome, raths, outgrabe.* After listening to the students' guesses for a few minutes, tell them that Alice in fact asked Humpty Dumpty about the meaning of the nonsense words in Verse 1 and she received the following answers:

brillig = four o'clock in the afternoon
slithy = active
tove = small animal, like a lizard
gyre = go round and round
gimble = make holes
wabe = grass-plot
mimsy = flimsy and miserable
borogove = a thin bird
mome = from home
rath = green pig
outgrabe (past tense of outgribe) = shout and whistle

Is there anyone who had several approximately correct guesses? Who succeeded in guessing the right parts of the words at least (nouns, verbs, adjectives, adverbs, etc.)?
4 Jabberwocky has been translated into many languages. Is there a translation in the students' mother tongue? If this is available, bring a

copy to class (or ask a volunteer to do so). Read out 'Jabberwocky' in translation (or ask one of the students to do it for you). How does the poem sound in comparison with the original? Which is more amusing?

5.2 In a dark dark wood

Summary:	This activity is aimed to enhance students' performing skills.
Level:	beginner – pre-intermediate
Time:	10–15 minutes
Preparation:	Make a copy for each student (or a transparency) of Box 44.

Procedure

1 Give each student a copy of Box 44.

> BOX 44
> In a dark dark wood
> There's a dark dark house.
> And in that dark dark house
> There's a dark dark room.
> And in that dark dark room
> There's a dark dark cupboard.
> And in that dark dark cupboard
> There's a dark dark shelf.
> And on that dark dark shelf
> There's a dark dark box.
> And in that dark dark box
> There's a GHOST!

Read out the rhyme in a scary way. Start out slowly and quietly, then gradually speed up and raise your voice; say 'ghost' at the top of your voice. Ask what makes the rhyme so spooky.

Suggested answer: Apart from the frightening scene, it is your delivery that makes it scary.

2 Read out the rhyme a second time and ask everyone to join in, imitating you as much as they can.

3 Now ask the class to read out the rhyme in chorus, with you producing an echo of some kind.
4 Divide the class into two teams of about equal size. Explain that Team A will say the rhyme in chorus, pausing briefly at the end of each line while Team B will play the 'echo', repeating the final word of each line. After a while, the two teams change roles.

Variation

Volunteers can draw the ghost that came out of the box at the end of the rhyme. They work on a large sheet of paper, and after cutting out the ghost, they paste it on a piece of cardboard. Others may like to bring a bedsheet to class to act as the ghost.

Acknowledgment

The echo idea comes from *The Inward Ear* by Maley and Duff (Cambridge University Press).

5.3 Old limericks – old people

Summary:	This activity presents three well-known limericks by Edward Lear.
Level:	intermediate – post-intermediate
Time:	10–15 minutes
Preparation:	Make a copy for each student (or a transparency) of Box 45. For the *Variation*, make a copy of Box 46 for each student.

Procedure

1 Tell the class that they are going to listen to three limericks while looking at three cartoons. Distribute the cartoons in Box 45. (Named after a city in Ireland, limericks are funny five-liners with a regular beat and a rhyme pattern. The three limericks in this activity were written by Edward Lear (1812–1888), the most famous author of limericks.)

© Cambridge University Press 2002

Read out the three limericks.

> 1 There was a young lady whose chin
> Resembled the point of a pin;
> So she had it made sharp,
> And purchased a harp,
> And played several tunes with her chin.
>
> 2 There was an old man who said: 'Hush!
> I perceive a young bird in this bush!'
> When they said: 'Is it small?'
> He replied: 'Not at all!
> It is four times as big as the bush.'
>
> 3 There was an old man who said: 'How
> Shall I flee from that horrible cow?
> I will sit on the stile,
> And continue to smile,
> Which may soften the heart of that cow.'

Ask which cartoon goes with which limerick.

Answers: A 3, B 1, C 2.

2 After you have pre-taught any unknown vocabulary, say the limericks yourself with students repeating them line by line. (N.B. 'Hush' and 'bush' do not rhyme when pronounced – they are rhymes only for the eyes.)

3 Recite the three limericks again a bit more slowly, but not so slow as to break the rhythm. This time, however, do not stop at the end of the line – students have to be just one word behind you, as if lip-reading.

Variation

In the box below, you find the same three limericks as above, but with the lines entangled. Give each student a copy. (N.B. You could do this activity before *Step 2*.)

BOX 46

There was a young lady whose chin (1.1)
When they said: 'Is it small?'
And continue to smile,
There was an old man who said: 'How (3.1)
He replied: 'Not at all!
And played several tunes with her chin.
I will sit on the stile,
So she had it made sharp,
I perceive a young bird in this bush!'
Which may soften the heart of that cow.'
Resembled the point of a pin;
It is four times as big as the bush.'
Shall I flee from that horrible cow?
There was an old man who said: 'Hush! (2.1)
And purchased a harp,

Students sort the lines into the correct order. The first line of each limerick has been supplied.

Follow-up

Encourage students to learn by heart the limerick they like best, and then present it to the class. Encourage them to do 'artistic' group presentations. That is to say, students who have learnt the same limerick should get into groups and decide who will say which line or part, when they will speak solo or in chorus, how fast or slow, loud or soft they will recite, etc. Incidentally, such artistic considerations may also apply to other activities in this section.

5.4 Witness reports

Summary:	Based on a limerick, students give eye-witness reports for journalists.
Level:	intermediate – post-intermediate
Time:	15–20 minutes
Preparation:	Make a copy of Box 47 for each student. For the *Variation*, make a copy of Box 48 for each student.

Procedure

1 Give everyone a copy of the limericks in Box 47, written by American poet Ogden Nash (1902–1971) (1) and British writer Frank Richards (1876–1971) (2):

BOX 47

1 A careless explorer named Blake
   Fell into a tropical lake.
   Said a fat alligator,
   A few minutes later:
   'Very nice, but I still prefer cake.'

2 Said a boastful young student from Hayes,
   As he entered the Hampton Court Maze:
   'There's nothing in it.
   I won't be a minute.'
   He's been missing for forty-one days.

© Cambridge University Press 2002

Pre-teach any unknown vocabulary. Read out the limericks, then ask students to choose the one they prefer.
2 Everybody prepares to tell the story described in one of the limericks, using their own words as if they had witnessed the accident. Ask them to adorn their story with funny details.
3 Students who have prepared reports on the same limerick form groups. Group members take it in turns to tell their version of the story. At the end, they identify the elements their stories have in common.

Follow-up

As a homework assignment, students write a newspaper article based on the limerick. In class, give students an opportunity for wider 'publication' of their articles. In other words, encourage them to read out their articles to the whole class. Alternatively, you may prefer to read all the articles in advance, choose the funniest ones and read only those out for entertainment.

Variation

It is worth doing this task *before* students have heard or read Ogden's limerick in Box 47. The limerick, consisting of the underlined words only, lies hidden in the newspaper article below. Can students reconstruct the five-liner in groups? Advise them to begin by finding the rhyming words. This is how the limerick begins: *A careless explorer ...*

BOX 48

Famous <u>Explorer</u> Dead

After the well-known explorer Jay <u>Blake</u> had not returned to the camp-site, his team-members went on <u>a</u> rescue mission. As they were walking beside <u>a</u> <u>tropical</u> <u>lake</u> <u>named</u> Knutnmga, they suddenly heard <u>a</u> strange sound. 'There he was,' <u>said</u> fellow-explorer James Whitney, 'a fifteen-foot <u>alligator</u>, staring at us. We were paralysed. <u>A</u> <u>few</u> <u>minutes</u> <u>later</u> the <u>fat</u> creature said in broken English: "You looking for friend, eh?" "Yes. Do you know where he is?" <u>I</u> asked. "Oh, <u>very</u> <u>nice</u> fella but <u>careless</u>." "<u>But</u> where is he, for God's sake?" "In me tummy. <u>Fell</u> <u>into</u> it, you know. <u>Still</u> <u>prefer</u> <u>cake</u> though ..."'

Acknowledgment

The limericks are from *The Penguin Book of Limericks* edited by Parrott (Penguin).

5.5 Two-way translations

Summary:	In a monolingual group, it is fun to translate a poem backwards and forwards.
Level:	post-intermediate – advanced
Time:	25–30 minutes
Preparation:	Make a copy of Box 49 for each pair of students. Cut up the limericks so that there is one for each student. For the *Extra*, make a copy of Box 50 for each pair of students. Again, cut up the limericks.

Procedure

1 Divide the class into two teams of equal size. Give each member of Team 1 a copy of one limerick and each member of Team 2 a copy of the other. Students should not show their limerick to anyone in the other team. As they read the limericks, help with any unknown words.

BOX 49

- >✂

There was a young fellow called Hall,
Who fell in the spring in the fall;
'Twould have been a sad thing,
Had he died in the spring,
But he didn't, he died in the fall.
  Anon.

- >✂

There was a young fellow of Perth,
Who was born on the day of his birth;
He was married, they say,
On his wife's wedding day,
And died when he quitted the earth.
  Anon.

---

2 Everybody translates their limerick into the mother tongue, makes a fair copy of their translation on a piece of paper, and then passes it on to a member of the other team.

Explain that translators are faced with two alternatives:

(a) They produce a literal translation; this will give their partner a better chance to approximate the original in *Step 3*.

(b) They produce a more artistic and therefore less precise translation; this will hinder their partner's work in *Step 3*, but is more likely to lead to funny English solutions.

3 Members of the other team turn the translations from the mother tongue back into English, trying to reproduce the AABBA rhyme pattern of limericks. Of course, they are not allowed to see the original limerick and can work only on the basis of the translation. On the other hand, if necessary, the person who produced the translation into the mother tongue may be asked for clarification. If you notice that certain students are running into difficulties, provide prompts.

4 The students who collaborated on this task pair up and check for discrepancies between their translation and the original version.

Extra

If students enjoyed doing the activity on the previous page, you may like to give them another two limericks for homework. To make things a bit easier for them, mention that the first limerick is based on a pun whereas the last line of the second one is unusually long.

BOX 50

There was a young girl, a sweet lamb,
Who smiled as she entered a tram.
   After she had embarked,
   The conductor remarked,
'Your fare.' And she said, 'Yes, I am.'

There was a young bard of Japan,
Whose limericks never would scan.
When told it was so,
He said: 'Yes, I know,
But I always try and get as many words into the last line as I possibly can.'

5.6 From verse to prose

Summary: Students translate a poem from the mother tongue into English.
Level: pre-intermediate – intermediate
Time: 10–15 minutes (in class)
Preparation: For the *Extra,* make a copy of Box 51 for each student.

Procedure

1 Choose a well-known poem in the students' mother tongue. Translate it into simple English prose. (If you don't share the students' mother tongue, ask a friend or colleague to help you with the rough translation.) For illustration, here is my translation of a poem written by a 19th century Hungarian poet:

> I went into the kitchen and lit my pipe. Better to say, I would have lit it if it had not already been alight. In fact, my pipe had nothing to do with the fact that I went into the kitchen. The reason why I entered was that I had spotted a pretty girl in there. etc.

Now read out your translation. As soon as somebody recognises the original poem, they should say the title aloud or quote it in the mother tongue – the discovery of the famous poem hidden in flat prose should lead to laughter!

2 At home, everybody thinks of a well-known poem and translates a couple of verses into English prose. To make recognition less easy, you may suggest translating verses from the middle or the end of the poem. Remind students to use a bilingual dictionary if necessary.

3 In class, students take it in turns to read out their translations. Meanwhile, the others quietly jot down the poets' names and the titles of the poems if they can. When everybody has had their turn, check the items one by one. Who has the highest number of correct guesses?

Extra

This activity is the reverse of the activity described above. Give out a copy of Box 51 to each student.

BOX 51
The Frog

What a wonderful bird the frog are
When he stand he sit almost;
When he hop he fly almost;
He ain't got no sense hardly;
He ain't got no tail hardly either.
When he sit he sit on what he ain't got almost.
  Anon.

As students read the poem on their own, they will discover that it is full of mistakes – help the class identify as many mistakes as possible. Afterwards, everybody should translate the poem into the mother tongue, using similar errors of both meaning and grammar.

5.7 Little Red Riding Hood

Summary:	This activity exploits a folk tale-turned-poem by Roald Dahl.
Level:	intermediate – post-intermediate
Time:	15–20 minutes
Preparation:	Make a copy of Box 52 for each student. Cut up the copies of the poem into three parts.

Procedure

1 Tell the class that they are going to read a poem written by Roald Dahl. (Roald Dahl's (1916–1990) parents were Norwegian, but he was born in Wales. He is famous for his bizarre short stories as well as his children's books. However, the poem 'Little Red Riding Hood and the Wolf' is no less striking than his stories.) Add that the poem is a paraphrase of the folk tale 'Little Red Riding Hood', and it actually begins in the middle of the tale. Give out the first part of the poem for everyone to read and help with any unknown vocabulary. So far, so good – the traditional storyline has not changed.

BOX 52

As soon as Wolf began to feel
That he would like a decent meal,
He went and knocked on Grandma's door.
When Grandma opened it, she saw
The sharp white teeth, the horrid grin,
And Wolfie said, 'May I come in?'
Poor Grandmamma was terrified,
'He's going to eat me up!' she cried.
And she was absolutely right.
He ate her up in one big bite.
But Grandmamma was small and tough,
And Wolfie wailed, 'That's not enough!
I haven't yet begun to feel
That I have had a decent meal!'
He ran around the kitchen yelping,
'I've *got* to have another helping!'
Then he added with a frightful leer,
'I'm therefore going to wait right here
Till Little Miss Red Riding Hood
Comes home from walking in the wood.'
He quickly put on Grandma's clothes,
(Of course he hadn't eaten those.)
He dressed himself in coat and hat.
He put on shoes and after that
He even brushed and curled his hair,
Then sat himself in Grandma's chair.
In came the little girl in red.
She stopped. She stared. And then she said,
'What great big ears you have, Grandma.'
'All the better to hear you with,' the Wolf replied.
'What great big eyes you have, Grandma,' said Little Red Riding Hood.
'All the better to see you with,' the Wolf replied.
He sat there watching her and smiled.
He thought, I'm going to eat this child.
Compared with her old Grandmamma
She's going to taste like caviare.

Then Little Red Riding Hood said, 'But Grandma,
what a lovely great big furry coat you have on.'
'That's wrong!' cried the Wolf. 'Have you forgotten
To tell me what BIG TEETH I've got?
Ah well, no matter what you say,
I'm going to eat you anyway.'
The small girl smiles. One eyelid flickers.
She whips a pistol from her knickers.
She aims it at the creature's head
And *bang bang bang*, she shoots him dead.

- ✂ - -

A few weeks later, in the wood,
I came across Miss Riding Hood.
But what a change! No cloak of red,
No silly hood upon her head.
She said, 'Hello, and do please note
My lovely furry WOLFSKIN COAT.'

2 Students work in groups and suggest how the story might continue. Can they think of an unexpected ending? While they are thinking, write these three sentences on the board:

> 1 Little Red Riding Hood produces a gun and shoots the Wolf dead.
> 2 She tells the Wolf a joke. It makes him laugh so much that he coughs up Grandma.
> 3 She tells him off for his macho behaviour. The Wolf slinks away in shame.

Ask students which of the three alternatives comes closest to their version. If their idea is even more far-fetched than those on the board, let them share it with the class.

3 Now give out the second part of the poem and again provide help with any unfamiliar words. After students have read the second part, ask if anybody has come up with the same idea as Dahl in *Step 2*.

4 The story could well end at this point, but the poet introduces yet another twist. What can it be? Students make guesses. Whose idea is the most original? Now give out the end of the poem and explain the meaning of any new words. Do students like the witty ending?

Variation

In a beginners' class, you could start by telling students that they are going to listen to a poem, without admitting that it is a paraphrase of

'Little Red Riding Hood'. Their job is simply to stand up the moment they think they have identified the well-known tale. Read out the poem. When most students are already standing, stop reading. Ask the first student who stood up to name the tale in their mother tongue. Put the English title on the board: 'Little Red Riding Hood and the Wolf'.

Follow-up

Ask students to turn the poem face down on their desk. Read it out to the class, so that you leave out the last word of every second line, which students shout out if they can. For example:

Teacher:	As soon as Wolf began to feel
	That he would like a decent ... ,
Students:	Meal!
Teacher:	He went and knocked on Grandma's door.
	When Grandma opened it, she ... ,
Students:	Saw! etc.

Incidentally, the same procedure can be followed with any rhyming poem after students have familiarised themselves with it.

Once the rhymes have been identified, students may deliberately wish to add non-rhyming synonyms to bring the poem 'down-to-earth'. For example, instead of *meal* and *saw* they can suggest *dinner* and *noticed*, respectively.

Acknowledgment

The poem is from *Revolting Rhymes* by Roald Dahl (Jonathan Cape and Penguin).

5.8 I wish I didn't talk so much

Summary:	This activity is structured around a poem concerned with wishes and 'non-wishes'.
Level:	intermediate – post-intermediate
Time:	20–25 minutes
Preparation:	Make a copy of Box 53 for each student.

Procedure

1 Ask students about their immediate wishes, both positive and negative. For example:

I wish I had a mobile phone.
I wish I didn't have to come to school every day.

2 Tell the class that the American poet Phyllis McGinley has lots of wishes. Give out copies of her poem in Box 53 and provide help with any unknown vocabulary. Then read out the poem.

BOX 53

Reflections at Dawn

I wish I owned a Dior dress
   Made to my order out of satin.
I wish I weighed a little less
   And could read Latin,
Had perfect pitch or matching pearls,
   A better head for street directions,
And seven daughters, all with curls
   And fair complexions.
I wish I'd tan instead of burn
   But most, on all the stars that glisten,
I wish at parties I could learn
   To sit and listen.

I wish I didn't talk so much at parties.
It isn't that I *want* to hear
My voice assaulting every ear,
Uprising loud and firm and clear
Above the cocktail clatter.
It's simply, once a doorbell's rung
(I've been like this since I was young)
Some madness overtakes my tongue
   And I begin to chatter ...

I wish I didn't talk so much
I wish I didn't talk so much
I wish I didn't talk so much,
   When I am at a party.

---

3 Go through Phyllis's wish list – all her wishes are positive except the last item. Ask the class:
   • Which of her wishes do you share?
   • Do you also worry that you talk too much at parties?
   • Do you talk too much in the English lesson, too? Why/not?

Follow-up

Some students might be prepared to compose their wishes into a funny poem. Encourage them to write it on a sheet of paper at home and then display it on a classroom wall.

Acknowledgment

'Reflections at Dawn' by Phyllis McGinley was first published in *The New Yorker*.

5.9 The pessimist

Summary:	Students approach the optimist–pessimist dilemma through a poem.
Level:	post-intermediate – advanced
Time:	20–25 minutes (in class)
Preparation:	Make a copy of Box 54 for each student. For the *Variation*, make a copy of Box 55 for each student.

Procedure

1 Distribute copies of the poem in Box 54. As students read the poem by Benjamin Franklin King (1857–1894), provide help with any new vocabulary.

BOX 54

Nothing to do but work,
   Nothing to eat but food,
Nothing to wear but clothes,
   To keep you from going nude.

Nothing to breathe but air,
   Quick as a flash 'tis gone;
Nowhere to fall but off,
   Nowhere to stand but on.

Nothing to comb but hair,
   Nowhere to sleep but in bed,
Nothing to weep but tears,
   Nothing to bury but dead.

Nothing to sing but songs,
   Ah, well, alas! alack!
Nowhere to go but out,
   Nowhere to come but back.

Nothing to see but sights,
   Nothing to quench but thirst,
Nothing to have but what we've got,
   Thus thro' life we are cursed.

---

2 What could the original title of the poem be? Allow students to think for a couple of minutes, before they share their guesses with their groupmates. Then each group chooses the title they think is the best. After you have listened to all the suggestions, supply the original title: 'The Pessimist'.

3 Since this is supposed to be a mock gloomy poem, students should read it out in a mock gloomy tone. It should be especially funny if groups recite the poem in chorus. Read out the poem so that the class have a model to imitate. After a few minutes' rehearsal time, groups take it in turns to do their recital.

4 But why despair? Let's look on the bright side of life by rehashing King's poem and give it the title 'The Optimist'. In its new version, the poem may begin like this:

> Plenty of work to do,
>   Plenty of food to eat,
> Plenty of clothes to wear,
>   To keep you from going nude. etc.

After you have written these four lines on the board, students try to write another verse in a similarly optimistic tone – possibly as a homework assignment. Back in class, volunteers come forward to recite their verse – in a manner which suits the happy message.

Variation

Instead of the original poem in Box 54, you may decide to distribute this mixed version of King's poem in *Step 1*.

BOX 55

Nothing to quench but work,
    Nothing to breathe but food,
Nothing to eat but clothes,
    To weep you from going nude.

Nothing to comb but air,
    Quick as a flash 'tis gone;
Nowhere to go but off,
    Nowhere to fall but on.

Nothing to bury but hair,
    Nowhere to keep but in bed,
Nothing to sing but tears,
    Nothing to wear but dead.

Nothing to stand but songs,
    Ah, well, alas! alack!
Nowhere to see but out,
    Nowhere to have but back.

Nothing to come but sights,
    Nothing to do but thirst,
Nothing to sleep but what we've got,
    Thus thro' life we are cursed.

Explain that all 17 infinitives in the poem got jumbled up. The students' task is to reconstruct the original poem in groups, moving the infinitives only.

Extras

1 The witticisms below spell out the difference between the pessimist and the optimist. Write on the board only the ones which suit your students' language and age level, then discuss them with the class:

> 1 An optimist invented the aeroplane; a pessimist invented the seat belts. (Anon.)
> 2 There is no sadder sight than a young pessimist, except an old optimist. (Mark Twain)
> 3 A pessimist is just a well-informed optimist. (Robert Mackenzie)
> 4 'Twixt the optimist and the pessimist
> The difference is droll:
> The optimist sees the doughnut
> But the pessimist sees the hole. (McLandburgh Wilson)

2 Students get into two teams, one consisting of optimists, the other of pessimists. Everybody chooses the team they wish to join. An 'optimist' begins by making a claim: 'In ten years' time, scooters will be so popular that even elderly people will use them.' To this a 'pessimist' may react with these words: 'On the contrary. In ten years' time, elderly people won't dare leave home for fear of being run over by these rapid scooters.' In turn, another optimist supplies a counter-argument, only to be opposed by another pessimist, and so on. When the two teams run out of arguments, someone should throw in a new topic – a funny one if possible. Changing groups is allowed at any point during the game.

Acknowledgment

The original version of the game in the *Extra 2* is from *Keep Talking* by Klippel (Cambridge University Press).

5.10 The disappearing song

Summary:	The activity is based on a popular action song.
Level:	beginner – pre-intermediate
Time:	5–10 minutes
Preparation:	Rehearse the song and the appropriate movements before the lesson.

Procedure

1 Tell the class that they are going to listen to an action song, that is, a song in which the words are accompanied by movements. Write the words of the song on the board:

> Head and shoulders, knees and toes,
> Knees and toes.
> Head and shoulders, knees and toes,
> Knees and toes.
> And eyes and ears and mouth and nose.
> Head and shoulders, knees and toes,
> Knees and toes.

2 Sing the song while pointing to the appropriate parts of your body (i.e. head, shoulders, knees and toes).

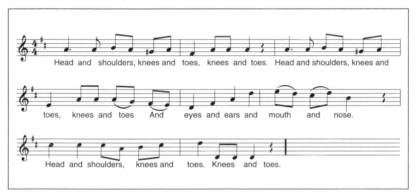

3 Sing and do the action song again, but this time slowly. Students repeat after you, line by line, action by action.
4 Once everybody has learnt to sing and perform fairly automatically, start singing the song again, but this time leave out the word *toes*. Students repeat the song in the same way. Next time around, you omit both *knees* and *toes* – and so on, until you have got rid of all four words.

Follow-ups

1 Students may like the idea of turning this into a competitive game. Everybody stands up and begins to sing the song: first in full, then leaving out the words one after the other. Those who either make a verbal mistake or perform the wrong action drop out and sit down.
2 Once the words have disappeared, it is fun to reconstruct the lyrics word by word, starting with the word which disappeared last (i.e. *head*). Finally, the class sing the song in full.

5.11 Billy Boy (and Lilly Girl)

Summary:	Students rewrite a traditional American song to make it politically correct.
Level:	intermediate – post-intermediate
Time:	15–20 minutes
Preparation:	Make a copy of Box 56 for each student. Bring to class a sheet of poster paper and some reusable adhesive.

Procedure

1 Give everyone a copy of the song in Box 56.

BOX 56

Oh, where have you been, Billy Boy, Billy Boy,
Oh, where have you been, charming Billy?
I have been to seek a wife, she's the joy of my life,
She's a young thing and cannot leave her mother.

Did she ask you to come in, Billy Boy, Billy Boy,
Did she ask you to come in, charming Billy?
Yes, she asked me to come in, there's a dimple in her chin,
She's a young thing and cannot leave her mother.

Can she bake a cherry pie, Billy Boy, Billy Boy,
Can she bake a cherry pie, charming Billy?
She can bake a cherry pie, quick as you can wink an eye,
She's a young thing and cannot leave her mother.

Can she make a feather bed, Billy Boy, Billy Boy?
Can she make a feather bed, charming Billy?
She can make a feather bed, while a-standing on her head,
She's a young thing and cannot leave her mother.

How tall is she, Billy Boy, Billy Boy?
How tall is she, charming Billy?
She is tall as any pine, and as straight as a pumpkin pie,
She's a young thing and cannot leave her mother.

How old is she, Billy Boy, Billy Boy?
How old is she, charming Billy?
She is sixty times eleven, twenty-eight and forty-seven,
She's a young thing and cannot leave her mother.

Playfully — Traditional — G — D7 — G — D7 — G

(Mother) 1. Oh,— where have you been, Bil - ly Boy, Bil - ly Boy, Oh,— where have you
2. Did she ask you to come in, Bil - ly Boy, Bil - ly Boy, Did she ask you to come

been, char - ming Bil - ly?— *(Billy) I have been to seek a wife, she's the
in, char - ming Bil - ly?— Yes, she asked me to come in, there's a

joy— of my life, She's a } young thing and can - not leave her mo - ther.—
dim - ple in her chin, She's a }

2 Discuss the lyrics with the class. Ask who the two characters are.
Answer: Billy and his mother.

If so, Billy's part had better be sung by male students while his
mother's part had better be sung by female students. Sing the song a
second time, with students joining in according to gender.

3 'Billy Boy' is a traditional American song, written at a time when
young ladies were expected not only to be pretty but also good at
housework. Times have changed, haven't they? Today, young men
also have to be ... well, if not pretty, then handsome, but more importantly, be prepared to do their fair share of the housework. Be that as
it may, the song needs bringing up to date. How about having the
dialogue conducted between, say, Lilly and her father? In that case,
the first stanza may run like this:

> Oh, where have you been, Lilly Girl, Lilly Girl,
> Oh, where have you been, charming Lilly?
> I have been to seek a guy, who is neither sad nor shy,
> He's a young thing and cannot leave his father.

Students rewrite the rest of the song, which requires little more than
changing *she* into *he* and *her* into *his*.

4 Students now sing the 'politically correct' version of the song in
compliance with the new roles.

Follow-up

Once in the mood for creative work, what about adding a couple of stanzas to the original song? To save time, set this writing task for homework; back in class, group members take turns singing the new lyrics. Having listened to one another, each group chooses one or two stanzas which they find the funniest, and neatly writes them on a sheet of paper. Collect all the sheets, stick them on poster paper, and display the collection on the wall. In case students get stuck, you can help them with a few ideas:

Did she/he sit close to you?

She/he sat as close to me as the bark upon the tree ...

Can she/he fry a dish of meat?

She/he can fry a dish of meat as fast as you can eat ...

Can she/he make a pair of britches?

She/he can make a pair of britches as fast as you can count the stitches ...

Can she/he bake a loaf of bread?

She/he can bake a loaf of bread with her/his nightcap on her/his head ...

5.12 I wonder who I am

Summary:	Students practise asking questions about musicians.
Level:	pre-intermediate – intermediate
Time:	10–15 minutes
Preparation:	Prepare name tags, one for each student. Bring to class some sticky tape or safety pins. Collect the names of well-known musicians from three categories: classics (such as Beethoven, Mozart or Chopin), oldies (such as Louis Armstrong, John Lennon or Ella Fitzgerald), as well as contemporary pop stars. Make sure that you only select names students are likely to have heard of. Collect as many musicians as there are students in the class and write their names on small pieces of paper.

Procedure

1 Write on the board a few types of questions students will be expected to ask:

> Am I alive?
> Am I a woman? man?
> Do I come from (Germany)?
> Am I a composer? conductor? singer?
> Do I play the guitar? the piano? the drums?
> Do I play/sing old music? pop songs?
> Do I play heavy metal? rap? rock? country?
> Have I released the song ('Yellow submarine')?
> Do you think my parents enjoy my songs?
> Do you like my performances?

2 Attach a name tag to each student's back with sticky tape or safety pins. Make sure that nobody can see their own name. There are two further rules: students may ask only (a) yes/no questions; (b) one question per partner. Everybody stands up and begins to circulate.

3 Those who have found out who they are go back to their seats. The game is over when most students are sitting. Anyone unable to discover their identity by the end of the game should tell the class all the information they have gathered. The others may give clues to help them guess.

Variation

Obviously, this game need not be limited to musicians – any celebrity or even people all the students know (like their teachers) may be substituted.

5.13 There was an old lady

Summary:	This song practises the names of animals and, incidentally, relative pronouns and purpose clauses.
Level:	pre-intermediate – intermediate
Time:	10–15 minutes
Preparation:	Make a copy of Box 57 and Box 58 for each student. (You could make a transparency of Box 57.)

Procedure

1 Distribute copies of the drawing in Box 57.

119

BOX 57

© Cambridge University Press 2002

As you call out the names of the animals one by one, students point to the animals, helping each other in pairs if necessary.

2 Encourage the class to answer the following questions before they listen to the song:

- What is the old woman about to do? (She is about to eat the animals.)
- Which one do you think she will swallow first? (The fly.)
- Why the fly? (Because it is the smallest of them all.)
- Which one will be the next victim? (The spider.)
- Why does she want to eat the spider? (Because the spider can then eat the fly.)
- After the spider, in what order will the old lady swallow the rest? (The bird, the cat, the dog, the goat, the cow, and finally the horse.)
- Will the old lady still be hungry after she has eaten them all? (Don't tell the class that she will eventually die of overeating.)

3 Give out the song in Box 58 and help students with any language difficulties.

BOX 58

1 There was an old lady who swallowed a fly,
  I don't know why she swallowed a fly,
  Perhaps she'll die.

2 There was an old lady who swallowed a spider
  That wriggled and jiggled and tickled inside her.
  She swallowed the spider to catch the fly,
  I don't know why she swallowed a fly,
  Perhaps she'll die.

3 There was an old lady who swallowed a bird,
  How absurd to swallow a bird!
  She swallowed the bird to catch the spider,
  She swallowed the spider to catch the fly,
  I don't know why she swallowed a fly,
  Perhaps she'll die.

4 There was an old lady who swallowed a cat,
  Fancy that! She swallowed a cat!
  She swallowed the cat to catch the bird ...

5 There was an old lady who swallowed a dog,
  Oh, what a hog! She swallowed a dog!
  She swallowed the dog to catch the cat ...

6 There was an old lady who swallowed a goat,
  She opened her throat and swallowed a goat!
  She swallowed the goat to catch the dog ...

7 There was an old lady who swallowed a cow,
  I don't know how she swallowed a cow.
  She swallowed the cow to catch the goat ...

8 There was an old lady who swallowed a horse,
  (Spoken) She's dead, of course.

Sing the song. Encourage everyone to join in as soon as they have understood how to sing the expanding verses.

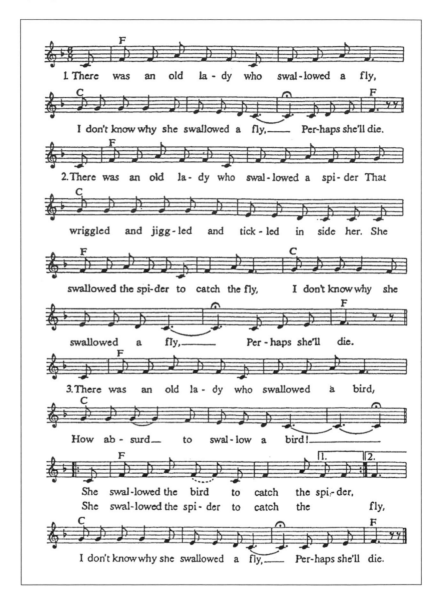

Variation

As you are singing for the first time, you may decide to stop after the first verse and ask students how they think the second verse will begin:

Students: There was an old lady who swallowed a spider.

Now stop after the second verse and ask about the beginning of the third verse:

Students: There was an old lady who swallowed a bird.

After singing 'How absurd to swallow a bird', pause again and wait for the class to add:

Students: She swallowed the bird to catch the spider,
She swallowed the spider to catch the fly,
I don't know why she swallowed a fly
Perhaps she'll die.

Do the same for the remaining verses. This is a playful way of learning the song by heart!

Follow-up

If students like this song, they may want to learn it by heart and sing the lines which begin with 'She swallowed' as fast as they can, only to slow down when singing 'I don't know why'.

6   Pictures and images

This section focuses on pictures, mostly cartoons. I love cartoons, both in my mother tongue and in English – provided I can understand them. The trouble is that they are often fraught with cultural connotations and make references to topical events with which I am not familiar. Thus I miss about two-thirds of the jokes and feel frustrated. However, the one third that I do comprehend gives me a great deal of satisfaction and often makes me laugh. The cartoons below are some of my favourites and I hope you like them, too. It is even better if they manage to move your students' imagination and motivate them to act out, draw and, at the same time, use the English language.

6.1 Don't panic!

Summary:	Students describe the emotions shown by faces.
Level:	beginner – pre-intermediate
Time:	5–10 minutes
Preparation:	Make a copy for each student (or a transparency) of Box 59.

Procedure

1 Give everybody a copy of the cartoon in Box 59.

124

After students have (hopefully) had a good laugh, ask what they think will happen next.

Answer: As the door slams, the lion's tail is caught. This may cause him to attack.

2 Put this list of adjectives on the board. Teach any unfamiliar words.

> bored   calm   funny   frightened   happy   kind   sad   serious
> surprised   unfriendly   worried

Ask students to describe the faces of the cartoon characters and the lion, using one or more of the adjectives.

3 In pairs, students compare their choices. Is there a consensus between the partners?

Follow-ups

1 Some students may like to draw a sequel to this cartoon for homework. In class, let them show their 'work of art' to the whole class.

2 Some people say jokes should never be explained: one either gets the punch line or doesn't. Still, you may ask students to discuss in groups what makes this cartoon funny. Needless to say, the same question may be asked for all the other cartoons in this section.

6.2 Sky-high with grimaces

Summary:	Cartoon strips without words can be quite amusing.
Level:	pre-intermediate – intermediate
Time:	10–15 minutes
Preparation:	Make a copy (or a transparency) of Box 60 and a copy of the cartoon strip in Box 61 with the last picture cut off. (Enlarge the cartoons if possible.)

Procedure

1 Invite eight volunteers to participate in a simple mime. Give the group leader the cartoon strip in Box 60 and ask this group to leave the room for a few minutes. Their task is to practise miming the activity as shown in the five pictures. You may suggest that those playing the passers-by should stand on the floor, the couple looking out of the window on a chair and the angel on a desk.

BOX 60

2 While the miming group is out in the corridor, keep the rest of the class occupied with the strip cartoon in Box 61.

BOX 61

Give out the strip cartoon, and tell the class that you have kept the sixth picture. What is in this missing picture? Students make guesses.
3 After a while, give out the last picture. Then ask:
  • Who can you see in the photo? (Probably the boy's sister.)
  • Before you saw the last picture, why did you think the boy was making faces? (Out of daftness.)
  • Now that you have seen the last picture, it's clear that he had a different motive. What exactly? (Probably to take revenge on his sister for something she had done to annoy him.)
  • What does the boy look like in the last picture? (Very satisfied.)
4 Call the rehearsing group back to perform the 'Look Up' cartoon strip in Box 60. Ask the others to explain why everyone is looking up.
  Answer: For no apparent reason, but as they say, 'One fool makes many.'

Follow-ups

1 'Revenge is sweet' runs the proverb. Can anybody in the class remember an incident in which they took revenge on someone? Are they willing to relate this incident, too? Was the revenge really sweet?

2 Most children are in the habit of pulling faces. Did students in the class use to practise this skill as children? Is there anybody bold enough to show their favourite grimace? As teenagers (or adults), do they still make faces on occasion? When was the last time they made a face? What urged them?

3 Referring back to the 'Look Up' cartoon, can anybody recall a situation in which they automatically imitated an individual or a group? Why did they do it? For example, in the 60s and 70s bananas were seldom available in Hungary. So whenever there was a long queue in the street, people knew that bananas were on sale and would join the queue automatically. Once it was my turn to order when I realised that this time it was some kind of perfume at a discount that people were queueing up for. I bought a bottle, just to save face ...

6.3 Doctor Rabbit

Summary:	Students turn the caption of a cartoon into a dialogue.
Level:	intermediate – post-intermediate
Time:	20–25 minutes
Preparation:	Make a copy (or a transparency) of Box 62. For *Follow-up 1*, make a copy of Box 63 for each student.

Procedure

1 Show the class the cartoon in Box 62.

BOX 62

'You said a moment ago that everybody you look at seems to be a rabbit. Now just what do you mean by that, Mrs. Sprague?'

© Cambridge University Press 2002

After students have looked at the cartoon, ask:
- Who are the two cartoon characters? (Mrs Sprague (the patient) and the psychiatrist.)
- Where is the scene set? (In the psychiatrist's consulting room.)
- Why is Mrs Sprague so surprised? (Because the psychiatrist has the head of a rabbit.)

2 In the caption, the psychiatrist asked a question. What could Mrs Sprague's answer be? And the psychiatrist's response after that? In pairs, students create an imaginary dialogue between the patient and the psychiatrist. If necessary, get them started by supplying the beginning of the dialogue:

Psychiatrist: You said a moment ago that everybody you look at seems to be a rabbit. Now just what do you mean by that, Mrs Sprague?
Mrs Sprague: But you *are* a rabbit, Dr Allen!
Psychiatrist: What makes you think so?
Mrs. Sprague: Your ears, for example. You have long ears, just like rabbits.
Psychiatrist: And long teeth as well, I suppose? ...

3 Once students have completed their dialogue, allow a few minutes for pairs to rehearse and memorise it. Afterwards, they take it in turns to act out their little scene.

Follow-ups

1 After the incident shown in the cartoon, both the psychiatrist and Mrs Sprague wrote a letter to a friend of theirs. Give a copy to everyone.

BOX 63
The psychiatrist's letter:
Dear Tom,
You won't believe what happened to me yesterday. We were just having our annual fancy-dress party at the clinic when my assistant came up to me and said ...

Mrs Sprague's letter:
Nicolette, my dearest Nicolette,
I am too upset to begin by asking about you and your family as usual. Yesterday, I went to see a psychiatrist. A psychiatrist? Oh no! A psychopath ...

Everybody chooses the letter they would prefer to continue writing at home. In the next lesson, neighbours swap their notebooks and read each other's letter. Anyone may recommend that their partner's letter is so funny that it is worth reading out to the whole class.

2 Ask a scribe to put both sentences of the caption on the board. Now get the class to suggest shortening the text by cutting out *one to three* words at a time. Each time the scribe wipes off the word(s) suggested for deletion. In the end, only one word is left on the board. At each step, the class reads out the receding caption in chorus. Notice that the shorter the sentence is, the bigger the role of intonation becomes.

Here is a possible solution:

You said *a moment ago* that everybody you look at seems to be a rabbit. Now just what do you mean by that, Mrs Sprague?

You said that everybody you look at seems to be a rabbit. *Now just* what do you mean by that, Mrs Sprague?

You said that everybody you look at seems to be a rabbit. What do you mean *by that*, Mrs Sprague?

You said *that* everybody you look at seems to be a rabbit. What do you mean, Mrs Sprague?

You said everybody you look at seems to be a rabbit. What do you mean, *Mrs Sprague*?

You said everybody *you look at* seems to be a rabbit. What do you mean?

You said everybody seems to be a rabbit. What do you mean?

Everybody seems to be a rabbit. What *do you mean*?

Everybody seems to be a rabbit. *What*?

Everybody seems *to be* a rabbit?

Everybody *seems* a rabbit?

Everybody a rabbit?

A rabbit?

Rabbit?

Now students move in reverse order, reconstructing the original text step by step. Another scribe writes the re-appearing word(s) on the board.

Acknowledgment

Follow-up 2 exploits an idea in Morgan and Rinvolucri's *Once Upon a Time* (Cambridge University Press).

6.4 Don't exaggerate!

Summary:	Students draw cartoons to illustrate hyperboles.
Level:	intermediate – post-intermediate
Time:	20–25 minutes
Preparation:	Make a copy of Box 64 for each student. Bring sheets of poster paper to class, one for each group.

Procedure

1 Write on the board this quotation by American humorist Robbie Shakes. Explain that *No hablo inglés* is the Spanish for *I don't speak English*.

> After twelve years of therapy my psychiatrist said something that brought tears to my eyes. He said, 'No hablo inglés'.

Ask what is funny about this saying.

Expected answer:
Although good psychiatrists talk little and listen a lot, it is hard to believe that a psychiatrist would only reveal his or her total lack of English after so many years.

In other words, this quote is based on an exaggeration or, to use a literary term, a hyperbole. (Check the pronunciation of *hyperbole*.)

2 Box 64 contains hyperboles which are frequently used in everyday English. Give everyone a copy of the list and then provide help with any unknown words and phrases.

BOX 64

over my dead body	one foot in the grave
white as a sheet	eighth wonder
innocent as a new-born baby	We were scared to death.
I'm starving.	Sheila is dressed to kill.
Stop that nonsense or I'll kill you.	I told you a million times, didn't I?
This child weighs a ton.	My brother is the biggest liar on Earth.
.....	.....
.....	.....
.....	.....

© Cambridge University Press 2002

Get students to suggest further hyperboles from their own stock of colloquial phrases in English and add them to the list in Box 64.

3 Divide the class into groups, so that in each group there is one 'artist' prepared to draw a simple sketch. Give the artist a sheet of poster paper. Group members choose a hyperbole from their list and 'guide the artist's hand' with their suggestions, as it were.

4 When the artists have finished drawing, they take it in turns to show their sketch to the whole class. Can the others identify the hyberbole?

Follow-up

At home, everybody thinks of 4–5 hyperboles in their mother tongue and translates them into English. In class, students take it in turns to read out the items in their collection, with the others copying in their notebooks the ones they like.

6.5 You've got cows

Summary:	This activity is based on a mad cow cartoon.
Level:	intermediate – post-intermediate
Time:	20–25 minutes (in class)
Preparation:	Make a copy (or a transparency) of Box 65. Have some reusable adhesive or sticky tape available.

Procedure

1 Show the class the cartoon in Box 65.

BOX 65

'Your disease is so rare that there's never been any TV movies about it.'

Jonny Hawkins Source: www.CartoonStock.com

© Cambridge University Press 2002

Ask the class what connection there is between rare diseases and TV movies. Can anyone remember any films based on illnesses? In the cartoon the man has a very rare disease called cows. One of the symptoms is tiny cowheads which start growing out of the body. Eager to find out more about cows, the doctor asks the man to describe his symptoms in the form of a diary. He supplies a set of questions to guide the man's thoughts. Students in groups collect three or four questions each. Provide a few triggers if necessary. For example:

- When did you first notice that there was something wrong with you?

131

- What were the initial symptoms?
- Has your condition worsened?
- Do you have any pain?
- Has anyone in your family had a similar disease, such as pigs or goats?
- Did you use to touch cows when you were a child?
- Do you drink a lot of milk?
- Why is cows such an unpleasant disease?
- Are you desperate enough to undergo an operation?

2 Groups read out their questions. Write the most salient ones on the board until you have collected about a dozen questions.

3 Everybody writes the man's imaginary diary on an A4 size sheet at home. In class, students read each other's diary in groups. Each group chooses the diary which they find the funniest, copies it in clear hand-writing, and sticks it on the wall for the whole class to enjoy.

Follow-up

Students may like to conceive of diseases which are as absurd as cows. They should give the disease a name and then either draw a patient suffering from this disease or describe the symptoms.

6.6 All wired up

Summary:	This activity compares high-tech cartoons.
Level:	pre-intermediate – intermediate
Time:	10–15 minutes
Preparation:	Make a copy for each student (or a transparency) of Box 66.

Procedure

1 Give everybody a copy of the cartoons in Box 66. Tell the class that all three cartoons are from the *Spectator*, a British magazine which has been in circulation for nearly 300 years.

'What's that?'

'Why can't you spend hours on the Internet like other kids?'

'He talks to himself.'

After students have had time to look at the three cartoons, encourage them to comment on them. Which of the cartoons do they find the funniest? Why? Do they know the term *snail mail*? (*Snail mail* refers to letters sent by ordinary post.)

2 Ask the class the following questions:
   * What is the common theme in the three cartoons in Box 66?
     (Telecommunication devices, such as the Internet, mobile phones, e-mail.)
   * Which of these gadgets do you have at home and at school?
   * Can you remember funny or annoying stories in connection with any of these devices?

Extra

Students bring to class as many cartoons as they can. (The captions may be in their mother tongue too if it is a monolingual class.) They display the cartoons on their desks. Students go around the classroom and look at the cartoons. They pick up cartoons which they believe are related, and mount these next to each other on the wall. If challenged, they explain what connects the items.

6.7 Children's games

Summary: This activity introduces a number of children's games, both past and present.
Level: pre-intermediate – intermediate
Time: 15–20 minutes
Preparation: Make a copy for each student (or a transparency) of Box 67 and Box 68.

Procedure

1 Give everybody a copy of the painting in Box 67. ('Children's games' was painted by Pieter Bruegel the Elder (1525–1569), a Flemish artist. The original can be seen in Vienna.)

BOX 67

© Cambridge University Press 2002

After students have perused the picture for a few minutes, ask these questions:

- In which century do you think the picture was painted? (16th century.)
- At a guess, how many children are there in the picture? (More than 230.)
- How many different games can you make out? Twenty? Forty? Even more? (About 90 different games.)
- Which of these games are popular today?
- Which did you like playing as a child?
- Do you still play games? What sort of games, for example?

2 The picture in Box 68 is an 'updated' version of Bruegel's painting: twelve modern games have been substituted for twelve old ones.

BOX 68

© Cambridge University Press 2002

Give out copies of the picture in Box 68. What exactly has changed? In pairs, students try to spot the changes and note them down. They may use the mother-tongue equivalents if they can't name certain games in English.

3 Stop the activity when the first pair signals that they have spotted all twelve games. Ask this pair to identify the games one by one. Write on the board the English equivalent of the games that they can name only in their mother tongue.

Answers: toy train, remote-controlled planes, one-armed bandit, pinball, monopoly, jigsaw puzzle, tin soldiers, dolls, teddy bears, biking, roller-skating, skateboarding.

Follow-up

Students describe where in the picture the modern games can be seen. You may wish to teach them these phrases:

in the foreground	in the top right/left-hand corner
in the background	in the bottom right/left-hand corner
in the middle	between ... and ...
next to ...	

Extra

Students interested in fine arts might like to choose a classic painting and make an updated caricature of this painting for homework. In class, encourage them to put both the original painting and its updated version on display.

6.8 Captionless cartoons

Summary: In this activity, students create captions and compare them with the missing originals.

Level: pre-intermediate – advanced

Time: 15–20 minutes

Preparation: Make a copy of Box 69 and remove the captions. (Enlarge the cartoons if possible.) Have some reusable adhesive or sticky tape and slips of paper ready.

Procedure

BOX 69

'And folklore has it they never forget! ...'

'I'm none too proud of that one. He thought I was taking his picture.'

'First the good news. His temperature has gone down.'

'That's the one officer, he did it!'

'He's wonderful with children ...'

'It's clues we're looking for, constable.'

1 Choose from the six *Punch* cartoons in Box 69 the ones you like and the class is likely to find funny as well. (You may replace the cartoons you have eliminated with some of your favourites.) Stick the cartoons on the wall in different parts of the classroom. Explain that each cartoon originally had a caption, and now the task is to guess what it could be. Give everyone some reusable adhesive or sticky tape and a few slips of paper.

2 Students stand up, walk around the classroom and look at all the cartoons. Everybody chooses one of them, devises a caption to match, writes the text on a slip of paper and glues it under the appropriate cartoon. Those who finish first can also create captions for other cartoons as well.

3 When students have run out of ideas, read out the original captions. Everybody tries to decide which caption goes with which cartoon. Paste the captions under those created by the class.

4 Everyone stands up again and checks the suggested captions underneath the cartoons. Are there any student-generated texts which are wittier than the originals?

Follow-up

Students vote for their favourite cartoon. You add up their votes and declare the cartoon with the highest number of votes 'The Best Cartoon'. If two cartoons happen to have received an equal number of votes, they can be joint winners. Remove all the cartoons from the wall, except the award-winning cartoon(s).

6.9 In my mind's eye ...

Summary:	Students visualise cartoons to match captions.
Level:	intermediate – post-intermediate
Time:	20–25 minutes
Preparation:	Bring to class several sheets of poster paper and some reusable adhesive or sticky tape. Make a copy of Box 70. (Enlarge the cartoons if possible.)

Procedure

1 Divide the board into three columns. Write the following captions at the top of each column:
   - Have you been going through my pockets again?
   - Typical! Not a single word in the manual what to do in a situation like this.

- Did Sir make a reservation?

Tell the class that these captions have been removed from existing cartoons. Which caption fuels their imagination most? Each student chooses one caption and then teams up with other students who have chosen the same caption. (There can be more than one group per caption.) They should arrange themselves so that there is at least one 'artist' per group.

2 Give each group a sheet of poster paper. Group members picture in their mind's eye the cartoon hidden behind the caption and share their ideas with their partners. Once the picture seems to have taken shape, the artist sketches it on the poster paper. When ready, she/he sticks the sketch in the appropriate column on the board.

3 When all the sketches are on the board, students admire the 'works of art'. Take a vote to find out which cartoon is the wittiest and the most suitable for each caption. Leave only those three cartoons on the board.

4 Stick the original cartoons under their caption. Invite everyone to the board to compare the pictures.

BOX 70

'Have you been going through
my pockets again?'

*Typical! Not a single word in the manual
what to do in a situation like this.*

Werner Wejp-Olsen Source: www.CartoonStock.com

'Did Sir make a reservation?'

Variation

If you want the class to engage in more talk, you could ask a spokes-person from each group to describe their sketch before putting it up.

6.10 Stupid questions – snappy answers

Summary:	We often get asked stupid questions – and, let's admit it, we often give stupid answers, too.
Level:	intermediate – post-intermediate
Time:	20–25 minutes
Preparation:	Make a copy for each group of students (or a transparency) of Box 71. (Enlarge the cartoon if possible.)

Procedure

1 Encourage students to recall either a stupid question they once asked, or the stupidest question they were asked. How did they respond to the question? Before students kick off, you may want to share with them some of your own experiences. The silliest question I ever asked was this: 'Oh, I'm so sorry. Have I hurt you?' – when in fact I had walked into my own reflection in a shop window.

2 Divide the class into groups and give each group the cartoon in Box 71.

BOX 71

© Cambridge University Press 2002

After you have helped with any unknown vocabulary, allow time for students to look at the cartoon. Then ask these questions:
- Where does the scene take place?
- Who do you think is asking the stupid question and who is giving the snappy answer?
- Which of the three answers is the snappiest?
- And the least snappy?

3 Students in groups should suggest a fourth (and possibly a fifth) snappy answer. Afterwards, they take it in turns to share their answer(s) with the whole class.

Follow-up

For homework, everybody should create a similar situation with a stupid question followed by a smart reply.

Extra

Referring back to *Step 1*, we are often asked stupid questions by foreigners about our culture. It is particularly irritating to be bombarded with stereotypes abroad, where we are stressed anyhow. For example, whenever I go abroad as a Hungarian, there is always someone who cannot help cracking this tired joke:

You Hungarians are always hungry, aren't you?

I usually feel tempted to answer something like this:

Yes, Hungarians are hungry all the time. So hungry in fact that we can't be bothered to cook. Normally, we eat everything raw: grass and grasshoppers, horseradish and horses – you name it. And we don't use forks, knives and spoons. We just eat with our hands. etc.

Get students in groups to conceive snappy answers to the typical questions that they are asked about their culture.

Acknowledgment

The idea in the Extra is from 'Exaggerating cultural stereotypes' from Davies and Rinvolucri's *Confidence Book* (Longman).

6.11 A cartoon exhibition

Summary:	Students pool their favourite mother-tongue cartoons and translate the captions into English.
Level:	intermediate – post-intermediate
Time:	15–20 minutes (in class)
Preparation:	Bring to class several sheets of poster paper and some reusable adhesive or sticky tape.

Procedure

1 At home, each student collects 4 or 5 cartoons from local newspapers and magazines. They should cut off the original captions, translate them into English and paste the English-language captions in their place.
2 In class, students pool their cartoons in small groups. While they correct and edit each other's work, go around to provide help.
3 Give each group a sheet of paper and some reusable adhesive or sticky tape. Group members select the cartoons which they find the wittiest. After mounting their favourites on the sheet, they stick them up on the wall.
4 Students walk around the classroom and look at all the cartoons.

Follow-up

Number each cartoon on the wall. Now everybody takes a pen and their notebook, and jots down the number of their favourite. They then take it in turns to say the number aloud. One student tallies the votes on the board. The five cartoons which receive the most votes are remounted on a sheet of 'Our Favourites'. Before the sheet is exhibited in the classroom, do a final check for language mistakes.

6.12 Please touch the exhibits!

Summary:	Students tidy up a cartoon exhibition.
Level:	beginner – advanced
Time:	10–15 minutes
Preparation:	Bring to class as many cartoons with captions as you can. (Needless to say, you should select pictures which suit the language level of your class.) Remove the captions from the cartoons and, before the lesson begins, use reusable adhesive or sticky tape to mount them all on the classroom walls, so that the corresponding items are placed in distant corners.

Procedure

1 When the lesson begins, invite students to the 'exhibition'. Ask them to observe and read the displayed items, and then find the matching pairs. Whenever they think they have found such a pair, they should remove the caption and stick it under the cartoon. If someone happens

to discover a mismatch, they should relocate the caption where they think it belongs. When all the captions and cartoons seem to have been matched, students sit down.

2 Go around and check whether all the items have been correctly matched up. If not, make any necessary adjustments. Finally, ask everyone to stand up again to enjoy the 'exhibition'; help with any comprehension difficulties.

Variation

To make the task trickier, your collection may include a few odd captions to which you 'forgot' to attach the cartoon. (Alternatively, or in addition, include some cartoons without captions.) At the end of the activity, pull the missing cartoons (and captions) out of your folder like a magician.

7 Stories and anecdotes

This section focuses on the world of story-telling. We all like listening to funny stories, don't we? And telling them? Well, the trouble is that not all of us are confident enough to tell stories in public. We non-native speakers of English are particularly reluctant to share our favourites because of our proficiency problems. However, with due practice non-native speakers may also become excellent story-tellers. I know quite a few of them. You do too, don't you?

7.1 Amazing titles

Summary:	This activity raises students' awareness of the importance of titles.
Level:	beginner – advanced
Time:	15–20 minutes
Preparation:	Make a copy of Box 72a, Box 72b or Box 72c for each student, depending on the level of the class.

Procedure

Every writer and publisher is conscious of the fact that a well-chosen title may help the book sell like hot cakes, just as a bad title may be a real turn-off. Ask what students think of the title *Laughing Matters*, for example. If they like it (as well as the activities in the book), let them have the author's e-mail address, so that they can send him their congratulations (medgyes@ludens.elte.hu). If they don't like it, make sure they never find out his whereabouts. Thank you.

1 Can anyone remember a witty title for a novel, a short story or a film? If it happens to be a title students have come across in their mother tongue, they should try to translate it into English. Does it lend itself easily to translation?

2 Steve Wright, author of *Book of the Amazing But True*, has found the following titles in his local library. He reports that all these books have been published in the past fifty years. Give out copies of Box 72a, Box 72b or Box 72c. Provide help with any new vocabulary.

BOX 72a beginner – pre-intermediate
A Handbook On Hanging
The Illustrated History of Metal Lunchboxes
Enjoy Your Pig
Be Bold with Bananas
Who's Who in Spaniels
.....
.....

BOX 72b pre-intermediate – post-intermediate
Keeping Your Tools Clean
Highlights in the History of Concrete
Frog Raising for Pleasure and Profit
The Development of Brain and Behaviour in the Chicken
Who's Who in Australian Embroidery
.....
.....

BOX 72c post-intermediate – advanced
Cesspools – a Do-it-yourself Guide
Manhole Covers of Los Angeles
Thermal Movements in the Upper Floor of a Multi-storey Car Park
Constipation and Our Civilisation
A Toddler's Guide to the Rubber Industry
.....
.....

Is it possible that these were meant to be serious titles? Which book would students fancy reading? Why?

3 There is space in the boxes for two more titles. Can students think of loony titles as a homework assignment? In class, encourage students to share their best ideas with the whole class.

Follow-ups

1 Everybody chooses the title they like best in Box 72, and writes an imaginary blurb of the book (the description on the back cover) for homework.
2 Some students may be willing to go to the local library and search for funny titles. Invite them to put the titles they have collected on the board for the whole class to enjoy.

Acknowledgment

The titles in *Step 2* have been slightly adapted from Wright's *Book of the Amazing But True* (Simon and Schuster).

7.2 The stone soup

Summary:	A folk tale is turned into a mime.
Level:	pre-intermediate – intermediate
Time:	20–25 minutes
Preparation:	none

Procedure

1 Tell the class that they are going to listen to a European folk tale entitled 'The Stone Soup'. Before you start reading, teach the following lexical items if necessary: *beggar, pot, stir, taste, salt, pepper, carrot, pantry, ingredients, ladle, bowl* and *(to) please*.
2 As you read out the story, mime appropriate actions. So when, for example, the narrator says 'a beggar knocked on an old woman's door', knock on the door or a desk.

> Once upon a time, a beggar knocked on an old woman's door to ask for some food. When the woman said she had nothing to give him, the beggar offered to make stone soup all the same. All he needed, he said, was a large pot, some water and a stone. The woman was surprised but gave him what he had asked for, and the man began to make the soup with the water and the stone. After stirring it for a while, he tasted the food and said that it was good but would be better if he added some salt and pepper. When the woman brought the salt and pepper, the man threw some into the pot. A little later he tasted the soup again and said that it could do with some carrots. The woman produced some nice carrots from the pantry ...

The cooking went on like this, the man asking for ingredients and the woman bringing them one after the other, until he found the soup tasty enough to eat. As he ladled the soup into the bowls, he put the stone into the woman's bowl to 'please' her.

3 In addition to a large pot, some water, a stone, some salt and pepper, and some carrots, the man asked for further ingredients. What else do students think was on his list? Put the suggestions on the board.
Possible answers: some cabbage, a bone, some flour, an onion, some butter, etc.

4 Divide the class into pairs. Tell students that this time round, while you are telling the tale, they are going to mime it in pairs, with Partner A playing the man and Partner B the old woman. Their job is simply to mime appropriate actions. If there is enough space, they may stand up, using the space around them as appropriate. As you are telling the tale, refer to the ingredients on the board. As often as possible, season your story-telling with these expressions:

Imagine that – soup from a stone!
This soup is good/tasty/rich, but it would be better/tastier/richer if we had some/a ... .
I think I have some/a ... .
This soup is just right. Let's eat!

Don't rush the narration – a folk tale needs time to unfold! For example, as the list of ingredients is expanding, repeat all the items. For example:
So the man stirred the pot with the creamy, yellow butter; and the yellow onions; and the fine, white flour; and the long, red bone; and the leafy purple cabbage; and the long, orange carrots; and the salt and the pepper; and the round, grey stone.

Variations

1 Groupwork. One student in each group takes over the role of the narrator, while the other two play the man and the woman. Write on the board the expressions in the box above.
2 To heighten the dramatic effect of their show, students may like to bring to class props: paper bowls and spoons, a big spoon and a big bowl, a stone and various food ingredients.
3 The show may become an absurd play if foodstuffs are replaced by non-edible objects, such as a shoestring or mud – especially if all these things are put into a real bowl to cook and stir.

147

Acknowledgment

I have adapted 'The Stone Soup' from *Using Folktales* by Taylor (Cambridge University Press).

7.3 Nasreddin anecdotes

Summary:	Nasreddin has entertained generations of Muslims – and people all over the world.
Level:	intermediate – post-intermediate
Time:	20–25 minutes
Preparation:	Make a copy of Box 73 for each group of students. Cut up the copies sentence by sentence. For *Extra 1*, make a copy of Box 74 for each student.

Procedure

1 Tell this Nasreddin anecdote to the class. (Nasreddin Hodja is a Muslim philosopher of the people, who embodied a mixture of silliness and shrewdness.)

> One of his neighbours found Nasreddin scattering crumbs all around his house.
>   'Why are you doing that?' he asked.
>   'I'm keeping the tigers away,' replied Nasreddin.
>   'But there aren't any tigers round here,' said the neighbour.
>   'That's right,' said Nasreddin. 'You see how well it works?'

2 Students suggest titles that would suit this anecdote. When you have heard several suggestions, supply the original title: 'No tigers'. It is certainly short, but is it any better than the students' ideas? Which side of Nasreddin's character does this story reveal, the silly or the shrewd?

3 In groups, students work with another Nasreddin story, entitled 'The Interrupted Dream'. Cut up the story in Box 73 and shuffle the slips of paper in each set. Provide a full set of 12 slips per group. Explain that the original anecdote consists of only nine sentences, so three sentences do not belong. Students lay the slips on their desk. They put the sentences in order and at the same time eliminate the three extra sentences.

Answer: The last three sentences in the box are the odd sentences out.

BOX 73

Nasreddin was taking a nap on the porch one hot summer day.

He dreamed that a stranger promised to give him ten pieces of gold.

The stranger placed them in Nasreddin's hand one by one.

However, when he reached the tenth piece, he didn't want to give it to him.

'Come on! What are you waiting for?' said Nasreddin.

'You promised me ten!'

Just then he woke up.

He immediately looked at his hand and saw that it was empty.

He quickly shut his eyes again, stretched out his hand and said, 'All right, nine's enough!'

'You're a very bad wife!' Nasreddin said angrily.

He worked on the engine day and night.

The stranger said: 'I can't solve this puzzle.'

---

4 Whenever a group signals that they are ready, go and check their solution. If it is not correct, ask them to carry on working. Continue like this until most of the groups have put the sentences in order and pinpointed the extra sentences. Finally, ask whether this anecdote exhibits Nasreddin's clever or daft side.

Follow-up

How could the three extra sentences be inserted so that the anecdote still makes sense? Obviously, this is only possible if the original story is altered and expanded. This is exactly what students have to do. They need not worry if their story turns out to be absurd – so much the better!

Extras

1 Give each student a copy of another Nasreddin story in Box 74. Students read the story ignoring the two missing sentences for the time being. Help with any new vocabulary.

BOX 74

People were always trying to play jokes on Nasreddin. One day the villagers invited him to give a sermon in their mosque to make a fool of him.

When he arrived in the mosque, he went to the pulpit and said: 'Do you people know what I'm going to talk about?'

'No, we don't,' the congregation replied.

'Then how can I talk to people as ignorant as you? You're wasting my time.' And he came down from the pulpit and went straight home.

The leaders went back to visit him and pleaded with him to preach to them the following Friday instead.

Again Nasreddin asked the same question but this time the villagers all answered, 'Yes, we do.'

'So why do you need me to talk to you at all?' asked Nasreddin scornfully, and he left the mosque and went home again.

The villagers begged him to come back again the following Friday. Eventually he agreed.

Again he asked the same question. This time the villagers replied, ... (1).

'In that case,' said Nasreddin, ... (2). And he went home yet again.

What can the two key sentences be? Write the three options for each on the board while students are reading. Students try to choose the most plausible answer in pairs.

1A	'Some of us do and some of us don't.'
1B	'We have got the answer at last!'
1C	'No, but we're dying to find out.'
2A	'there's no point in me preaching, is there?'
2B	'ask Allah!'
2C	'let the ones who know tell the ones who don't!'

In the end, supply the key.

Answers: 1A, 2C.

2 Many fables, anecdotes and tales end with a moral. Students should discuss the moral of the three Nasreddin tales.

Acknowledgment

I have borrowed the Nasreddin story in *Extra 1* from Maley's *Short and Sweet* (Penguin English).

7.4 The sages of Chelm

Summary:	These stories illustrate Jewish folk humour.
Level:	intermediate – post-intermediate
Time:	25–30 minutes
Preparation:	none

Procedure

1 Tell the class this story from Chelm. (Chelm is a mythical town somewhere in Europe, inhabited by simpletons.)

> Kohn, the water carrier, was returning home one evening when a stranger rushed up to him and slapped his face.
>   'Take that, Meyer!' shouted the attacker.
>   Kohn picked himself up from the street and stared at the man. Suddenly he burst out laughing.
>   'Meyer, what are you laughing at?' exclaimed the other. 'I just knocked you down.'
>   'The joke is on you,' said Kohn. 'I'm not Meyer!'

The phrase 'The joke is on you' may not be easy to understand. Ask who can explain or perhaps translate it into their mother tongue. Can anyone describe another situation or tell a joke which would end with this punch line?

2 Here is another Chelm story. Pre-teach these words and phrases (and any others if necessary): *rock the cradle, boil over, preserved fruit, rat poison, ankle, violent tug, scream, mutter, make a scene.* Read out the story, but stop just before the punch line after 'What shall I do now?'

Hirschler's wife was preparing to go to market and was telling
her husband what to do:

'Whenever the baby wakes up, rock the cradle,' she told him.
'And be sure to watch the milk on the stove so that it doesn't
boil over.' Then she remembered how much her husband liked
preserved fruit. 'And don't touch that jar on the shelf,' she
warned. 'It's rat poison.'

Now, Hirschler wanted to read and at the same time mind his
wife's words. He had an idea. He tied one end of a rope to his
ankle and the other end to the cradle. So he was able to rock the
cradle, watch the milk and meanwhile read his book. This
worked quite well for a while, but suddenly he saw the milk
rising. As he jumped forward to pull the pot off the stove, he
gave the cradle such a violent tug that it turned over and the
baby fell out, screaming at the top of his voice.

At that moment he heard his wife entering the house. 'Good
heavens,' Hirschler muttered as he pictured his wife making a
terrible scene. 'What shall I do now?'

3 Students get into groups and make up a witty ending to the story. After
   finding a suitable punch line, they share it with the rest of the class.
4 After listening to students' suggestions, pre-teach the words *moan* and
   respect. Then finish by reading out the punch line:

He quickly jumped into bed. When Hirschler's wife came into the
room and saw what had happened, she began to shout at him.
First, Hirschler just listened without moving at all. Then he
moaned: 'Please, have a little respect for my final hours!'

'What?!' the wife exlaimed.

'Yes, I'm waiting for the end. I just ate the poison in the fruit jar.'

Follow-up

Each culture has its own witty folk tales. Can students remember one or
two stories in which silliness and shrewdness mingle to create fun?

Extra

If students liked the two Chelm stories in this activity, tell them a third
one just for their entertainment:

Simon the winemaker was deeply disturbed about a strange event that had occurred that morning, so he went to the rabbi for an explanation.

'It's a fact that whenever a poor man such as I drops a slice of bread, it always falls butter-side down,' began Simon.

'Yes, that's true,' agreed the rabbi.

'Well, today I dropped my bread and it fell butter-side up!'

'What? That's impossible!' exclaimed the rabbi. 'I never heard of such a thing!'

'But it happened!'

The rabbi thought for some time. At last he smiled as he found the simple truth.

'Simon, go home and don't worry,' he said. 'You buttered your bread on the wrong side!'

7.5 British anecdotes

Summary:	Here is a sample of 20th century British anecdotes.
Level:	intermediate – post-intermediate
Time:	10–15 minutes
Preparation:	Make a copy of Box 75 for each group of students.

Procedure

1 Put students into groups and give each group a copy of the anecdotes in Box 75. Help them with unfamiliar words, expressions and other comprehension difficulties, and provide information about the people mentioned. (Spike Milligan (1918 –): Irish writer and performer, most famous for his BBC comedy series 'The Goon Show'; Evelyn Waugh (1903–1966): English novelist, whose books include 'Decline and Fall' and 'Brideshead Revisited'; Sue Townsend: became famous with 'The Secret Diary of Adrian Mole, aged 13³/₄' and its sequels.)

> **BOX 75**
>
> 1 A cabinet minister was dining with King George VI at Buckingham Palace in the late 1940s. The king asked his guest if he would like a cigar. 'Oh no, thank you,' the minister said. 'I only smoke on special occasions.'
>
> 2 A famous actor, who was boring his listener with a never-ending monologue about his latest performance in a play, suddenly interrupted himself. 'But I'm talking all about myself,' he apologized. 'Let's talk about *you*. How did you like me in the part?'
>
> 3 Arriving at a restaurant well after last orders had been taken, a famous radio and TV quizmaster persuaded the staff to find him something to eat. Just as he was eating the last bit of food, he overheard one waiter say to another, incredulously, 'He's eaten it!'
>
> 4 The comic Spike Milligan had great admiration for the English novelist Evelyn Waugh. Once Milligan saw Waugh coming out of his club. He went up to him and asked for his autograph. Waugh scribbled on a bit of paper and handed it to Milligan, who thanked him and went home. When he looked at what Waugh had written on the paper, it said, 'Go away.'
>
> 5 After years of poverty, Sue Townsend had two books which were bestsellers and she was wearing a new coat. She was looking in at the window of an elegant restaurant in London to see if her friends had arrived there yet. A bagman came along, carrying about thirteen carrier bags and a bottle of sherry in his hand, and stood by Townsend. He sighed deeply and said, 'Ah, it's not for the likes of us.'

2 Which of the five anecdotes do students like best? Take a vote to find out. Ask a few students to justify their choices.

Extras

1 Write the end of this anecdote on the board and explain the meaning of any unknown words and phrases:

> The note said: 'You're drunk. Leave the room at once.' The butler put the note on a silver tray and presented it to the guest of honour, the British Foreign Secretary.

Tell the class that only the opening sentence is missing. What can it be? When all the suggestions have been put forward, write the original sentence on the board. Here it is:

> At an elegant London party in the 1920s, the hostess slipped a drunk butler a note.

2 For homework, everybody should create a funny story which consists of no more than five sentences. In class, they take it in turns to read out their story without the beginning. The others try to guess the beginning.

Acknowledgment

The anecdotes in this activity have been adapted from *The Guinness Book of Humorous Anecdotes* by Rees (Guinness Publishing).

7.6 The hobbyhorse

Summary:	Some people are great story-tellers – like this person.
Level:	intermediate – post-intermediate
Time:	40–45 minutes
Preparation:	Make a copy (or transparency) of Box 76. Enlarge the drawing if possible. Make a copy of Box 77 for each student.

Procedure

1 The anecdote on the next page is divided into three parts. When you get to the end of each block of text, stop reading. Before you start reading the story, teach any unknown vocabulary items in the first block of text and show the drawing of the hobbyhorse in Box 76.

This is a story about a Hungarian writer in the 1930s, a good-looking man, who loved having fun and playing practical jokes. He was invited to a party, and he thought that he would be funny by … Anyway, he decided to wear his bathing suit to the party and to take a hobbyhorse with him – you know, the thing that looks like a broomstick with a horse's head at the end. Perhaps it was a fancy-dress party in the first place. He would take his overcoat off when he got there and jump around shouting, 'Hey-ho, hey-ho, the riders come and go'. So, on the evening of the party, he walked up to his hosts' apartment block, but by mistake

----

he rang the wrong doorbell. A maid opened the door – these were the days when there were maids – and said, 'Good evening'. The maid took his overcoat, and as you might expect, was shocked when she saw the man's bathing suit and hobbyhorse. But the writer, of course, expected the maid to be flabbergasted. She stood there with his overcoat in her hands looking absolutely petrified. Meanwhile, he opened the door and went into a room where

----

an elderly couple were having dinner. They were sitting at the table, the two of them, silently eating their meal. And when he saw this scene, the writer realised that something was wrong. But it was too late – inertia carried him forward and he jumped around the room, shouting at the top of his voice, 'Hey-ho, hey-ho, the riders come and go'. The elderly couple looked at him as if they had seen an apparition. The writer then returned to the entrance hall, where the maid was still standing with his overcoat. He slipped his coat on and left the apartment.

BOX 76

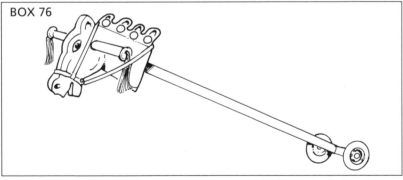

Ask these questions:
- Did you have a hobbyhorse when you were a child? Is it a typical gift for children these days? Do you have a hobbyhorse – in the figurative sense of the word? (A 'hobbyhorse' in the figurative sense is an opinion on a subject that you talk about frequently, usually for a long time.)
- Have you ever been to a fancy-dress party? What did you wear? What was the most interesting costume you saw? If you were going to go to such a party, how would you like to dress up?

2 Students listen to the first part of the story. Then ask what mistake they think the writer made. Obviously, he rang the wrong doorbell. Once this has been clarified, ask the class to guess:
- Did anyone answer the bell?
- If yes, who was it, a man or a woman?
- How did this person react to the arrival of the 'uninvited guest'?
Students discuss their ideas in groups, then share some of the funniest ones with the whole class.

3 After you have read the second part of the story, ask students what they think happened next. There are five alternatives offered in Box 77, but anyone may forward an even more bizarre idea, and write it in the box as a sixth alternative.

BOX 77

1 The room was full of his friends, all riding hobbyhorses.
2 A beautiful lady came to embrace him.
3 An elderly couple were having a quiet dinner.
4 The room was empty. When the writer said 'Good evening', there was no answer except for the echo of his voice.
5 As soon as he entered, a witch sprang at him.
6 .....

In groups, students discuss which alternative is (a) the most plausible, and (b) the strangest. After each group have made their choice, they suggest how the situation came about. A scribe in each group records their best suggestion and then reports it to the class.

Possible answers:
1 All his friends came to the wrong place by accident.
2 The beautiful woman was in fact waiting for him – the prince on the 'white horse'.
3 The elderly couple were having their anniversary dinner – the husband had surprised his wife by inviting her favourite writer.
4 He suddenly woke up and realised that he had fallen asleep in his armchair at home.
5 The witch was not a real one but another guest dressed up as a witch.

4 Students listen to the final part of the anecdote. Then ask the following questions:
  • Who was the most embarrassed character in the story: the writer, the maid, or the elderly couple?
  • In such a situation, would you have behaved the same way as the writer?
  • What did the writer do after leaving the flat, do you think?
  • Suppose he joined his friends at the fancy-dress party. Did he tell anyone what had happened to him downstairs? Why/not?
  Students answer these questions in groups and then share their ideas with the whole class.

Follow-up

It is no easy thing to tell an embarrassing story. Nevertheless, volunteers may like to tell a story in which they got into an awkward situation or witnessed someone else's predicament. If you are short of time, you may decide to give this as a homework assignment.

Extra

Small children keep asking 'why' questions, often getting on their parents' nerves. Divide the class into pairs for a role-play. In each pair, one student is 'the child', the other one 'the parent'. The parent begins to tell 'The hobbyhorse' in the first person singular, with the child constantly interrupting her/him. The parent answers all the questions, but becomes increasingly impatient. The dialogue may begin like this:

Parent: Once I was invited to a fancy-dress ball.
Child: Why were you invited?
Parent: Because the hosts were good friends of mine ... I decided to ride a hobbyhorse at the party.
Child: Why a hobbyhorse?
Parent: Because I thought that would be funny ...

Acknowledgment

I heard 'The hobbyhorse' from Ádám Nádasdy.

7.7 Urban myths

Summary: The contemporary world is no less rich in legends than earlier ages.

Level: intermediate – post-intermediate

Time: 20–25 minutes

Preparation: Make a copy of Box 78a and Box 78b for each student.

Procedure

1 A special feature of urban myths is that they are presented as true, though they may never have happened. But even if they are true stories, they probably have been embellished and exaggerated as they have travelled on from person to person, country to country, language to language. Urban myths are often rude and/or cruel, using lots of colloquial and slang expressions. The story presented here is an exceptionally innocent example. After you have read this story at home, prepare to tell it to the class, using your own words.

Dirty dog

A politician at the last general election was visiting his large constituency and came to a house with a vicious-looking pit bull terrier outside. He hated dogs and was a bit hesitant as he pressed the doorbell, but he was given a warm welcome by the people of the house.

They told him they always voted for him anyway and invited him in for a cup of tea. He was feeling pretty tired and accepted their offer, stepping past the pit bull.

The dog followed him into the room and lay down showing its teeth and staring at him from the middle of the floor.

He was enjoying his cup of tea as much as he could with the dog there, chatting with his hosts about local issues, when the dog stood up, lifted its leg and completely wetted the carpet. His hosts looked at the dog briefly, then carried on talking.

The politician was a bit surprised, but as no one else said anything, he just wondered a bit about what kind of supporter he was attracting. Each to their own, he decided.

After a good chat, the candidate finished his cup of tea, thanked the family, and made his way out of the door. He'd just taken a few paces outside when he heard someone call out behind him:

'Excuse me, aren't you going to take your dog with you?'

Tell the story as well as you can. Ask if students liked it. Why/not? Who can summarise it?

2 Ask students to think of a funny urban myth they have heard, but add that they won't have to tell the story off the cuff – it is a homework assignment. Should anyone complain that they cannot think of a story worth telling, help them out with either the story in Box 78a or the one in Box 78b.

At home, everybody gets ready to tell their story in their own words. None of the stories should be longer than two minutes. In class, students in groups tell each other the stories they have prepared, and then choose the one they find the funniest. The best can then be told to the whole class.

BOX 78a

The deer-stalker

A friend of mine recalls a man at his office who was quite high-up but a big-headed old fool, and therefore unpopular with his workmates. One day, he was browsing in the local market and came across a Sherlock Holmes-style deer-stalker hat, which he bought and wore to work, to everyone's quiet amusement.

Unfortunately for him, a few days later, two of his colleagues went to the same market stall, and decided to buy two more identical hats – one in the largest size available, the other the smallest.

The next day, the man hung his deer-stalker up in reception as usual. The two colleagues took it off its hook, replacing it with the large one they'd bought. At the end of the day, the old fool picked up the hat and put it on. He was quite surprised to find that it was far too big, but he didn't think much about it and went home with the hat resting on his ears.

The next day, they replaced the largest hat with the smallest ... and so they went on, day after day for weeks – sometimes leaving the guy's original hat for a few days – until eventually the confused old fool paid a visit to his doctor, convinced that his head was expanding and contracting like a balloon.

BOX 78b

Wrong ring

A friend of a former colleague told me about an incident that
recently happened to his boss on a train. The boss was feeling
pleased at claiming a four-seat table for himself and settled down
to a nice quiet journey reading his book. The whistle blew and as
the train pulled out, a loud yuppie went into the carriage and
threw his bags down on the table, collapsed into the seat
opposite, immediately took out his mobile phone and began a
loud, silly conversation – 'buy ... sell ... take a check ... hyper!' –
that sort of thing.

The quieter man couldn't believe his misfortune and tried to
ignore the stupid city type, but he was so noisy, ringing people
up and rustling papers and shouting 'Yah ... yah ... yah ...' into
the phone all the time, that the boss couldn't take any more and
left for another part of the train.

He'd just sat down when an old man opposite him went pale
and groaned. He was having a heart attack and collapsed on the
floor. The guard arrived as passengers tried to come to the old
gent's aid, and he explained that they'd have to wait until the
next station before they could phone as the train's
communication lines were down.

'I know someone with a phone!' said the boss happily, 'we can
ring ahead and have an ambulance waiting for him at the
station.'

So the guard, the boss and some other concerned passengers
marched back down the carriage. The yuppie was still in mid-
conversation when the guard cut in to explain the situation and
ask him, as it was an emergency, if they might have the use of his
mobile phone.

At first the yuppie waved them away as if he was busy, still
talking down the line. But when they persisted and got
increasingly agitated, he threw the phone down, went red in the
face and looking down mumbled, 'You can't. It's only a fake
phone.'

Variations

1   Invite a volunteer to tell their story, facing the class. Before they begin,
however, warn them of a plot. During their monologue, you will be
writing adjectives on the board behind their back, and the class will
respond as suggested by the adjectives. So if you write 'bored', for

example, everybody will be yawning and dozing off. Having finished their story, the volunteer will have to try identifying the swings of mood.

Other useful adjectives are:

angry	ecstatic	enthusiastic	impatient	jubilant	puzzled
silly	unhappy	uninterested	worried		

2 In this variation, students do not tell their story straight away, but leave it to their classmates to make up a story. To help guesswork, everybody should bring to class a rucksack containing objects to serve as clues. In class, the first student comes forward, fishes the objects out of her/his rucksack in the order that they get referred to in the story, places them on the floor, then tells the beginning of the story. After she/he has stopped, anybody who has an idea may continue – and so on, until a full story is created. Finally, the owner of the story relates the original version of the story, pointing to the objects on the floor as she/he mentions them during her/his narration. When she/he has finished, another volunteer comes forward with her/his rucksack.

Acknowledgments

The stories in this activity have been adapted from *Urban Myths* by Healey and Glanvill (Virgin Publishing).

7.8 Story relay

Summary:	Students make up a story sentence by sentence.
Level:	beginner – pre-intermediate
Time:	10–15 minutes
Preparation:	none

Procedure

1 Everybody should think of a simple story they have heard recently. Allow about five minutes for preparation.
2 Call on a student. Instead of telling the full story, however, Student A should only say the opening sentence. For example:

Student A: My uncle is a terribly vain man.

Now Student A points to Student B, who adds a sentence which is related to the first one:

Student B: He is so vain that his colleagues decided to play a trick on him.

It is Student B's turn to call on Student C, who, after supplying her/his sentence, asks Student D to continue, and so on. Anyone unable to keep the story going drops out.

3 After the story has been rounded off, the 'owner' of the story (Student A) tells her/his story from beginning to end. Surely it is very different from what the class have produced!

Variations

1 This activity can be made particularly enjoyable if the story is recorded on tape sentence by sentence.
2 Bring to class pictures of all sorts. Before each turn-taking, produce a picture on which the next student has to base her/his sentence.

7.9 Can you imagine?

Summary:	This activity practises how to tell a flat story in an entertaining way.
Level:	pre-intermediate – intermediate
Time:	20–25 minutes
Procedure:	Make a copy of Box 79 for each student.

Procedure

1 Read out the first version of this story, making it sound as dull as possible:

> I had a lovely time this morning. I woke at half past six. I got out of bed and went to the bathroom. I washed my hands and face, cleaned my teeth, and then got dressed. After I had had a sandwich and a cup of coffee, I kissed my mum and dad, and left home round half past seven. Mum waved good-bye to me from the kitchen window. The weather was a bit chilly, but sunny. It took me about five minutes to arrive at the bus stop. Just as I got there, the bus turned round the corner. It was almost full, but I managed to find an empty seat in the back.

Ask whether students enjoyed your story. No wonder they didn't: it was a trivial story told in a boring fashion!

2 Now read out the second version of the story. It is the same story and yet it is quite different. What has made the change? Can students identify certain phrases which jazzed up the text?

> I had a lovely time this morning! This is hard to believe, but I woke up at half past six. You'll never guess what happened next. I got out of bed and went to the bathroom. Can you imagine? I washed my hands and face, cleaned my teeth, and then got dressed. But wait, there's more! After I had had a sandwich and a cup of coffee, I kissed my mum and dad, and left home round half past seven. Mum waved good-bye to me from the kitchen window. Strangely enough, the weather was a bit chilly, but sunny. It took me about five minutes to arrive at the bus stop. Believe it or not, just as I got there, the bus turned round the corner. And that's not the end of it! It was almost full, but I managed to find an empty seat in the back. I couldn't believe my eyes!

3 Give out the phrases in Box 79.

> **BOX 79**
> This is hard to believe, but ...
> You'll never guess what happened next ...
> Can you imagine?
> But wait, there's more!
> Strangely enough, ...
> Believe it or not, ...
> And that's not the end of it!
> I couldn't believe my eyes/ears!

Run through the list and explain the meaning of the phrases if necessary.

4 Everyone has a few minutes to compose a simple story and then add the expressions in Box 79. Students relate their stories in pairs.

Extra

Suppose that the class is on a school trip, travelling on a long and boring train journey. Sitting in compartments for four passengers, they pass away the time by telling each other the stories created in *Step 4*. While one person is speaking, the other three should react:

(a) with a lack of interest if the story is told flatly:
  e.g. Hmm, Really? Well, Interesting, I see.

(b) with enthusiasm if it is told with dramatic force:
  e.g. Oh no! Gosh! Amazing! Oh dear! Fantastic! You're kidding! Wow!

164

Remind students that intonation usually carries more weight than even the most expressive phrase!

Acknowledgment

Ideas for this activity have been borrowed from 'You'll never believe this!' in Dörnyei & Thurrell's *Conversation and Dialogues in Action* (Prentice Hall International).

7.10 Call my bluff!

Summary:	This activity is concerned with 'professional' liars.
Level:	pre-intermediate – advanced
Time:	30–35 minutes
Preparation:	Make a copy of Box 80a, Box 80b or Box 80c, depending on the level of the class. If there are more than 15 students in the class, make several copies for groupwork.

Procedure

1 Introduce the topic of lying with these jokes:

> Doctor, you've got to help me. Everyone thinks I'm a liar.
>   I find that hard to believe.
>
> I'm not saying he's a liar. Let's just say he lives on the wrong side of the facts.
>
> What you're saying is as false as the teeth you're saying it through!

Then ask the following questions:
- Do you know people who never tell lies?
- Why do people lie?
- What was the biggest lie you have ever heard?
- Do you often lie?

2 'Professional' liars have good acting skills. Although lying is the last skill we want to develop, 'Call my bluff!' is an innocent game, eliciting lots of laughter, as a rule. This version of the well-known party game is based on dictionary definitions.

Divide the class into groups of three. Give each group three definitions of the same word. Help with any unknown words and phrases.

BOX 80a pre-intermediate – intermediate

--✂

1 BLOCK
   (F) A slip you receive as you pay in a shop. 'Take your block, madam.'
   (T) The distance between two street crossings. 'It's just three blocks to the store.'
   (F) A ticket the police give you when you park in the wrong place. 'Oh no, not another block!'

--✂

2 NOVEL
   (F) A short story. 'Have you read E.G. Brixton's new collection of novels yet?'
   (F) A colloquial form of *not very well*. 'How are you, Jim?' 'Novel.'
   (T) A long written story. 'Maugham wrote a lot of novels and short stories.'

--✂

3 SYMPATHETIC
   (F) Nice. 'He's just a charming, sympathetic man!'
   (T) Understanding. 'Why aren't you a little bit more sympathetic, Clare?'
   (F) Full form of *pathetic*, i.e. *useless*. 'How can you be so (sym)pathetic?! Let me do it!'

--✂

4 GYM
   (T) A special hall in which you do physical exercise. 'Where's the P.E. class today: in the gym or outdoors?'
   (F) sports shoes; 'Mum, where did you put my gyms?'
   (F) a special type of secondary school; short for *gymnasium*. 'Does she still attend the gym?'

--✂

5 LATELY
   (T) Recently, these days. 'I've been feeling ill lately.'
   (F) After the expected time. 'Sue came home lately because she had a great time at the disco.'
   (F) Last. 'Not again! Why are you always the lately to arrive.'

BOX 80b intermediate – post-intermediate

1 MARK
- (F) A particular type of product. 'What mark is this car? A Peugeot or a Toyota?'
- (F) Remaining money in the set phrase *mark and dark*. 'If you deduct the expenses, we'll be left with $200 mark and dark.'
- (T) Dirt. 'I can't get these marks out of my T-shirt.'

2 HYMN
- (T) A song of praise to God. 'We shall now sing a hymn for those who have died.'
- (F) The masculine third person plural until the 17th century. 'O, be hallowed Hymn who dieth for the motherland.'
- (F) The official song of a nation. 'Whenever I hear the hymn of Hungary, I feel like crying.'

3 STRAIGHTFORWARD
- (T) Honest. 'Jack is tough, but always straightforward and fair.'
- (F) Straight on. 'Go straightforward this road and take the second street on your right.'
- (F) An attacking player in a team, such as football. 'Manchester United paid 25 million pounds for Friganti, the Italian straightforward.'

4 INFLUENCE
- (F) The full form of *flu*, the infectious disease. 'I'm sorry, Kevin, but I'm in bed with a bad influence.'
- (T) The power to have an effect on things or people. 'Van Gogh had a great influence on generations of artists.'
- (F) Name of several popes. 'Influence VI (1588–1610) was one of the greatest popes in the Vatican.'

5 PLUG
- (F) A colloquial form of *matter* in the set phrase: 'What's the plug, man?'
- (F) A small insect that lives on people's skin and hair. 'Just imagine! I had to take Maggie to the doctor with plugs.'
- (T) A thing used for connecting a piece of electrical equipment to the main supply of electricity. 'Make sure you turn the television off at the plug.'

Laughing Matters

BOX 80c post-intermediate – advanced

- ✂

1 OOMPH
   (T) If you say that someone or something has oomph, you mean that they are energetic and exciting. 'There's no buzz, there's no oomph about the place.'
   (F) This word is uttered when someone is hit or struck by something. 'Oomph! That hurt!'
   (F) An oomph is a unit of weight used in Britain. There are 23 oomphs in a pound. 'Give me four oomphs of sugar, please.'

- ✂

2 SEVER
   (F) If you are sever, you are ill. Sever is often used in the set phrase 'sick and sever'. 'There were no doctors to treat the sick and sever.'
   (F) Sever is an outdated form of several; it is used with *in* after the word to which it refers. 'Henry VIII was not the only British monarch who had wives in sever.'
   (T) To sever something means to cut it completely off. 'Glen severed his right foot in a motorbike accident.'

- ✂

3 SIDEBURNS
   (F) Sideburns are a special kind of desert ant; they have a poisonous sting.
   (T) If a man has sideburns, he has a strip of hair growing down the side of each cheek. 'I like guys with long sideburns.'
   (F) If a building has suffered sideburns, it means that the central frame has survived and only the edges were destroyed. 'With sideburns only, the damage was less than $50,000.'

- ✂

4 WHINNY
   (F) Whinny is the main character in Milne's *Whinny-the-Pooh*.
   (T) When a horse whinnies, it neighs softly. 'The girl's horse whinnied.'
   (F) A whinny person is extremely thin, in a way that you find unattractive. 'He was quite a whinny little boy.'

- ✂

5 ILL-TEMPERED
   (T) If you describe someone as ill-tempered, you mean they are angry or hostile. 'He sounded like an ill-tempered child.'
   (F) An ill-tempered person has a body temperature that is higher than 38°C. 'John is ill-tempered. Call the doctor at once!'
   (F) If a car is ill-tempered, it is either not serviced at regular intervals or it has been repaired with unskilled hands. 'Poor Helen! She's bought the most ill-tempered car I've ever seen.'

© Cambridge University Press 2002

168

3 No matter whether their definition is true or false, everybody keeps this a secret and reads out their definition as seriously as possible. The class listen to all three definitions, and then try to guess which is the correct answer. When everyone has had their turn, ask which students are considered to be the smartest 'liars' by their classmates.

4 Challenge students to create their own pool of definitions at home, at least one word per student. Students should bear three things in mind:
   1 Use a monolingual dictionary.
   2 Select unfamiliar words.
   3 Choose the distractors (F) so that they sound as plausible as the true definition (T).

In class, students take turns presenting their definitions.

Extras

1 On the subject of lying, volunteers prepare to tell a simple story. It may be either a true story or made up. The teller should keep a straight face and answer any questions while relating the story. In the end, the audience should guess whether or not the story is true.

2 Somebody writes three sentences on the board describing experiences they have had: two of the sentences are true and one is false. The other members of the class ask the scribe questions about each experience. When enough evidence has been collected, the class tries to identify the false sentence.

7.11 Mumble-jumble

Summary:	Students turn up the volume of their mumble.
Level:	intermediate – post-intermediate
Time:	15–20 minutes (in class)
Preparation:	none

Procedure

1 At home, each student prepares a funny anecdote. This may be a story that happened to them or someone else, but it should not be a well-known story. Everyone rehearses their story until they can tell it fluently, humorously and by heart. The duration of each story should be between two and three minutes!

2 In class, explain the rules of the game: Everybody begins to mumble their story to themselves. When they have been mumbling for about half a minute, you interrupt by calling on someone. This person goes on telling their story out loud for about half a minute while the others just listen. At a given signal, the class mumble resumes until you pinpoint another individual, and so on.
3 Before the real show begins, offer students the opportunity to rehearse their mumble, but stop the activity when the three minutes are up. Warn those who have finished in less than two minutes as well as those who would have needed more than three minutes to keep to the time limit.
4 Now the curtain rises! After four or five students have been given the floor to speak aloud, stop the activity. Ask which of the snippets was the most stimulating. Encourage this student to tell her/his story in full.

Variation

In a multilingual class where students do not share the same mother tongue, they may enjoy listening to each other's stories told in the mother tongue. Ask the story-tellers to choose a simple story or folk tale, and tell it to the class. Remind them that they can help understanding by (a) speaking slowly; (b) inserting frequent pauses; (c) imitating the voice of the characters in the story; and (d) gesticulating a lot. After the volunteers have finished their stories, encourage the class to try and tell the gist of the stories.

Acknowledgment

This is an adapted version of an activity I learnt from Mario Rinvolucri.

7.12 Buzz off!

Summary:	How we say something can be as important as what we say.
Level:	post-intermediate – advanced
Time:	30–35 minutes (in class)
Preparation:	Make a copy of Box 81 and Box 82 for each student.

Procedure

1 The following extract is from Bill Bryson's (1951–) entertaining travel book *The Lost Continent: Travels in Small Town America*. The author, after having lived in England for many years, returns to his

home-state, Iowa, to revisit places from his youth. As he drives
aimlessly around the countryside, he happens to stop at a small town
called Littleton. Give everybody a copy of Box 81 to read at home.
Pre-teach any new vocabulary, but don't make a fuss about the fancy
ice creams and the endless list of berry pies.

BOX 81

It was the friendliest little place I had ever seen. I went into the
Topic of the Town restaurant. The other customers smiled at me,
the lady at the cash register showed me where to put my jacket,
and the waitress, a plump and dimpled little lady, couldn't do
enough for me. It was as if they had all been given some kind of
marvellous tranquilliser.

The waitress brought me a menu and I made the mistake of
saying thank you. 'You're welcome,' she said. She brought me
some cutlery wrapped in a paper napkin. I hesitated, but I
couldn't stop myself. 'Thank you,' I said. 'You're welcome,' she
said. Then came a placemat with Topic of the Town written on
it, and then a glass of water and then a clean ashtray, and then a
little basket of Saltine crackers wrapped in cellophane, and at
each we had our polite exchange. I ordered the fried chicken
special. As I waited I became uncomfortably aware that the
people at the next table were watching me and smiling at me in a
deranged fashion. The waitress was watching me, too, from a
position by the kichen doorway. It was all rather unnerving.
Every few moments she would come over and top up my iced
water and tell me that my food would only be a minute.

'Thank you,' I'd say.

'You're welcome,' she'd say.

Eventually the waitress came out of the kitchen with a tray the
size of a table-top and started setting down plates of food in front
of me – soup, salad, a platter of chicken, a basket of steaming
rolls. It all looked delicious. Suddenly I realised that I was starving.

'Can I get you anything else?' she said.

'No, this is just fine, thank you,' I answered, knife and fork
plugged in my fists, ready to lunge at the food.

'Would you like some ketchup?'

'No thank you.'

'Would you like a little more dressing for your salad?'

'No thank you.'

'Have you got enough gravy?'

There was enough gravy to drown a horse. 'Yes, plenty of
gravy, thank you.'

'How about a cup of coffee?'

'Really, I'm fine.'

'You sure there's nothing I can do for you?'

'Well, you might just buzz off and let me eat my dinner,' I wanted to say, but I didn't, of course. I just smiled sweetly and said no thank you and after a while she withdrew. But she stood with a pitcher of iced water and watched me closely the whole meal. Every time I took a sip of water, she would come forward and top up my glass. Once when I reached for the pepper, she misread my intentions and started forward with the water pitcher, but then had to retreat. After that, whenever my hands left the cutlery for any reason, I would semi-mime an explanation to her of what I was about to do – 'I'm just going to butter my roll now' – so that she wouldn't rush over to give me more water. And all the while the people at the next table watched me eat and smiled encouragingly. I couldn't wait to get out of there.

When at last I finished the waitress came over and offered me dessert. 'How about a piece of pie? We've got blueberry, blackberry, raspberry, boysenberry, huckleberry, whortleberry, cherry berry, hair berry, chuckberry and berry-berry.'

'Gosh, no thanks, I'm too full,' I said placing my hands on my stomach. I looked as if I had stuffed a pillow under my shirt.

'Well, how about some ice-cream? We've got chocolate chip, chocolate fudge, chocolate ripple, chocolate-vanilla fudge, chocolate nut fudge, chocolate marshmallow swirl, chocolate mint with fudge chips, and fudge nut with or without chocolate chips.'

'Have you got just plain chocolate?'

'No, I'm afraid there's not much call for that.'

'I don't think I'll have anything then.'

'Well, how about a piece of cake. We've got –'

'Really, no thank you.'

'A cup of coffee?'

'No thank you.'

'You sure now?'

'Yes, thank you.'

'Well, I'll just get you a little more water then,' and she was off for the water jug before I could get her to give me my bill. The people at the next table watched this with interest and smiled a smile that said 'We are completely off our heads. How are you?' [...]

2 Students in groups discuss which parts of the excerpt they found particularly funny.

3 Now distribute the dialogue in Box 82. After students have read it, they practise it in pairs until they have learnt it by heart. Remind them that, for the sake of contrast, the 'waitress' in each pair should be overpolite whereas the 'customer' should gradually lose patience.

BOX 82

Waitress:	Can I get you anything else?
Customer:	No, this is just fine, thank you.
Waitress:	Would you like some ketchup?
Customer:	No, thank you.
Waitress:	Would you like a little more dressing for your salad?
Customer:	No, thank you.
Waitress:	Have you got enough gravy?
Customer:	Yes, plenty of gravy, thank you.
Waitress:	How about a cup of coffee?
Customer:	Really, I'm fine.
Waitress:	You sure there's nothing I can do for you?
Customer:	Well, you might just buzz off and let me eat my dinner.

© Cambridge University Press 2002

Variations

1 Polite forms tend to be longer than less polite ones. Students may alter the text of the dialogue in *Step 3* by making the exchanges so polite as to be sarcastic. The box below contains a few useful expressions to use:

I'm terribly sorry to disturb you, but ...
I hate to bother you again, but ...
I wonder if you'd care for ...
I was wondering if you'd fancy ...
I hope you don't mind me asking ...
Thank you so much, sir/madam, but the real credit should go to ...

Oh, how kind of you!
Lovely idea, thank you.
That would be very nice indeed.
Not just at the moment, thank you.
That was a really delicious meal.
You've done a marvellous job.

---

2 Suppose the dialogue is meant to be impolite. Students should reduce the length of the same dialogue. How short can they make it?

Suggested dialogue:
Anything else?
  No.
Ketchup?
  No.
Dressing?
  No.
Enough gravy?
  Plenty.
Coffee?
  No.
Anything else?
  Buzz off.

Now get students to practise this telegraphic dialogue.

Acknowledgment

The extract is slightly adapted from Bryson's *The Lost Continent: Travels in Small Town America* (Penguin Books).

7.13 Catch-22

Summary:	We sometimes get into catch-22 situations in which we simply can't win.
Level:	post-intermediate – advanced
Time:	25–30 minutes (in class)
Preparation:	Make a copy of Box 83 for each student.

Procedure

1 Can students think of typical catch-22 situations from their own experience? Are any of them funny? After thinking for a few minutes, encourage them to share their stories and ideas with the rest of the class. Tell the class this bitter joke which describes such a no-win situation.

> The fox and the wolf are walking in the forest. When they see Little Rabbit approaching, the fox says, 'Let's beat him up!'
>
> 'Good idea,' agrees the wolf, and indeed they give the rabbit a good spanking. Little Rabbit asks them: 'What have I done to make you so angry?' The fox replies: 'Well, you're not wearing a hat, are you?'
>
> The next day Little Rabbit puts on his hat, just to be on the safe side. He meets the fox and the wolf once again. The fox says to the wolf: 'Let's beat him up!' And they do. Poor Little Rabbit asks: 'Why did you beat me up this time?' 'Because you're wearing a hat,' the fox replies. 'But yesterday the trouble was I wasn't wearing one!' 'Tough,' says the fox.

Ask what the moral of the sad story is.

Suggested answer: There are situations in life where you are bound to lose – no matter what.

2 The phrase *catch-22* was coined by Joseph Heller, and it is in fact the title of his famous American wartime novel. Has this book been translated into the students' mother tongue? (Joseph Heller (1923–2000) served as a bombardier during the war. His novel *Catch-22*, first published in 1961, is based on his wartime experiences. His other novels include *Something happened*, *God knows* and *Good as Gold*.) Tell the class that the story is set on a small Mediterranean island during World War II. Captain Yossarian, the main character, is a bombardier in the US Air Force. His mad commander is willing to sacrifice his soldiers in order to get promotion. In an attempt to save his life, Yossarian asks the army doctor to ground him as unfit for flying. But there's a catch there – catch-22, as it will turn out from the passage.

3 Give out the extract from Heller's novel for reading at home. Pre-teach the key vocabulary.

BOX 83

'You're wasting your time,' Doc Daneeka was forced to tell him.

'Can't you ground someone who's crazy?'

'Oh, sure. I have to. There's a rule saying I have to ground anyone who's crazy.'

'Then why don't you ground me? I'm crazy. Ask Clevinger.'

'Clevinger? Where is Clevinger? You find Clevinger and I'll ask him.'

'Then ask any of the others. They'll tell you how crazy I am.'

'They're crazy.'

'Then why don't you ground them?'

'Why don't they ask me to ground them?'

'Because they're crazy, that's why.'

'Of course they're crazy,' Doc Daneeka replied. 'I just told you they're crazy, didn't I? And you can't let crazy people decide whether you're crazy or not, can you?'

Yossarian looked at him soberly and tried another approach. 'Is Orr crazy?'

'He sure is,' Doc Daneeka said.

'Can you ground him?'

'I sure can. But first he has to ask me to. That's part of the rule.'

'Then why doesn't he ask you to?'

'Because he's crazy,' Doc Daneeka said. 'He has to be crazy to keep flying combat missions after all the close calls he's had. Sure, I can ground Orr. But first he has to ask me to.'

'That's all he has to do to be grounded?'

'That's all. Let him ask me.'

'And then you can ground him?' Yossarian asked.

'No. Then I can't ground him.'

'You mean there's a catch?'

'Sure there's a catch,' Doc Daneeka replied. 'Catch-22. Anyone who wants to get out of combat duty isn't really crazy.'

There was only one catch and that was Catch-22 which specified that a concern for one's safety in the face of dangers that were real and immediate was the process of a rational mind. Orr was crazy and could be grounded. All he had to do was ask; and as soon as he did, he would no longer be crazy and would have to fly more missions. Orr would be crazy to fly more missions and sane if he didn't, but if he was sane he had to fly them. If he flew them he was crazy and didn't have to; but if he didn't want to he was sane and had to.

Yossarian was moved very deeply by the absolute simplicity of this clause of Catch-22 and let out a respectful whistle.

'That's some catch, that Catch-22,' he observed.

'It's the best there is,' Doc Daneeka agreed.

4 In groups, students discuss the contradiction in the Heller passage. Can they suggest a way out of the jam? How do they think the novel will end?

Answer: Yossarian succeeds in escaping.

Acknowledgment

The extract is from Heller's *Catch-22* (Dell Publishing Co., Inc.).

7.14 The mini-novel

Summary:	Students develop a mini-novel from an opening sentence.
Level:	pre-intermediate – intermediate
Time:	10–15 minutes (in the first class)
Preparation:	Have large sheets and some reusable adhesive at the ready.

Procedure

1 Write these three sentences on the board:

> Vivienne had only one thing on her mind as she crept along the cornfield.
> Jake looked quite bored, but penguins often do.
> When we entered the hotel, Santa Claus lay dead on the floor.

Tell the class that these are the first sentences of three (imaginary) novels. Which one has whetted their appetite to read the whole book? If none of them sound interesting, give students a few minutes to think of a better opening sentence in groups. When several ideas have been put forward, vote for the most popular.

2 Invite the class to write a mini-novel on the basis of the first sentence. This project task may continue for several weeks. From lesson to lesson, students take it in turns to add two or three sentences to the passage, and stick them (in legible handwriting) on the wall under one another. Before each lesson, everybody goes up to the current passage, reads it, and decides who will write the next part. Funny twists are welcome! The student left last to add their bit should bring the mini-novel to an end. (Whenever you feel that the novel is becoming somewhat tired or clumsy, you could introduce an unexpected twist yourself.)

Variation

Any author may embellish their sequel with an illustration or a collage.

Follow-up

Once the mini-novel is complete, it could be typed up and copied, so that everybody can have their own copy. This may well be the first tangible result of teamwork for some students!

Acknowledgment

The idea of the mini-novel comes from Lee's *Language Teaching Games and Contests* (Oxford University Press).

8 Sketches and dialogues

Everyday conversation typically consists of dialogues between two or more people. In an attempt to reproduce authentic communication, coursebooks are also full of dialogues, but it has to be admitted that few of them are funny.

A sketch is a special form of dialogue; it is usually short and trivial, but it has always been an essential and valuable part of comic entertainment. The tradition of presenting a witty dramatic piece is almost as old as comedy itself. In most sketches, two characters enter into a funny conversation but, quite often, the interaction is non-verbal as in mimes and silent movies. Typically, comedy sketches ridicule ordinary human faults and weaknesses. What I particularly like about them is that it is often the underdog that takes the upper hand – unlike in real life.

8.1 Group mime story

Summary:	This activity develops observation skills through non-verbal communication.
Level:	beginner – pre-intermediate
Time:	10–15 minutes
Preparation:	none

Procedure

1 Students get into groups of 6–8 and stand in a circle. Student A thinks of something and mimes it to the student next to her/him. For example, she/he pretends to pick up a 'thing' and shows what it is by the way she/he holds it, her/his facial expressions and what she/he does with it. Then she/he passes the 'thing' on to Student B, who decides what she/he thinks the 'thing' is and handles it accordingly. This person then hands it over to Student C – and so on round the group. The last person should add an obvious ending to the imaginary story, such as letting the 'thing' fly away or dropping it. Throughout the mime, no verbal clues are allowed!

2 After the mime, group members identify what they thought the 'thing' was. After agreeing on a final scenario, they rehearse the mime.

3 Groups take it in turns to act out their mime while the other groups watch and then try to make sense of the scene. At the end of each mime, the spectators make guesses.

Variation

Should a group need a trigger, whisper an idea from this bank:

a snake   a baby   mercury   a heavy trunk   a bird a hot cup of tea   a soft cushion   contact lenses a bottle of perfume   a wet sponge

Extra

In another circle game, Student A hands Student B a 'thing', saying, 'This is a cat.' Somewhat surprised, Student B asks: 'A what?' Student A repeats: 'A cat.' Student B then passes the thing to Student C, saying 'This is a cat', followed by the surprised exclamation of Student C: 'A what?', and so on. When the thing comes back to Student A at the end of the circle, she/he says: 'This is a cat', but then starts off another thing (a bat or whatever), but this time in the opposite direction. Now both things go around the circle in opposite directions and, soon enough, a third thing will begin to go around as well, and so on. When different things meet up, complications will arise – and laughter in their wake!

Acknowledgment

The idea described in the *Extra* is from *The Oxford Guide to Word Games* by Augarde (Oxford University Press).

8.2 Silent movie scripts

Summary:	Students write and then mime a silent movie sketch.
Level:	pre-intermediate – intermediate
Time:	20–25 minutes
Preparation:	none

Procedure

1 Slapstick comedies are based on humorously embarrassing and clumsy situations. Ask if students like such comedies. Do they prefer

sketches with or without words? Do they have any favourites? What makes people laugh in such movies?

2 In old silent movies, special gagmen were employed, whose job was to write jokes and funny lines for the script. Would students make good gagmen (and gagwomen, of course)? Here is a chance for them to try! Read out the beginning of this story:

> Three gangsters are chasing a boy. They want to catch him because he saw them rob an old millionaire in his house. As the boy is running down a narrow lane, he notices that one of the thugs is waiting for him at the end of the lane ...

In groups, students design the script for the next few takes. Obviously, the aim is to save the boy's life and make the gangsters look stupid. The scribe in each group jots down the sequence of events. Note that this is a silent film, so no dialogue is required.

3 Once the script has been written, each group member takes the role of a character in the sketch and then the rehearsals begin.

4 Show-time! Groups take it in turns to perform their little scenes. After each performance, the audience describe what they have seen.

Possible answer:
Halfway down the street, there is a crossing. Just as the boy gets there, a cyclist passes by. The boy jumps on the frame of the bike and dashes off. The four gangsters shake their fists after him in frustration.

Variation

The scriptwriters might derive inspiration from some background music which suits the atmosphere of the scene. So have some scary music available if possible, and play it during both the writing process and the show.

Extra

Here are a few more story frames to help groups who are short of ideas:

> A girl is sitting on a bench reading a magazine, with a vicious-looking dog sitting at her feet. A boy approaches and sits down close to her. He tries to chat her up, but the girl ignores him. The boy becomes more and more aggressive ...

> It is sunset on the beach. A man has lost his car key in the sand. He lies down, hoping that he will spot the key glittering in the sun. A few yards away, a group of youngsters watch him with growing interest ...

> A couple are hopelessly looking for something in their messy living-room. The man looks behind the bookshelves and the woman opens a box of matches. An elephant hides behind a big sofa, laughing to himself ...

Acknowledgment

The idea of script writing is borrowed from *When in Britain* by Nolasco and Medgyes (Oxford University Press).

8.3 Charades

Summary:	This popular team game can be played in several variations.
Level:	beginner – intermediate
Time:	20–25 minutes
Preparation:	none

Procedure

1 Divide the class into two teams of about equal size. Give each team a word which can be broken down into two meaningful one-syllable words. Depending on the language level of the class, here are three lists:

beginner	*pre-intermediate*	*intermediate*
forest (for+rest)	music (mew+sick)	exact (eggs+act)
foreign (for+in)	comfortable (come+	survive (serve+I've)
letter (let+her)	for+table)	phantom (fan+Tom)
person (pair+son)	peaceful (peas+full)	literature (litter+richer)
	notice (no+tease)	

Both teams design and then act out three sketches, each consisting of one or two sentences: one sketch is based on the first syllable, one on the second syllable and one on the full word. (The word could also consist of three or four syllables, but then the number of scenes increases too.) Note that the spelling of the two bits does not have to combine exactly into the full word; as long as the sounds are roughly right, the word can pass. On the other hand, the key item should be casually but clearly mentioned in the scene. For example, Team A chooses 'forest' (= for + rest). The first scene might be a shop where the shop assistant asks: 'What can I do for you?' In the second scene, an exhausted student at the end of the day talks to a friend: 'All I need is a good night's rest'. The third may be a scene from Hansel and Gretel as they talk about going out into the forest. The job of Team B is to watch and guess the word. If they succeed in doing so, they then take a turn. If they don't guess the word, Team A can have another go.

2 After a while, instead of you supplying the word, students choose their own words.

Variation

In a well-known variation of 'Charades', the title of a play, novel, film or piece of music is to be mimed. Divide the class into two teams. Everyone prepares a title for the other team and writes it on a slip of paper. The slips are pooled and the game begins. For example, Liz from Team A draws a slip – it happens to be the novel *The Lord of the Flies* by William Golding. She begins by showing her partners in Team A that the title consists of five words and then goes on to show that she will mime the fifth word first. She makes flapping movements with her hands as if flying. Someone in her team says 'fly'. Through gestures, Liz urges her partner to alter the word *fly* slightly. Another team member gets it right: *flies*. Liz nods her head as a sign of approval. Now she indicates that next she will mime the second word in the title, and so on. Each turn may take a maximum of three minutes. The team which succeeds in guessing a title scores one point. The game finishes when everybody has had a turn to mime. The winner is the team with the higher score.

N.B. Certain signals are allowed throughout the game. Thus students may:
1 nod their head for *yes* and shake it for *no*;
2 hold up the number of fingers representing the number of words in the title or the number of syllables in each word;
3 indicate whether a word is short or long by holding their hands close together or far apart;
4 agree on certain signs to indicate a play, a novel, a film and a piece of music, respectively.

On the other hand, they are not allowed to speak, write, touch or point at an object.

8.4 I'm a little deaf

Summary:	We often ask for repetition – especially people with hearing problems.
Level:	pre-intermediate – intermediate
Time:	10–15 minutes
Preparation:	Make a copy of Box 84 for each student.

Procedure

1 Start your lesson speaking very quietly, so that students cannot hear what you are saying. While they look at you puzzled, carry on muttering as you write these phrases on the board:

> Pardon?
> I beg your pardon?
> Sorry?
> I'm sorry?
> What?

Some students will realise that they have to use the phrases on the board. When they ask you to repeat what you have said, raise your voice for a while, but then turn your voice down again to provoke pleas for repetition.

2 Give everybody a copy of the dialogue in Box 84. Ask two volunteers to play the role of the two gunmen while you act as the shopkeeper. Read out the sketch.

> **BOX 84**
> *The elderly shopkeeper hums a song to herself. Enter two gunmen.*
> Gunman A: Put your hands up!
> Shopkeeper: Sorry?
> Gunman A: Put your hands up!
> Shopkeeper: You'll have to speak up. I'm a little deaf, you see.
> Gunman B: Put your hands on your head!
> Shopkeeper: Put what on your head?
> Gunman B: Hands!
> Shopkeeper: I see, bands. Rubber bands. For your hair, right?
> Gunman A: No, you fool, we want your money!
> Shopkeeper: No problem. We've got very good honey.

Gunman A:	I said money, not honey. Look! *(Shows a bunch of banknotes.)*
Shopkeeper:	*(Snatches the banknotes from his hand and quickly counts them.)* Twenty, forty, sixty, eighty dollars. Five dollars a jar. That'll be sixteen jars of honey.
Gunman B:	We want your money!!!
Shopkeeper:	I'll bring them in a second. Anything else, love?
Gunman A:	*(to Gunman A)* It's no good. We'll never get it. Let's go.
Gunman B:	You're right. *(The two gunmen leave.)*
Shopkeeper:	*(Runs after them.)* But you've left your honey behind!

© Cambridge University Press 2002

Ask the class what the two words are that the shopkeeper misheard.
Answers: hands/bands and money/honey.

3 Students read out the dialogue in groups of three. They can then rehearse it for a class performance.

Extras

1 Students get into pairs and stand in opposite corners of the classroom. Explain that everyone is going to conduct a telephone conversation with their partner, all at the same time. As this will produce a lot of noise, the partners might have to keep asking for repetition, using the phrases on the board.

2 In this game, students in pairs carry on a conversation, in which they are only allowed to ask questions. If a student makes a statement or runs out of questions, she/he is out of the game. The winners of the first round pair up again for a second round. The game goes on like this until there are only two players left; the one who wins the final round is the winner. For example:

Student A:	How old are you?
Student B:	Why are you so curious?
Student A:	We all are, aren't we?
Student B:	But what if I tell you my age?
Student A:	Why, is this such an embarrassing question?
Student B:	Who said it is?
Student A:	Then tell me please, would you?
Student B:	Would you believe me if I told you that I'm twenty-five?

Laughing Matters

>Student A: What?!
>Student B: Twenty-five.

Student B lost the game, because she/he responded with a statement.

Acknowledgment

I found *Extra 2* in *101 Word Games* by McCallum (Oxford University Press).

8.5 Repeats

Summary: This funny dialogue is a reminder of a children's game.
Level: intermediate – post-intermediate
Time: 20–25 minutes
Preparation: Make a copy of Box 85 for each student.

Procedure

1   Pre-teach any unknown words in the dialogue in Box 85. Now ask the following questions:
    • Is it customary for children in your country to tease a friend by repeating everything she/he says?
    • Can you think of other ways of pulling someone's leg?
    • As opposed to children, how do teenagers and adults annoy one another?
    • Do you remember deliberately irritating your friends, siblings or parents when you were a child?
    • Are you still a nuisance sometimes?

2   With a volunteer read out the 'Repeats' sketch; you take Prothero's part. When you have finished, ask the class to explain what was going on.
    Answer: One character was teasing the other one by repeating him all the time.

3   Give out the sketch in Box 85. Students might like to practise it in pairs.

BOX 85
A party scene. Wilkins approaches Prothero.
Prothero: Hello.
Wilkins: Hello.
Prothero: Nice day.
Wilkins: Nice day.
Prothero: Warmer than yesterday.
Wilkins: Warmer than yesterday.
Prothero: Look, would you mind not repeating everything I say?
Wilkins: Sorry. Awfully sorry. My name's Arthur Williams by the way.
Prothero: Hello. I'm George Prothero.
Wilkins: Hello. I'm George Prothero.
Prothero: You said you were Arthur Williams.
Wilkins: You said you were Arthur Williams.
Prothero: Oh my God. You're doing it again.
Wilkins: Oh my God. You're doing it again.
Prothero: Look, would you mind not repeating everything I say?
Wilkins: Sorry. Awfully sorry. (Pause.) I bought a calendar in Tamworth yesterday.
Prothero: That's better.
Wilkins: That's better.
Prothero: Oh no.
Wilkins: Oh no.
Prothero: Stop it.
Wilkins: Stop it.
Prothero: Look, I find it very irritating when you keep repeating what I say. It's silly.
Wilkins: Sorry. Awfully sorry. I have this little problem, you see. I repeat what people say three times, and then I don't repeat them once, and then I repeat them three times again, and then I don't repeat them once again, and then I repeat them three times again, and then I don't repeat them again.
Prothero: My God, that's awful.
Wilkins: My God, that's awful.
Prothero: The thing to do is to get through my next two remarks quickly. Shoes.
Wilkins: The thing to do is to get through my next two remarks quickly. Shoes.
Prothero: More shoes.
Wilkins: More shoes.

Prothero:	Good. Now perhaps we can get some sense. How long has this dreadful complaint been going on?
Wilkins:	Good. Now perhaps we can get some sense. How long has this dreadful complaint been going on?
Prothero:	You've just repeated me a fourth time.
Wilkins:	Yes, I think it must be getting worse.
Prothero:	I believe you're a fraud.
Wilkins:	I believe you're a fraud.
Prothero:	I'll fox you. To go with a monkey from Baden Baden to Wagga Wagga through Addis Ababa or back is enough to make a geisha commit hari kiri.
Wilkins:	I'll fox you. To go with a monkey from Baden Baden to Wagga Wagga through Addis Ababa or back is enough to make a geisha commit hari kiri.
Prothero:	Rumanian dalmatians hate Tasmanian alsatians and Tasmanian dalmatians hate Rumanian alsatians. Tasmanian alsatians hate Rumanian dalmatians but Rumanian alsatians like Tasmanian dalmatians. Tasmanian alsatians hate Rumanian alsatians but Rumanian alsatians like Tasmanian alsatians. So Tasmanian alsatians hate Rumanian alsatians and dalmatians but Rumanian alsatians don't hate Tasmanian dalmatians or alsatians.
Wilkins:	(after a pause) Sometimes I only repeat things twice.
Prothero:	You're a fake. I'm not talking to you.
Wilkins:	You're a fake. I'm not talking to you.
Prothero:	*(To party at large)* That man's a fake.
All:	That man's a fake.
Prothero:	Oh no.
All:	Oh no.

Extras

1 Students of similar height pair up and face each other. Student A begins to gesticulate and grimace. Student B tries to mirror her/his partner's movement as closely as possible. If the two students are smart enough, observers will find it difficult to tell who is the 'person' and who is the 'mirror'. After a while, the roles are reversed.

2 Choose a taped monologue of medium difficulty and speed, preferably one that the class is already familiar with. Students listen to it

once, so as to get the hang of it. For the second listening, they voice-over the monologue after the speaker, with a delay of not more than two or three words. They should not worry if they become tongue-tied on occasion. Instead of stopping and correcting themselves, they should try to catch up with the speaker. In another variation of this exercise, students in groups can try getting their tongues around texts with more than one speaker.

Acknowledgments

This slightly adapted sketch by David Nobbs was selected from *The Book of Comedy Sketches*, edited by Muir and Brett (Elm Tree Books). The idea of the first extra is from *Mentor Courses* by Malderez and Bodóczky (Cambridge University Press), while the second one is from *The Non-Native Teacher* by Medgyes (Hueber Verlag).

8.6 Yuk, yuk ...

Summary:	Tastes are different – what is appetising to some people may be repulsive to others.
Level:	intermediate – post-intermediate
Time:	15–20 minutes
Preparation:	Make a copy of Box 86 for each student.

Procedure

1 Tell the class that in colloquial English if people like the food, they may say *yum yum*, but if they don't like it, *yuk yuk* is an appropriate reaction. Is the following dialogue *yum yum* or *yuk yuk*? With a volunteer act out the dialogue in Box 86, inserting the following words into the spaces: 1 cold worm soup; 2 a pair of socks stuffed with fried mice; 3 cooked in cucumber sauce; 4 sweet and sour water; 5 a mud roll with plums inside, sprinkled with ashes. You take the role of the host!
2 Yes, it is *yuk yuk!* Ask what disgusting dishes the guest was offered. If necessary, repeat the dialogue, pausing after each dish so that students can identify them.
3 Give everyone a copy of the incomplete dialogue in Box 86. The task is to fill the gaps with dishes students hate to eat.

BOX 86

Host: Hello, nice to see you. You're just in time for a meal I've prepared.

Guest: Mm, I'm starving.

Host: Great! I've cooked some of my favourite dishes. Have some ..... (1) for a starter.

Guest: Well, just a little please. It really looks most interesting.

Host: Yes, doesn't it?... Don't you like your starter?

Guest: Well, it isn't quite what I'm used to, but very nice, all the same.

Host: OK. Now here's the main course.

Guest: That's enough, thank you.

Host: You'll love it. It's ..... (2), ... (3).

Guest: Oh really? May I have some tap water?

Host: Why not try ..... (4) instead?

Guest: Oh fine.

Host: And now for the dessert. Can I have your plate please?

Guest: Stop, stop! That's too much. What exactly is this?

Host: It's ..... (5).

Guest: Well, I don't think I could ... Er, will you excuse me for a moment? *(runs out to the bathroom, feeling sick.)*

---

4 In pairs, students practise the dialogue. Those who created the dialogues with the funniest dishes can read them out to the whole class.

Variation

Students may find their national dishes tasty, but not all foreigners do. For instance, my foreign friends have often been repelled by some of the typical Hungarian dishes I love, such as cold fruit soup with whipped cream, blood sausage or sweet pasta with poppy seed. Students in groups fill in the gaps on the worksheet with national dishes foreigners are known to dislike. When they have agreed on the courses, they read out their dialogues to the whole class.

8.7 Life in a village

Summary:	The situations listed in this activity may call for both wicked gossiping and innocent reasoning.
Level:	intermediate – post-intermediate
Time:	20–25 minutes
Preparation:	Make a copy of Box 87 for each student.

Procedure

1 Give everybody a copy of the situations in Box 87. Students read through the list and speculate about the situations. Help with any unknown vocabulary.

> **BOX 87**
> 1 At 7 am, a police car stopped outside the Greggs' house. Two policemen got out and rang the doorbell several times, but nobody answered. About ten minutes later they left.
> 2 At 9 am, the postman entered Mrs Wilkinson's house and two hours later he was still there.
> 3 At around noon, twelve-year-old Alan climbed up the tree in old Mrs Henley's garden, picking cherries and stuffing them into a plastic bag.
> 4 At 5 pm, the two Alderson boys were running down the field. It looked as if the field had caught fire.
> 5 At 11 pm, a shriek was heard. The next moment Mrs West was running down the street in her dressing gown, with Mr West running after her with what looked like an axe in his hand.
> 6 At 2 am, a car stopped across the street. Two men got out, dragging a huge sack towards the river.
>
> © Cambridge University Press 2002

2 Students imagine that they all live in this village and witnessed the scenes described in Box 87. However, while one half of the class are well-intentioned neighbours, the other half are rumour-mongers and gossips. Everybody should choose to belong to either the naive or the nasty team, and then collect arguments either for or against the neighbours. As such a debate requires the use of certain modal auxiliaries, put these phrases on the board and practise their use:

> must have
> can't have
> could have
> might have
> may have
> was/were probably

3 Before team discussion begins, urge everyone to argue as passionately as they can. Exaggerated stresses, gestures and tones are welcome! Here is a sample dialogue on the basis of the first situation:

Bad guy A:	They must have been at home. They just didn't want to let the police in.
Good guy A:	Why wouldn't they? The Greggs are such a nice family!
Bad guy B:	Dad being a burglar? Is that what you'd call a nice family?
Good guy B:	All right, all right. He was a burglar once. 15 years ago. Since then, he has become a very decent man.
Good guy C:	Actually I saw the family leave home the night before. They may have gone to visit a relative.
Bad guy C:	They can't have left home, because ...

Extra

By the way, does anyone know the definition of *gossip*? Well, a gossip is a person with a keen sense of rumour ... Sorry. Pun: rumour vs. humour.

Acknowledgment

I came across this idea in *The Standby Book*, edited by Lindstromberg (Cambridge University Press).

8.8 The bunny

Summary:	Turn a simple dialogue into a weird one!
Level:	pre-intermediate – intermediate
Time:	15–20 minutes
Preparation:	Make a copy of Box 88a and Box 88b for each student.

Procedure

1 Ask for volunteeers. Give one pair a copy of Box 88a and another pair a copy of Box 88b and get the students to read out their dialogues. As students will have noticed, there is something wrong with these dialogues. What is it? Where do the scenes take place? Who are the characters? If necessary, ask the volunteers to read out their dialogue again.
   Answer: The lines of the two dialogues got entangled.

2 Give everybody a copy of both Box 88a and Box 88b.

BOX 88a
Man:	Good morning, madam. Can I help you?
Woman:	Why are you so cold, love?
Man:	I beg your pardon?
Woman:	Aren't I your bunny any more?
Man:	I'm sorry, but we don't sell animals here. This is a computer shop.
Woman:	Oh, I'm so sorry.

BOX 88b
Man:	Morning, Mary.
Woman:	I'd like to buy a bunny, please.
Man:	Am I?
Woman:	I said, a bunny!
Man:	Your bunny? Not after what happened last night.
Woman:	Gosh, of course it is!

In pairs, students put the lines in the correct order.

Answers: The correct versions run as follows:

Man:	Good morning, madam. Can I help you?
Woman:	I'd like to buy a bunny, please.
Man:	I beg your pardon?
Woman:	I said, a bunny!
Man:	I'm sorry, but we don't sell animals here. This is a computer shop.
Woman:	Gosh, of course it is!

Man:	Morning, Mary.
Woman:	Why are you so cold, love?
Man:	Am I?
Woman:	Aren't I your bunny any more?
Man:	Your bunny? Not after what happened last night.
Woman:	Oh, I'm so sorry.

3 Volunteers read aloud the two dialogues as they might have sounded in real life.

Extras

1 Students might like to create a similarly entangled pair of dialogues at home. In class, they practise their dialogues in pairs and then read them out.

2 Another possible source of fun is to reverse the order of the lines of a dialogue in a standard coursebook. Here is an example (in which the two lines of each pair have been reversed):

Policeman:	A little. How can I help you?
Pat:	Oh, good afternoon. Do you speak English?
Policeman:	You've lost your camera?
Pat:	Well, I've lost my camera.
Policeman:	Stolen? When? Where?
Pat:	Well, actually it's been stolen.
Policeman:	Well, you were lucky!
Pat:	I was in Grinzing, waiting for the bus, when suddenly I noticed I hadn't got my camera. It was in my pocket.
Policeman:	Yes, some people lose all their money, their passports ... sometimes their jewellery too. Was it an expensive camera?
Pat:	Lucky?
Policeman:	Yes, I understand that. Well, we must make a report. But I'm afraid you probably won't see your camera again.
Pat:	No, not very, just an ordinary camera. But I'm not rich, you know! I'm only a student.

Students choose a dialogue from their coursebook and change the order of the lines. Can the others recognise the unit in which the dialogue occurred?

Acknowledgment

The dialogue in *Extra 2* is from *Criss Cross* by Ellis, Laidlaw and Medgyes (Hueber Verlag).

8.9 What a small world!

Summary:	This activity introduces students to the world of clichés.
Level:	intermediate – post-intermediate
Time:	15–20 minutes
Preparation:	Make a copy of Box 89 for each student. Bring a large sheet of poster paper and a few felt pens.

Procedure

1 The 'Hello' sketch is an extract from a longer sketch, originally performed by two British comedians, Pete and Dud. Peter Cook (1937–1995) was a British comedian known for his dry sense of

humour. His partner, Dudley Moore (1935–), is also famous as a jazz pianist and a movie actor. If necessary, pre-teach any unknown vocabulary items. Then ask for a volunteer and read out the dialogue with her/him, taking the role of Dud yourself. Stop four lines from the bottom, after *ehm*. Ask students how they think Dud will finish his sentence. If nobody can guess, supply the word *before*. Then finish reading out the dialogue.

2 Give out copies of the dialogue in Box 89 and ask everyone to read it. Point out that the situation is quite ordinary and all the sentences are predictable – except for the one which ends with *before*. If students would enjoy reading aloud the dialogue in pairs, give them a few minutes to practise it.

BOX 89

Pete: Hello.
Dud: Hello.
Pete: How are you?
Dud: I'm terribly well. And you?
Pete: I'm terribly well as well.
Dud: Well, I must say you're looking awfully fit.
Pete: Oh, I'm feeling pretty fit, actually.
Dud: Yes.
Pete: Isn't it amazing us bumping into each other like this?
Dud: Yes. I mean, here of all places.
Pete: Here of all places. I mean, I haven't seen you since ... er ...
Dud: Oh, God, hold on a second.
Pete: When was it?
Dud: We haven't seen each other ...
Pete: ... er ... Oh, God!
Dud: ... er ... Oh, God! Oh, we haven't seen each other ... ehm ... before.
Pete: That's right. We've never ever seen each other before, have we? You've never seen me.
Dud: And I've never seen you. What a small world!

---

3 'What a small world!' Everyday language use is full of such clichés. Ask students what a cliché is. (A cliché is an expression that has been used so often that it has lost most of its impact. When I was a kid, for example, my mother often used to tell me: 'Life is not cottage cheese down to the bottom', which is the same as: 'Life is not a bed of roses.') Can students think of any other clichés in English? If they get stuck, there is a box of clichés on the next page; use the ones which best suit your students' language level.

the long and short of it	Big deal!
read between the lines	My lips are sealed.
free as a bird	She's not my cup of tea.
last but not least	It sells like hot cakes.
crystal clear	Just speak for yourself!
with all my heart	Life is not a bed of roses!

4 Do these clichés have mother-tongue equivalents? What are they? Students can collect funny clichés in their mother tongue and make a literal translation of them. Stick a large sheet of poster paper on the wall for everyone to write their items on. When the sheet is full, students read the collection and translate the clichés back into the mother tongue.

Acknowledgment

The extract in this activity is from a sketch by Peter Cook and Dudley Moore.

8.10 And it's a big IF!

Summary:	This activity combines fun with practising the second conditional.
Level:	intermediate – post-intermediate
Time:	15–20 minutes
Preparation:	none

Procedure

1 Tell the class this joke about the mother and her good-for-nothing son:

Mother:	If you weren't so lazy, you could get a job.
Son:	Why?
Mother:	Because if you had a job, you'd get paid.
Son:	So?
Mother:	So if you got paid, you could save money.
Son:	What for?
Mother:	If you saved enough, you wouldn't have to work any more.
Son:	But I'm not working now!

Ask students who they think is right, the mother or the son? Why?

2 The mother in the previous joke kept using the conditional. This game focuses on the same grammar point. Supply an 'if' clause and ask the class to finish it. Here is an idea to show how the chain works:

Teacher: If I were a teacher, I'd ...

Student A: If I were a teacher, I'd give every student the best mark.

Student B: If I gave every student the best mark, they'd love me.

Student C: If they loved me, the principal would learn about it.

Student D: If the principal learnt about it, he'd raise my salary.

Student E: If he raised my salary, I'd be able to take my class on a canoe trip – and so on.

Here are a few more triggers to use:

> If
>
> I had to write a dialogue for homework, I'd write about ...
> I went to live in another country, I'd choose to live ...
> I were a boy/girl (i.e. the opposite sex), ...
> I were a genius, ...
> I could make a wish, ...
> I won one million dollars in the national lottery, ...
> I were elected the prime minister of my country, ...
> I failed the school-leaving exam in English, ...
> I were a musical instrument, ...
> I could choose what or who to be in my next life, ...

Variation

The chain activity in *Step 2* can also be done in writing. Give each student a sheet of paper and organise them into groups. Student A in each group invents a trigger like the ones in the box, writes it at the top of the sheet, and passes it on to the next student in the group. Student B writes a possible result on the second line, hands the sheet to Student C, who writes down the next event in the chain, and so on. When the chain comes to an end, another student in the group triggers off a new chain.

Acknowledgement

I found the activity described in *Step 2* in *Grammar Practice Activities* by Ur (Cambridge University Press).

8.11 Talking objects

Summary: Students make their drawings engage in a dialogue.
Level: pre-intermediate – intermediate
Time: 25–30 minutes
Preparation: Have several bits of chalk available.

Procedure

1 Draw an object in the middle of the board; it can be anything and your drawing need not be artistic. Then invite about 10–12 students to draw something else on the board; any object is acceptable except people. Warn the 'artists' that they should not take more than two minutes to draw a simple sketch of the object. To save time, let several students draw at the same time. When all 10–12 drawings have been put up, get students to identify each object.

2 In pairs, students choose two objects from the board and write a weird dialogue between them. Each dialogue should consist of about 5–6 exchanges. The basic rule of the game is that they must not mention the name of the object, but there should be certain tell-tale signs about 'who' is talking to whom. After each pair have completed their dialogue, they practise reading it aloud.

3 Pairs take it in turns to read out their dialogue, with the others guessing which items on the board are talking to each other. However, the audience must not shout out their guesses before the dialogue has been read out to the end.

Variation

If several students in the class dislike drawing, ask them to place an object in the middle of the floor. You are likely to have more unusual items if you tell the class in advance to bring something funny to school.

Acknowledgment

The idea of the collective picture is borrowed from *Once Upon a Time* by Morgan and Rinvolucri (Cambridge University Press).

8.12 Mad libs

Summary:	The mad lib is an entertaining way to review and practise parts of speech.
Level:	intermediate – post-intermediate
Time:	15–20 minutes
Preparation:	Make a copy of Box 90 and Box 91 for each student.

Procedure

1 Explain that in a mad lib, there is a story or a dialogue with gaps waiting to be filled in. However, the player is not shown the frame of the text until she/he has provided the words, so she/he can't know whether and how they will fit in. Thus the resulting text is completely mad – true to the name of the game. The only assistance available to the player is that the type of word for each gap is identified. Distribute the list in Box 90 and ask everyone to fill in each gap with an appropriate word. Point out that words 1 and 4, and 5 and 6 are the same. The more weird the suggestions, the better!

BOX 90			
1 surname	=	11 age	=
2 job	=	12 age	=
3 verb+ing form	=	13 animal	=
4 surname	=	14 country	=
5 verb+ing form	=	15 language	=
6 verb+ing form	=	16 town	=
7 adjective	=	17 point in time	=
8 animal	=	18 number	=
9 adjective	=	19 point in time	=
10 animal	=		

2 Now give out the incomplete text in Box 91. Working on their own, students copy the words in Box 90 into the gaps in Box 91.

BOX 91

Man: Hello.

Woman: Mr Dowdy?

Man: Speaking.

Woman: I'm calling to ask about the job that's advertised in the Brinton Tribune.

Man: Oh yes, Ms ... Could you tell me your name please?

Woman: (^{1}_____)

Man: Certainly. May I ask what qualifications you have?

Woman: I'm a (^{2}_____).

Man: So that's why your English is so good! Any other skills you may have?

Woman: I have advanced (^{3}_____) skills.

Man: That's wonderful! I have to admit, Ms ...

Woman: (^{4}_____).

Man: ... , I have to admit that this job involves a lot of (^{5}_____).

Woman: Oh, that's no problem. I love (^{6}_____)!

Man: What about your family? Wouldn't they mind? ... By the way, do you have any children?

Woman: Yes, a (^{7}_____) (^{8}_____) and a (^{9}_____) (^{10}_____).

Man: How old are they?

Woman: (^{11}_____) and (^{12}_____).

Man: And who could look after them while you're away, if I may ask?

Woman: My (^{13}_____).

Man: I see ... And which country would you like to visit in particular?

Woman: Well, it's hard to say. (^{14}_____) perhaps.

Man: That's great! Do you speak (^{15}_____), by any chance?

Woman: Yes, I went to school in (^{16}_____) for three years.

Man: Fantastic! ... What is the earliest date you could start work?

Woman: Any time, Mr Dowdy. I'm free at the moment.

Man: How about (^{17}_____)?

Woman: That suits me fine ... Oh, one final question. What would my salary be?

Man: (^{18}_____) dollars a year.

Woman: Oh ... er ... I'd like to discuss your offer at home, Mr Dowdy. May I call you back (^{19}_____)?

3 Students in groups read out their version of the dialogue. Whose is the most bizarre? This student should read out her/his version to the whole class.

Follow-up

Students may be interested to read the original job phone interview.

Suggested dialogue:

Man:	Hello.
Woman:	Mr Dowdy?
Man:	Speaking.
Woman:	I'm calling to ask about the job that's advertised in the Brinton Tribune.
Man:	Oh yes, Ms ... Could you tell me your name please?
Woman:	<u>Brlik.</u>
Man:	Certainly. May I ask what qualifications you have?
Woman:	I'm a<u>n English teacher</u>.
Man:	So that's why your English is so good! Any other skills you may have?
Woman:	I have advanced <u>typing</u> skills.
Man:	That's wonderful! I have to admit, Ms ...
Woman:	<u>Brlik.</u>
Man:	... , I have to admit that this job involves a lot of <u>travelling</u>.
Woman:	Oh, that's no problem. I love <u>travelling</u>!
Man:	What about your family? Wouldn't they mind? ... By the way, do you have any children?
Woman:	Yes, a <u>big boy</u> and a <u>little girl</u>.
Man:	How old are they?
Woman:	<u>Twelve</u> and <u>four</u>.
Man:	And who could look after them while you're away, if I may ask?
Woman:	My <u>husband</u>.
Man:	I see ... And which country would you like to visit in particular?
Woman:	Well, it's hard to say. <u>Egypt</u> perhaps.
Man:	That's great! Do you speak <u>Arabic</u>, by any chance?
Woman:	Yes, I went to school in <u>Cairo</u> for three years.
Man:	Fantastic! ... What is the earliest date you could start work?
Woman:	Any time, Mr Dowdy. I'm free at the moment.
Man:	How about <u>next Monday</u>?
Woman:	That suits me fine ... Oh, one final question. What would my salary be?
Man:	<u>1,500</u> dollars a year.
Woman:	Oh ... er ... I'd like to discuss your offer at home, Mr Dowdy. May I call you back <u>next week</u>?

8.13 The pancake

Summary:	Students are given the opportunity to dramatise and perform a folk tale.
Level:	pre-intermediate – advanced
Time:	more than 60 minutes (in class)
Preparation:	Make a copy of Box 92 for each student.

Procedure

1 Distribute copies of 'The pancake' in Box 92 and ask students to read it. Help with any unknown vocabulary.

BOX 92

Once upon a time, there was a mother who had seven little boys – seven hungry little boys. One day, the mother began to make a very big pancake – a huge pancake – to feed her sons. The seven hungry little boys watched the pancake as it cooked, crying how hungry they were, and asked impatiently whether it was ready to eat. The mother said that it was just turning golden and she would still have to toss it. She took  the frying pan in both hands and tossed the pancake high in the air. Then she held out the frying pan to catch the pancake as it turned in the air. Meanwhile, the pancake realised that it shouldn't wait until its other side was golden too, or the seven hungry little boys would eat it. It decided to run away from the seven hungry little boys.

So, as the mother tossed the pancake up in the air, it flipped over, missed the frying pan and landed on the floor. Then it rolled away on its edge, like a very big penny, out the door and down the road. The mother ordered the pancake to stop, and ran after it with her frying pan still in her hand. Faster and faster rolled the pancake, with the seven hungry little boys running behind their mother. They shouted that they wanted to eat it. It is little wonder that the pancake didn't want to be eaten.

Soon the pancake passed a man, who said what a delicious pancake it looked and asked if he could eat it. The pancake said that a mother couldn't catch it, seven hungry little boys couldn't catch it, so this man wouldn't be able to catch it either. The man joined in behind the seven hungry little boys and the mother, and they all ran after the big pancake. The pancake rolled on faster and faster, past a cat, a cock, a duck, a cow, one after the other.

Finally the pancake passed a pig. The pig asked where it was going in such hurry. The pancake answered that it was running away from a mother, seven hungry little boys, a man, a cat, a cock, a duck and a cow, because they all wanted to eat it. Running along beside the pancake, the pig said that of course the pancake didn't want to be eaten up. Soon they came to a river. When the pancake admitted it couldn't swim, the pig said that he'd take it across the river, and all the pancake would have to do was to get onto his snout. As soon as the pancake rolled onto the pig's snout, the pig opened his mouth and gobbled it up. And it *was* a delicious pancake! So the mother and the seven hungry little boys and the man and the cat and the cock and the duck and the cow never *did* catch the big pancake!

203

2 Explain that students have to convert the story into a play. This involves changing indirect speech into direct speech, past tense into present tense, and representing as many narrative comments as possible with dialogue and actions. At home, everybody prepares a dramatised version of the tale. Note that the third paragraph in Box 92 is condensed and waiting for students to expand the dialogue between the pancake and the animals one by one.

3 In class, students get into large groups. There are 15 characters in the story, but you can increase or decrease the number of children to fit in with the number of students in your class. Group members compare their plays and compose a final one.

4 It is now time to put the different versions of the play on the stage! Each cast should identify suitable props, and then rehearse their production before and after lessons during the week. Finally, the groups take it in turns to perform their play.

Variation

Depending on the language level of the class, you may decide to give prompts for the scriptwriters, selecting from the ones in the box below:

Boys:	We're hungry!
	Is it ready to eat?
Mother:	It's just turning golden.
	I still have to toss it.
Pancake:	I mustn't wait until my other side is golden.
	Those seven hungry little boys will eat me.
	I will run away from the seven hungry little boys.
	I don't want to be eaten.
	A mother couldn't catch me.
	Seven hungry little boys couldn't catch me.
	I won't let *you* catch me.
	They all want to eat me.
	I can't swim.
Boys/mother:	Stop! Stop!
	We want to eat you.
Man/animals:	You look like a delicious pancake.
	Please let me eat you.
Pig:	Where are you going in such a hurry?
	Of course you don't want to be eaten up.
	I'll take you across the river.
	Get onto my snout.

Follow-up

The class may decide to perform the best production for another class in the school or to an audience of family, friends and teachers.

Extra

You can find other tales and stories for dramatisation almost everywhere – three excellent sources for EFL/ESL teachers are: *Using Folktales* by Taylor (Cambridge University Press), *Once Upon a Time* by Morgan & Rinvolucri (Cambridge University Press), and *Storytelling with Children* by Wright (Oxford University Press).

Acknowledgment

I have borrowed the idea of dramatisation from *Using Folktales* by Taylor (Cambridge University Press).

9 Errors and failures

'No one is listening until you make a mistake,' I heard somebody say, and it is true in a certain sense. Day in, day out, we make all sorts of mistakes, big and small, those of pronunciation, spelling, grammar and vocabulary. We often come across wrong signs, ads and headlines, and we often say things we didn't mean to say, but then it's too late to take them back. Mind you, although language learners make a lot more mistakes than native speakers, natives are not exempt, either. Even foreign language exports, oops, experts are prone to occasional slips of the tongue.

But errors go well beyond language use; we spend lots of time, energy and money on plans that go awry in the end. Successes don't come easy, failures do. Successes seldom provide humour, failures often do. Great discoveries are no sources of humour, useless inventions may make us laugh. Accurate predictions elicit appreciation, false ones make us smirk. Which, I trust, does not mean that we gloat over other people's bad luck. As a matter of fact, laughter can be a sign of sympathy and genuine commiseration. Be that as it may, the topic of this section is funny errors and failures.

9.1 It makes all the difference!

Summary:	This activity is based on misprints – a letter is changed, missing or added.
Level:	intermediate – post-intermediate
Time:	15–20 minutes
Preparation:	Make a copy of Box 93 and Box 94 for each student.

Procedure

1 One small typo can make all the difference! Distribute copies of Box 93. Each sentence has just one letter wrong. Can students spot the mistakes? Stop the activity when the first student indicates that she/he has found them all.

BOX 93

1 They lived happily even after.
2 It's better to slow down then get a ticket.
3 Today's special: Frozen soap with mushrooms.
4 Rivaldino was sent off for licking Figo on the knee.
5 Enjoy the desert on your own: Hire a cat to take you there!
6 I always find it intriguing to watch News for the dead on TV.
7 Have you ever thought of changing your wife? I bet you have. Who hasn't?
8 Jack will be highly honoured; he will be deceived even by the Prime Minister.
9 Mrs Bentley passed away yesterday at the age of 93. She was loved by all who knew her will.

Check the answers with the class.

Answers: 1 ever, 2 than, 3 soup, 4 kicking, 5 car, 6 deaf, 7 life, 8 received, 9 well.

2 Give everybody a copy of Box 94. Can students find mistakes in these sentences? No wonder they can't, because all the sentences are correct. But can they make them wrong? There are two alternative routes to do so: they should either add (+) or delete (–) one letter. Students work in pairs.

BOX 94

1 For Rent: 6-room heated apartment. (–)
2 The Executive Director was changed yesterday, because the company had failed to increase productivity. (–)
3 The patient slipped into a coma yesterday. (+)
4 Get rid of ants: Zap does the job in 24 hours. (+)
5 My wife was charged with careless driving. (–)
6 First you have to insert the money and then choose the kind of coffee you want, and not the other way round. (+)
7 Close your book when the teacher tells you. (–)
8 All the passengers will be accommodated with host families. (+)
9 Good teachers always try to bring out the best in their students. (+)

Check the solution together. There is more than one way of changing the sentences, but here are some suggestions:

Answers: 1 hated, 2 hanged, 3 comma, 4 aunts, 5 carless, 6 monkey, 7 Lose, 8 ghost, 9 beast.

Follow-up

Students may like the idea of creating wrong sentences to challenge their partner. First they should find a word to contort; for example, *hello* may be reduced to *hell*. Then they place *hell* in a sentence; for example, 'I stopped at the pub to say hell to my friends.' After everybody has created two or three sentences with one 'misprint' each, they take it in turns to show their sentences to a partner, who tries to correct them.

Extra

According to *The Guinness Book of Records*, the record for newspaper misprints was set by the well-known British daily *The Times*. On page 19 of the 22 August 1978 edition there were 97 misprints in a single column. The passage concerned 'Pop' (Pope) Paul VI. But of course every language abounds in funny misprints. Can students remember a few in their mother tongue?

9.2 Are you sure, sir?

Summary:	As we non-natives know well enough, English is not a phonetic language.
Level:	intermediate – post-intermediate
Time:	20–25 minutes
Preparation:	Make a copy of Box 95 for each student.

Procedure

1 Learners of English are always complaining that there are no rules for correct pronunciation. However, this complaint is only partially legitimate. Tell the class this anecdote:

> Once a famous phonetician came to give a lecture at our university. He emphasised that in fact there are numerous rules of pronunciation. For example, he said, if the first letter in a word is an 's' followed by a vowel, it should always be pronounced as [s] and never as [ʃ]. There is only one exception to this rule, he added: the 's' in *sugar* should be pronounced as [ʃ]. At this point, a student asked: 'Are you *sure*, sir?'

Check whether students have understood the anecdote.

Answer: Sugar is not the only exception – *sure* is another one. But surely there are no more ... *Issue* and *tissue*, for example, don't count as 's' is not the first letter of the word.

2 The poem below is full of surprises; I would be very surprised if it weren't. Distribute copies of Box 95. Sorry, wait! First check the pronunciation of each word you are uncertain about – better be on the safe side! Now give out the poem written by an anonymous poet.

BOX 95

1 I take it you already know
2 Of *tough* and *bough* and *cough* and *dough*?
3 Some falter (but I think not you)
4 On *hiccough, thorough, trough* and *through.*
5 Well done! And now you wish, perhaps,
6 To learn of less familiar traps?

7 Beware of *heard*, a dreadful word,
8 That looks like *beard* and sounds like *bird*.
9 And *dead*: it's said like *bed*, not *bead*
10 For goodness sake, don't call it *deed*!
11 Watch out for *meat* and *great* and *threat*,
12 They rhyme with *suite* and *straight* and *debt*.

13 A *moth* is not the moth in *mother*,
14 Nor *both* in *bother*, *broth* in *brother*;
15 And *here* is not a match for *there*,
16 Nor *dear* and *fear* for *bear* and *pear* –
17 And then there's *dose* and *rose* and *lose*;
18 Just look these up, with *goose* and *choose*.

19 Now *cork* and *work*; and *card* and *ward*;
20 And *font* and *front*; and *word* and *sword*,
21 And *do* and *go*; and *thwart* and *cart* –
22 Come, come, I've hardly made a start!
23 A dreadful language? Full of tricks?
24 I'd mastered it when I was six!

Students underline every italicised word they know and put it on the board. All right, but can they pronounce it too? Correct their pronunciation if necessary.

3 Everyone will learn one line of the poem by heart, while you keep those lines which do not contain any words in italics. That is to say, give away 17 lines and reserve seven for yourself (lines 1 + 3 + 5 + 6 + 22 + 23 + 24). If there are more than 17 students in the class, some of them should share the same line. After you have given out the numbers, read out the poem line by line. Students in charge of a

certain line, repeat it correctly and then learn it by heart. Warn everyone that they will have to say their line not only correctly but loudly and rhythmically as well.

4 Time for the show! Begin to beat the rhythm and then say the first line. Practise the recital as long as students enjoy it.

Follow-up

Collect a few words that students notoriously mispronounce. Ask them to write two-liners around those words in groups or at home.

9.3 Vot a relef!

Summary:	Here is an Internet initiative to simplify English spelling.
Level:	intermediate – post-intermediate
Time:	15–20 minutes
Preparation:	Make a copy of Box 96 for each pair of students.

Procedure

1 Hand out the extract in Box 96 and read out the first paragraph. Supply the meaning of any unknown words and concepts.

BOX 96

Officials in the European Union have often pointed out that English spelling is unnecessarily difficult. What is clearly needed is a programme to get rid of these difficulties. The programme would, of course, be run by an international EU committee.

In the first year, for example, the committee would suggest using 's' instead of the soft 'c'. Sertainly, sivil servants in all sities would reseive this news with joy.

At the same time, the hard 'c' could be replased by 'k' sinse both letters are pronounsed alike. This would klear up konfusion in the minds of klerikal workers, and keyboards kould be made with one less letter.

In the sekond year, it kould be announsed that the troublesome 'ph' would be written 'f'. This would make words like 'fotograf' twenty per sent shorter in print.

In the next fase, more komplikated changes would bekome possible. Governments would enkourage the removal of double letters which have always made akurate speling difikult ...

We would al agre that the horible mes of silent 'e' in the languag is disgrasful. Therfor, in the third year, we kould drop thes and kontinu to read and writ with les hasl. By this tim it would be thre years sins the skem began and peopl would be reseptiv to steps sutsh as replasing 'th' by 'z'. Perhaps zen ze funktion of 'w' kould be takn on by 'v', vitsh is, after al, haf a 'w'. Shortly after zis, ze unesesary 'o' kould be dropd from vords kontaining 'ou'. Similar arguments vud of kors be aplid to ozer kombinations of leters.

Kontinuing zis proses yer after yer, ve vud hav a reli sensibl ritn styl. Zer vud b no mor trubls or difikultis and evrivun vud find it ezi tu understand etch ozer. Ze drem vud finali kum tru.

Vot a relef!

2 In pairs, students look over the various phases of the spelling programme and discuss the changes. Help viz any unnon vokabulary and vords zat at first glans lok unrekognizabl. Oops! Help with any unknown vocabulary and words that at first glance look unrecognisable.

Follow-ups

1 As a homework assignment, students recreate the whole text with conventional English spelling. Thus, *klerikal*, *hasl* and *vud*, for example, will become *clerical*, *hassle* and *would*, respectively.
2 Students could turn a text of their own choice into simplified English, and then get their partner to decipher it in class.

Extra

Speaking of spelling, let me share with you one of my favourite quotes: 'You cannot help respecting anybody who can spell Tuesday, even if he can't spell it right.' (Anon.)

9.4 **Teeth and beeth**

Summary:	Inconsistencies in the use of English grammar and vocabulary are all too frequent.
Level:	pre-intermediate – intermediate
Time:	10–15 minutes
Preparation:	none

Procedure

1 Some people say that English is a crazy language. If students listen to the examples you read out, they may agree. Teach them any new words.

> There is no ham in hamburgers.
> English muffins were not invented in England.
> Quicksand can work quite slowly.
> Guinea pigs are neither pigs nor from Guinea.
> If the plural of tooth is teeth, why isn't the plural of booth beeth?

2 Turn to the sentences below. As you read them out fairly fast, give enough time for everyone to write down the missing word in each. Students must not shout out their solutions – this is a writing task.

> Boxing rings are in fact ... . (square)
> Writers write, but grocers don't ... . (groce)
> If the past of *teach* is *taught*, then the past of *reach* is ... . (raught)
> How can the weather be as hot as hell one day and as ... as hell another? (cold)
> If a set is more than one, how come you only get one ... ? (TV)
> There are no apples in ... . (pineapples)
> Fingers don't fing and hammers don't ... . (ham)
> French ... were not invented in France. (fries)

3 Read out the same sentences again and check the solution. Who has the highest score?

Follow-ups

1 Can students find similar paradoxes in English? Once they have collected three or four examples, they take turns following the procedure described in *Step 2*.

2 But isn't every language 'illogical'? Isn't the students' mother tongue full of contradictions, too? In pairs, students collect three or four odd cases from their mother tongue and then share them with the class.

9.5 Mistakes all around

Summary: This is an authentic collection of signs, notices and advertisements from all over the world.
Level: pre-intermediate – post-intermediate
Time: 10–15 minutes
Preparation: Make a copy of Box 97a, Box 97b or Box 97c for each student, depending on the level of the class.

Procedure

1 Give out copies of Boxes 97a, 97b or 97c. Students read the sentences on their own.

BOX 97a pre-intermediate
1 Drop your pants here for best results.
2 Special – Turkey $2.35, Chicken or Beef $2.25, Children $2.00.
3 Elephants please stay in your car.
4 We take your bags and send them in all directions.
5 Out of business. Thanks to our customers.
6 Toilet out of order. Please use floor below.
7 Wanted – man to take care of cow that does not smoke.

© Cambridge University Press 2002

BOX 97b intermediate
1 Please remove all your clothes when the light goes out.
2 Mountain inn: Special today – no ice cream.
3 Please do not feed the animals. If you have suitable food, give it to the guard on duty.
4 Illiterate? Write today for free help.
5 Specialist in women and other diseases.
6 We can repair anything. (Please knock hard on the door – the bell doesn't work.)
7 Doll: Laugh while you throw up.

© Cambridge University Press 2002

> BOX 97c post-intermediate
> 1 We do not tear your clothing with machinery. We do it carefully by hand.
> 2 Our wines leave you nothing to hope for.
> 3 The river is inhabited by crocodiles. Swimming is prohibited. Survivors will be prosecuted.
> 4 Free pick-up and delivery. Try us once, you'll never go anywhere again.
> 5 We exchange anything – bicycles, washing machines, etc. Why not bring your wife along and get a wonderful bargain?
> 6 A desk suitable for lady with thick legs and large drawers.
> 7 No children allowed in the maternity ward.

2 In what kinds of places were these signs put up? Students guess in pairs.

Answers:

Box 97a: 1 launderette, 2 restaurant, 3 safari park, 4 airline ticket office, 5 shop, 6 office building, 7 job advertisement.

Box 97b: 1 launderette, 2 restaurant, 3 zoo, 4 literacy course, 5 doctor's office, 6 repair shop, 7 toy shop.

Box 97c: 1 launderette, 2 restaurant, 3 safari park, 4 car rental, 5 swap shop, 6 antique shop, 7 hospital.

3 What led students to guess correctly? Discuss the tell-tale signs with the whole class. What exactly went wrong? How could the signs be put right?

Answers:

Box 97a:

1 Leave your pants here for best results.
2 Special – Turkey $2.35,Chicken or Beef $2.25, half portion $2.00.
3 Wild elephants. Please stay in your car.
4 We deliver your bags anywhere in the world.
5 Out of business. Thanks for your understanding.
6 Toilet out of order. Please use the toilet downstairs.
7 Wanted – non-smoker to take care of cow.

Box 97b:

1 Please collect all your clothes when the light goes out.
2 Mountain inn: Special today – but no ice cream.
3 Please do not feed the animals. Leave your food with the guard on duty.
4 Illiterate? Call us today for free help.
5 Specialist in diseases including women's diseases.
6 We can repair anything. (Please knock hard on the door.)
7 Doll: Laughs while you throw her up in the air.

Box 97c:
1 We do not tear your clothing with machinery. We wash it carefully by hand.
2 The best wines you can taste.
3 The river is full of crocodiles. Swimming is prohibited. Offenders will be prosecuted.
4 Free pick-up and delivery. Try us once and you'll be hooked.
5 We exchange anything – bicycles, washing machines, etc. Why not come along and get a wonderful bargain?
6 A desk with thick legs and large drawers – suitable for ladies.
7 No children allowed to visit the maternity ward.

9.6 Enjoy your stay!

Summary: All the odd notices in this activity have been found in hotels and restaurants.
Level: intermediate – post-intermediate
Time: 10–15 minutes
Preparation: Make a copy of Box 98a or Box 98b for each student, depending on the level of the class.

Procedure

1 Use either the sentences in Box 98a or those in Box 98b. (Needless to say, advanced classes may enjoy both lists.) Students read their list in pairs.

BOX 98a intermediate
1 If you consider our help impolite, you should see the manager.
2 If this is your first visit to our country, you are welcome to it.
3 Guests are expected to complain at the office between the hours of 9 am and 11 am daily.
4 A room with a view on the sea or the backside of the country.
5 Do not enter the lift backwards and only when lit up.
6 Ladies are requested not to have children in the bar.
7 To move the cabin push button for the wishing floor.
8 If you want just condition of warm in your room please control yourself.

BOX 98b post-intermediate
1 In case of fire do your utmost to alarm the hotel porter.
2 The manager has personally passed all the water served here.
3 You are invited to take advantage of the chambermaid.
4 As for the trout served you at the hotel you will be singing its praise to your grandchildren as you lie on your deathbed.
5 It is forbidden to steal hotel towels please. If you are not person to do such thing is please not to read notis.
6 If you wish for breakfast, lift the telephone and ask for room service. This will be enough for you to bring your food up.
7 Contact the concierge immediately for informations. Please don't wait last minutes then it will be too late to arrange any inconveniences.
8 If your order is not satisfactory please return the product to the counter and we will replace it with a smile.

© Cambridge University Press 2002

2 Ask students which sentences made them laugh and which ones did not. Were there any misunderstandings which they could not catch? Clarify any ambiguities.

Suggested answers:

Box 98a
1 The unintended message is that the manager is even less polite than the staff.
2 *You are welcome to it* is a sarcastic invitation to something unpleasant.
3 Of course nobody *must* complain during this time.
4 *Backside* means that part of our body on which we sit.
5 Are we supposed to enter the lift when it is dark?
6 No woman is likely to deliver a baby in the bar, surely?
7 Correctly: *to the floor where you wish to go.*
8 Adjust the control, that is.

Box 98b
1 *Alarm* means *frighten* – *alert* would be the right word here.
2 *Pass* also means *urinate* and not only *ensure that the water is safe.*
3 *Take advantage*? Well, well ... sexual connotations.
4 This suggests that you will die if you eat the trout served here.
5 Whether or not you read this notice has nothing to do with honesty.
6 *Get your food*, because *bring up your food* means that it makes you sick.
7 Who on earth would like to feel inconvenient? It is rather that you want to prevent inconvenience.
8 Thanks for your smile! But can I get my money back?

Follow-up

You may wish to spend some time analysing the causes of errors in terms of grammar, vocabulary and idioms.

9.7 You can't be serious!

Summary:	Faulty logic, self-contradiction or sheer silliness may give rise to laughter.
Level:	intermediate – post-intermediate
Time:	15–20 minutes
Preparation:	Make a copy of Box 99 for each student.

Procedure

1 Distribute the sentences in Box 99 for students to read on their own. Help with any unknown vocabulary.

BOX 99

1 At least half our customers who fly to New York come by plane!
2 A verbal contract isn't worth the paper it's written on.
3 If we don't succeed, we run the risk of failure.
4 How would you like to write my autobiography?
5 The best cure for insomnia is to get a lot of sleep.
6 I watch a lot of football on the radio.
7 I suppose you think that on our board half the directors do the work and the other half do nothing. As a matter of fact, gentlemen, the reverse is the case.
8 Some reporters said I don't have any vision. I don't see that.

© Cambridge University Press 2002

2 Ask the class what makes these sentences ridiculous. Where does logic falter in each? Is it possible that all this nonsense is due to slips of the tongue? Which of them may have been meant to be funny?
Suggested answer:
Quote 2 is known to be a wisecrack by the movie mogul, Samuel Goldwyn, but quotes 3 and 5 may also be tongue-in-cheek remarks.

3 All the quotes on the next page are alleged to have been said by politicians. The students' task is to rate these gaffes on a five-point 'stupidity scale' (5 being the most stupid). Read the quotes out sentence by sentence.

1 I was recently on a tour of Latin America, and the only regret I have was that I didn't study Latin harder in school so I could converse with those people.
2 (in Bogotá, Colombia) Now would you join me in a toast to the people of Bolivia ... no, that's where I'm going ... to the people of Brazil?!
3 Hawaii's always played a very pivotal role in the Pacific. It is in the Pacific. It's part of the United States that is an island that is right here.
4 I didn't say that I didn't say it. I said that I didn't say that I said it. I want to make that very clear.
5 Those who survived the San Francisco earthquake said, 'Thank God I'm still alive.' But, of course, those who died, their lives will never be the same again.

4 Check the scores. Individuals whose judgments are very different from the rest should justify their assessment.

9.8 Hot off the press

Summary: Newspaper headlines sometimes make us exclaim: 'What?'
Level: advanced
Time: 25–30 minutes (in class)
Preparation: Make a copy of Box 100 and Box 101 for each student.

Procedure

1 Give each student the handout in Box 100. Everybody reads the headlines on their own and marks the ones which they cannot understand. Students form groups to disambiguate the bloopers. If problems persist, provide help.

BOX 100
Fried Chicken Cooked in Microwave Wins Trip
Woman Improving After Fatal Crash
Jail May Have to Close Doors
Typhoon Rips Through Cemetery: Hundreds Dead
Extinct Animals May Lose Protection
Students at Colleges Grow Older
Memorisation Ability Attributed to Brain Use
October is Breast Awareness Month
Juvenile Court to Try Shooting Defendant
War Dims Hope for Peace
If Strike Isn't Settled Quickly, It May Last a While
Local Secondary School Dropouts Cut in Half

© Cambridge University Press 2002

2 When all the meanings have been clarified, each students chooses one headline. They have a twofold homework assignment to carry out. With reference to their favourite headline, they write (1) a serious report based on what the event really was, and (2) a funny report based on the 'spoof' meaning. Each report should be brief, consisting of not more than three sentences. You may illustrate the task with the example in Box 101.

BOX 101
'Memorisation Ability Attributed to Brain Use'

1 An interesting development in brain study was reported in the autumn issue of the Indian science journal *Mindset*. On the basis of a survey including over 300 subjects, Professor Pradesh Ganaharaja from the University of Abigael established that those who had used his battery of memory exercises were able to retain unrelated words 50% more effectively than those who had not jogged their memories.

2 Pradesh Ganaharaja from the University of Abigael, India, came to the conclusion that mice use their brains to remember the names of cats in the neighbourhood. Professor Ganaharaja's concept seems to shatter earlier theories which linked mice's memory-storing capability to the size of their ears. If he doesn't get the Nobel Prize for this ground-breaking discovery, we can't imagine who will.

© Cambridge University Press 2002

3 In groups, students entertain one another with their brief reports. Each group singles out one set of reports (serious plus funny) which they find the wittiest. The author reads out her/his composition to the whole class. The class could choose a winner, whose dual report will go up on the wall for public display.

Extra

Though not in connection with headlines, this newspaper apology in Lederer's collection makes one look twice.

> We would like to point out that the previous writer on the subject, who was referred to as Miss Turner, was in fact Ms Turner, not Mrs Davis as we stated last week.

Put this nonsense on the board and get students to fathom it out.

Acknowledgment

The extracts in this activity are authentic. They are quoted in *Fractured English* and *Anguished English* by Lederer (Pocket Books).

9.9 Sad consequences

Summary:	This is a variation of the party game 'Consequences'.
Level:	beginner – pre-intermediate
Time:	10–15 minutes
Preparation:	Have several A4-size sheets available.

Procedure

1 Give Player 1 a blank sheet of paper. She/he writes down a man's name (somebody the class know), followed by the word *and*, folds the paper so that the name is hidden, and passes it on to Player 2. (N.B. The same folding and passing procedure is carried out in subsequent steps as well. No one is allowed to open any of the folds until the final entry has been recorded!)
2 Player 2 chooses a woman's name (again someone familiar to the class), followed by the word *met*.
3 Player 3 identifies the place where they met. (The preposition is *at* or *in* according to the place.)
4 Player 4 writes *He said* and then quotes the man.

5 Player 5 writes *She said* and then quotes the woman.
6 Player 6 provides an unhappy consequence, beginning with *And so they.*
7 Player 7 unfolds the folded paper and reads out the story – which is bound to be totally absurd! To illustrate the task, you may like to write this example on the board:

> Arnold Swarzenegger <u>and</u> Tanya (a girl in the class) <u>met</u> <u>at</u> a disco. <u>He said,</u> 'Marry me.' <u>She said,</u> 'Do you also like Geography?' <u>And so they</u> set the school on fire.

Variations

1 The same game may be based on the use of the past conditional, like this:
<u>If</u> Swarzenegger <u>and</u> Tanya <u>had met</u> <u>at</u> a disco, <u>he would have said,</u> 'Marry me.' <u>She would have said,</u> 'Do you also like Geography?' <u>And so they would have</u> set the school on fire.
2 If you want to keep more people busy, you may turn this class activity into groupwork, each group ideally consisting of seven people.
3 With this game, you can also practise reported speech. In this case, instead of *He said* and *She said*, you will have *He asked if* and *She answered that.*

9.10 Useless inventions

Summary:	An invention may be brilliant – and yet totally useless.
Level:	intermediate – post-intermediate
Time:	20–25 minutes (in class)
Preparation:	Make a copy of Box 102 for each group of four students.

Procedure

1 Record books give accounts of outstanding feats but never mention any failures – although the number of aborted attempts is sure to exceed successful ones. Thomas Edison, the most versatile inventor ever, had this to tell a reporter:
> Results! My man, I have gotten a lot of results. I know 50 thousand things that won't work.

(American inventor Thomas Alva Edison (1847–1931) is most famous for the light bulb, but had more than a thousand patents during his lifetime. Incidentally, the conclusion of a Parliamentary Committee's report on whether Edison's light bulbs would ever be relevant to Britain was this: 'Unworthy of the attention of practical or scientific men.')

2   There are descriptions of four inventions in Box 102. Cut up the handouts and give each student one description. Those who have the same invention should form groups, read the text and help each other to get the hang of the device as well as to understand the language of the description. Provide assistance if necessary.

BOX 102

1   A cereal bowl

Cereals are customarily eaten with milk. The trouble is that crispy cereals become soggy if they are mixed with milk for more than a few seconds. Ugggh! This smart bowl keeps the cereal and the milk in separate containers.

2   Wearable seating apparatus

Where can you sit if there isn't a chair around? On the wet and/or dirty ground? Not any more! This portable apparatus solves the problem. Equipped with a padded support, it can be worn around your waist with a belt.

3   A protective coat for sheep

Many sheep are lost because of cold weather. Why don't we protect them with a coat? Sewn to its wool, this coat covers the back and sides of the sheep but leaves two openings: one for the head and one for the rear.

4   Book rests

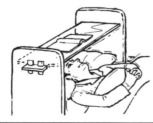

I find it tiring to hold a book when lying in bed. You too? This device not only frees your hands, but it also enables you to read with your head facing upwards and not to the side. You can see through transparent material.

3 As a homework assignment, students create their own invention. They draw their invention on a piece of paper and simultaneously explain its purpose, using their own words and possibly adding their own ideas. Their aim is to persuade manufacturers, i.e. their partners, to buy the product.
4 In class, students take it in turns to talk their peers into buying their product. Who is the smartest salesperson?

Follow-up

Some students may like the idea of designing their own invention or gadget and making it as useless as can be! After they have prepared a description at home, they present it to the whole class. Whose is the most useless of all?

Extra

These three quotations are related to the topic of failure. Write them on the board and then discuss their meaning with the class:

---

1 It's not enough to succeed. Others must fail. (Gore Vidal)
2 I'm a connoisseur of failure. I can smell it, roll it round my mouth, tell you vintage and the side of the hill that grew it. (Giles Cooper)
3 When you reach my age and you find yourself eating light bulbs for a living, you know you've made some bad career moves along the way. (Matt Hely, 46, on his life as a circus performer, *Newsweek*)

In this regard, you may like to mention this:

Eric II, King of Denmark, passed away in 1104. He was known as Eric the Memorable. No one can remember why.

Acknowledgment

The four inventions have been selected from *Great British Inventions* by Tanner (Fourth Estate). The third quote in the *Extra* is from *Newsweek*.

9.11 The art of being wrong

Summary:	We often say things we wish we hadn't said.
Level:	post-intermediate – advanced
Time:	25–30 minutes
Preparation:	Make a copy of Box 103 and Box 104 for each student.

Laughing Matters

Laughing Matters

Procedure

1 'Being wrong is a natural gift. You cannot learn it. Some of us have a particular genius in this direction,' says Stephen Pile, author of *The Book of Heroic Failures*, and then provides a long list of examples. Box 103 contains a sample of patently wrong judgments and predictions. Give everyone a copy of this list.

BOX 103

Literature

1 'Shakespeare's name, you may depend on it, stands absolutely too high and will go down.' (English poet Lord Byron)
2 'My dear Sir, I have read your manuscript. Oh, my dear Sir.' (a publisher's rejection letter to playwright Oscar Wilde)
3 'No reader interest.' (a publisher's rejection letter on Frederick Forsyth's most widely read book, *The Day of the Jackal*)

Art

4 'Rembrandt is not to be compared in the painting of character with our extraordinarily gifted English artist, Mr Rippingille.' (19th-century art critic)
5 'He has no talent at all, that boy. Tell him please to give up painting.' (French artist Edouard Manet on the great impressionist Auguste Renoir)
6 'It's the work of a madman.' (art dealer on Picasso's famous 'Desmoiselles d'Avignon')

Music

7 'Deprived of beauty, of harmony, and of clarity of melody.' (contemporary musicologist on Johann Sebastian Bach)
8 'Far too noisy, my dear Mozart. Far too many notes.' (Emperor Ferdinand after the first performance of 'The Marriage of Figaro')
9 'We don't like their sound. Groups of guitars are on the way out.' (Decca Recording Company rejecting the recording of the Beatles in 1962)

As students read the quotes, help them with any language difficulties. In discussing these regrettable quotations, ask what may have led the critics to those stupid statements. Ignorance? Jealousy? Bad taste? Snobbery? Anything else?

2 The world of science is not exempt from blunders either. Great discoveries and inventions have repeatedly been labelled as rubbish – as is evidenced by the list in Box 104. Give each student a copy to read.

Help with any unknown words.

BOX 104

1 'Animals, which move, have limbs and muscles; the earth has no limbs and muscles, hence it does not move.' (Scipio Chiarimonti, Professor of Philosophy and Mathematics at the University of Pisa, proves in 1633 that the Earth is a cauliflower)

2 'I am tired of this sort of thing called science. We have spent millions on that sort of thing for the last few years, and it is time it should be stopped.' (a US senator in an effort to cut off funding for the Smithsonian Institute in Washington in 1861)

3 'An amazing invention – but who would ever want to use one?' (US President Rutherford Hayes about the telephone in 1876)

4 'Everything that can be invented has been invented.' (Director of the US Patent Office in 1899).

5 'I can accept the theory of relativity as little as I can accept the existence of atoms and other such dogmas.' (Professor Ernst Mach in 1913)

6 'For the majority of people, smoking has a beneficial effect.' (Los Angeles surgeon in 1963)

© Cambridge University Press 2002

3 In groups, students single out a great scientific achievement of the 20th century. Their task is to write a silly statement about this achievement in the style of the quotes in Box 104. When all the statements have been devised, a spokesperson in each group reads out what they have written with a mock serious face.

4 Needless to say, we don't have to wait for others to make silly statements. We say plenty of daft things ourselves, don't we? While most of our blunders have no direct consequences, a few of them do. The next one surely did. Legend has it that during the Battle of Spotsylvania in 1864 General John Sedgwick looked at enemy lines and said: 'They couldn't hit an elephant at this dist ...' Ask students why he left his sentence unfinished.

Answer: He was hit and killed, so he left his sentence unfinished, which would have been: 'at this distance'.

Acknowledgment

The quotations were borrowed from two sources: from *They Got it Wrong! The Guinness Book of Regrettable Quotations* compiled by Milsted (Guinness Publishing), and from *The Book of Heroic Failures* by Pile (Macdonald Futura Publishers Ltd).

9.12 A daft letter

> *Summary:* Who wouldn't dream of getting into 'The Guinness
> Book of Records' some day?
> *Level:* post-intermediate – advanced
> *Time:* 30–35 minutes
> *Preparation:* Make a copy of Box 105 for each student.

Procedure

1 Has anyone in the class come across *The Guinness Book of Records*?
Is there a mother-tongue edition as well? (Brought out every year, *The
Guinness Book of Records* contains details of all sorts of records. Not
all the records are serious and many record rather daft achievements.)
Some people do their utmost to get into the *Guinness Book of
Records*, even at the cost of making idiots of themselves – like the guy
in the following letter. Give everyone a copy of Box 105 to read.
Provide help with any unknown vocabulary.

BOX 105

> P.O.Box 9369
> Colo. Springs, CO
> 80932
> September 15, 2001

Records Review Committee
The Guinness Book of World Records
460 Park Avenue South
New York, NY 10016

Dear Record Keepers,

Since I was a small kid growing up in Millsboro, Delaware
(pop.1,233), I have excitedly welcomed the new Guinness Book
of World Records each year. When it would arrive at our house
I would disappear into the attic for several days, fascinated
with the various records and achievements! My parents (Ed and
Agnes) would bring my meals to me as I memorised page after
page of information. I was very popular at school, as I knew
the answers to all sorts of obscure questions. Hip, hip, hooray
for the Guinness heroes!

I never dreamed that my name could appear in your book, but that all changed recently! On September 12, 2000 I decided to engage in an activity that would push me to my physical limit, as well as (hopefully) get me in your record book! I decided to pick up my cat, Jess (she weighed only seven pounds), and carry her around for as long as I could. I began to carry her about for sixteen hours a day, releasing her only to sleep.

Yes, while I ate, shopped, showered and worked (I'm a used bookstore owner), Jesse was constantly in my arms! OK, there were some difficult times – holding Jesse over her litter box was a problem – but as a rule, we got along famously! My girlfriend (Cynthia) left me in January, because she could never understand my devotion to your publication, nor my strong desire to be a part of it. In time, Jesse became quite happy with our arrangement, even jumping into my arms as I climbed out of bed each morning. Unfortunately, Jesse, getting no exercise to speak of, ballooned to sixteen pounds. My biceps grew to 22 inches, adjusting to the tremendous task at hand. In April I met my new girlfriend (Grace), and the three of us could often be seen walking about town, happy as can be. I promised to marry Grace when my 'cat carrying' ended, and our wedding is due next August!

Please write to me quickly and give me the news – good or bad!

Purrfectly frank,

Paul Rosa

Paul C. Rosa

P.S. Please send a (XL) T-shirt.

2 Is Paul Rosa serious? Is it possible that this letter reports on a fake record designed for fun? Encourage students to justify their views.
   Answers: Here are a few tell-tale signs that Paul may well be mad or kidding: He supplies unnecessary details, such as the population of his town and his parents' first names. His closing lines (Purrfectly frank) are also strange, let alone the request for a T-shirt in the postscript.

3 Who in the class would like to get into *The Guinness Book of Records*? Can they think of a record they would fancy for themselves? Students in groups should think of a ridiculous attempt to get into the Book. Once they have agreed on a stunt, they should work the details out and prepare to describe it to the whole class. The activity ends with the group reports.

Follow-ups

1 Challenge students to write a letter to *The Guinness Book of Records*, reporting on their achievement in the mock-serious style of Paul. They should write their letter legibly on a sheet of paper and display it on the wall for the whole class to enjoy.

2 Did Paul eventually make his way into *The Guinness Book of Records*? Sadly, no. Read out the answer he received from an editor:

Facts on File, Inc.
460 Park Avenue South
New York, NY 10016–7382

October 29, 2001

Paul C. Rosa
P.O.Box 9369
Colo. Springs, CO 80932

Dear Mr Rosa

Thank you for your inquiry concerning your 'record' proposal to be included in *The Guinness Book of Records*. This is a most unusual story and I believe it is the first of its type that we have received. For this reason it is very difficult for me to be able to say whether or not you have established any kind of record. While I certainly do not underestimate your proposal, I do think this item is too specialised for a reference book as general as *The Guinness Book of Records*. I'm afraid that unique occurrences, interesting peculiarities, or 'firsts' are not necessarily records and therefore are rarely included in the book.

I am sorry that I cannot be more positive at this stage, however all letters are kept on file for possible future reference. Thank you again for your inquiry and interest in *The Guinness Book of Records*.

Sincerely yours,

Denise Jack

Denise G. Jack
Editorial Assistant
U.S. edition

Acknowledgment

The two letters have been adapted from *Idiot Letters* by Rosa (A Main Street Book, Doubleday).

9.13 The belly-dancer

Summary:	Bring a coursebook text alive by adding a twist to it!
Level:	post-intermediate – advanced
Time:	20–25 minutes (in class)
Preparation:	Make a copy of Box 106 and Box 107 for each student. Have number tags and some reusable adhesive ready.

Procedure

1 I hope coursebook authors will not take offence if I say that not all their texts are inspiring. What should we do if we come across a boring reading passage? The recipe is simple: invigorate it by giving it a spin! Since every text is different, there are no generalisable tips on how to ginger up uninspiring texts, but perhaps this activity will clarify what I mean. Here is a standard job advertisement which many coursebooks include:

BOX 106

RECEPTIONIST/GENERAL ASSISTANT

for busy 3 star hotel in Brighton. Applicants must be mature and keen, with a minimum of one year's experience. An excellent salary, a uniform and your own bedroom will be provided. Please supply a recent photograph and C.V. to:

Jim Burlington
Thistle Hotel, Brighton
Tel: 0487 276955

Give everybody a copy of the advertisement in Box 106 to read, but first supply the meaning of any unknown words and expressions. (Brighton is a seaside town in the South of England. C.V. is short for Latin 'curriculum vitae', in which the applicant is expected to describe her/his qualifications, previous career, professional interests, hobbies, etc.)

2 In coursebooks, you will also find letters to illustrate the conventions
of application. These applications tend to be just as ordinary as the
advertisement itself. Now comes the twist! Why don't we add an
outrageous application – like the one in Box 107 – to the ordinary one?

BOX 107

Gül Baba
Moon Lodge
Rye, Surrey

24 October 2001

Dear Jim (if I may),

I am writing to apply for the job of Receptionist/General
Assistant, which you advertised recently in Hotel & Catering
Magazine.

I am 86 years old. I dropped out of school after 6 years of
elementary school. Since I left my last regular job 31 years ago
as a dog trainer, I have had several years' experience as a belly-
dancer. Last year I won second prize in the 'over 80' category at
the local belly-dancing contest.

I am interested in working as a receptionist in your hotel as I
love talking to young (and not so young) ladies, and – who
knows? – I might even show my real talent in the hotel bar one
day (or rather one night ...).

I enclose a photograph and a full curriculum vitae, and I would
be happy to send any further details you may require.

I very much look forward to meeting you, Jim.

Take care!

عّول بابا

Gül Baba

P.S. 'Wow!' – I hear you say as you look at my attached photo.

Students read Gül Baba's application while you help with any new
vocabulary items.

3 At home, everybody writes a letter of application advertised for the job at the Thistle Hotel. The letters can be even more out of the ordinary than Gül Baba's.
4 Collect all the letters, stick them on the wall with reusable adhesive and number them. During the break, students read all the applications and choose their favourite. Next lesson students vote for the applicant to whom they think the job should go.

Variation

Students administer an oral interview, instead of offering someone the job merely on the strength of their application. After nominations for the three shortlisted candidates have been made, the candidates are asked to leave the classroom, and subsequently called in one by one. Any 'board member' may ask questions relating to the points mentioned in the candidate's letter of application and then grade each of them on a five-point scale (5 is best). Once all the candidates have had their turn, the job is offered to the candidate with the highest score.

9.14 The Secret Society of Incompetents

Summary:	Here is an opportunity for students to apply to a society of incompetents!
Level:	pre-intermediate – intermediate
Time:	10–15 minutes (in class)
Preparation:	Make a copy of of Box 108 for each student.

Procedure

1 Being able to mock one's own weaknesses is a virtue. Anybody with an adequate degree of self-criticism may become a member of the 'Secret Society of Incompetents', *SeSocIncom* for short. Explain to the class that the Society dates back several centuries, and some of the greatest figures of history have been members, so it is a great honour to belong. The Society sets two chief missions before itself: (a) to record in detail stupid things, both orally and in writing, and (b) to recruit new members. Those students who would like to join in should fill in the application form in Box 108. Tell the class that you will leave the forms on your desk and anybody may take a copy if they toy with the idea of applying. Application is strictly voluntary!

BOX 108
MEMBERSHIP APPLICATION FORM
SeSocIncom

Name: _____

Address: _____

Main area of incompetence: _____

Other areas of incompetence: _____

The most stupid statement I have made: _____

_____

The silliest prediction I have made: _____

The biggest mess I have caused: _____

_____

Examinations failed: _____

Other comments: _____

_____

I declare my intention of joining *SeSocIncom*:

Date: _____   Signature: _____

2 Those who have decided to apply should fill in the form at home, and
   secretly return it in the next lesson. After you have collected the forms,
   appoint one student to be the temporary spokesperson for the Society.
   Give this person the list of candidates, and ask her/him to convene the
   first secret meeting. During this meeting, the candidates check each
   other's application form and elect dignitaries, including a President, a
   Secretary, a Treasurer, a Scribe, a Jester, a Musician and an Artist.
   Obviously, the candidates found most incompetent by their peers
   should be appointed to the highest posts. As a first step, the Artist
   should take on the job of designing a beautiful membership card.
   When it is ready, help with photocopying. To mark the official foundation of the class branch of the Society, the President awards the
   membership cards.
3 From then on, members work out their own local rules, never losing
   sight of the Society's two chief missions. They may invite or consult
   you from time to time, and occasionally hold meetings open to the
   whole class.

10   Children and schools

To devote a chapter in this book to children and school-life is a fairly obvious choice. After all, all of us were children at some point in our lives – usually not long after birth! We may have changed a little in our appearance over the years, but surely most of us have preserved the child in our souls.

And we all used to go to school, too, didn't we? Who can forget their school-days – for better or for worse? Pranks, poor excuses, bloopers, copycats, snappy boys and cheeky girls, the chewing gum – all sorts of fun? Oh yes, and irresistible laughter above all.

10.1 What a change!

Summary:	Recognising a classmate in a baby photo may give rise to a few laughs.
Level:	pre-intermediate – intermediate
Time:	10–15 minutes
Preparation:	Have some reusable adhesive ready.

Procedure

1 Students bring to school a baby or nursery-school photo of themselves in an unsealed envelope. Warn students not to show each other the photos before the lesson. Collect in the envelopes with the photos inside, mix them up, then ask everyone to draw one envelope. As they look at the photo, students identify the person in the photo and write a short description on the envelope. For example:

   This is Greg. He has the same curly hair.

   Now everyone puts the photo back into the envelope and passes it on to a neighbour, who will:

   (a) either confirm the previous assumption:

   Of course it's Greg! The same blue eyes, too.

(b) or contradict it:

Nonsense! It's Ben. Look at his head. It's as round as a ball.

The envelopes are passed on like this for a few more rounds.

2 Take the photos out of the envelopes and stick them on the wall with their envelopes attached underneath. With their pens at the ready, students go and look at the photos, and tick off the guesses with which they agree (but, of course, leaving out their own photo).

3 Everybody then goes up to their own photo and signs their name at the bottom of the envelope.

Extra

You may wish to supply a few useful phrases to describe people above the neck:

HEAD	big, long, oval, round, square
FACE	happy, lively, pale, pretty, sad, smiling
EARS	close to the head, large, small, sticking out
EYES	bright, close together, large, round, wide
HAIR	curly, dark, fair, long, short, straight, thick, wavy
NOSE	crooked, curved, long, short, snub

Follow-up

To discuss issues concerning photography, you could ask students these questions:

• Do you like taking photos?
• Which do you prefer: taking photos or posing for them? Why?
• What do you think of this quotation?

'No one is as ugly as their passport photo.' (Arthur Bloch)

• What is the message of this joke:

Friend: My, that's a beautiful baby you have there!

Mother: Oh, that's nothing – you should see his photograph!

• Picture yourself sightseeing. When you see something beautiful, do you first take pictures of the sights and then admire them, or vice versa? Why?

Acknowledgment

The main activity is an adapted version of a game in Lee's *Language Teaching Games and Contests* (Oxford University Press).

10.2 Excuses, excuses

Summary: This activity takes stock of certain forms of school misbehaviour and the excuses students like to offer.
Level: intermediate – post-intermediate
Time: 20–25 minutes
Preparation: Make a copy of Box 109 for each student.

Procedure

1 Children misbehave at school in different ways. What are the most common discipline problems? Referring to their own experiences, the class discuss typical problems.
2 I have singled out three types of misbehaviour with three excuses provided for each and one left open. Distribute copies of Box 109.

BOX 109

1 Excuses for being late for school:
 • The bus had a puncture and we had to push it into the garage.
 • I stopped to help an old lady across the road and she was so slow that it took more than ten minutes.
 • I was here much earlier, but no one else was, so I went home again thinking school was cancelled.
 • .....
2 Excuses for not handing in homework:
 • Dad thought my essay was so good that he sent it off to a magazine.
 • I handed in my homework and left it on your desk. Have you lost it?
 • My brother filled my pen with vanishing ink, and when I got up this morning all my writing had vanished.
 • .....
3 Excuses for not going to school:
 • There's a bully at school who says he's going to get me.
 • There were so many children in bed with flu that the principal closed the school for the week.
 • There was chewing gum on my chair and I was stuck to it.
 • .....

Students get into groups. After reading the three excuses in Box 109, they offer one more for each type of misbehaviour and write it in the gap.

3 Here is a four-step activity:
- Everybody grades all twelve excuses on a five-point scale (5 for the funniest).
- In groups students choose the excuse which scored highest for each type of misbehaviour.
- Group leaders report back on their choices.
- You summarise the results and announce the funniest excuse for each type of misbehaviour.

Extra

Students try to guess the punch line of this joke:

> It was Monday morning and Mum was having a tough time preparing her son for another week at school.
> 'I'm not going to school today,' Jimmy said.
> 'What's up this time?' Mum asked.
> 'Nobody likes me. The teachers don't like me. The kids don't like me. I just don't want to go anymore,' he complained.
> 'Pull yourself together,' said his mother. 'You've just got to go. You're ... .'

Answer: You're 40 years old and the headmaster of the school.

Acknowledgment

The book I consulted for this activity is *How to Handle Grown-ups* by Jim and Duncan Eldridge (Beaver Books).

10.3 Telltales and others

Summary:	Certain children are unpopular among their peers.
Level:	beginner – pre-intermediate
Time:	5–10 minutes
Preparation:	Make a copy of Box 110 for each student. For *Extra 1*, make a copy of Box 111 for each student.

Procedure

1 Read out the three children's rhymes in Box 110. Ask what the three rhymes have in common.
Answer: They poke fun at certain types of children.

The three key words are *telltale*, *liar* and *cry-baby*. Who can infer their meaning from the little rhymes?
Answers:
telltale – a child who tells adults about other children's secrets or bad behaviour
liar – someone who tells lies
cry-baby – a child who cries very frequently

2 Distribute the three rhymes in Box 110. Give students a few minutes to memorise one of them. As they say the rhyme, they poke a finger at one of their friends in a jocular manner.

BOX 110
1 Telltale tit,
   Your tongue will be slit;
   And all the dogs in the town
   Will have a little bit.

2 Liar, liar,
   Your pants are on fire;
   Your nose is as long
   As a telephone wire.

3 Cry-baby, cry,
   Put your finger in your eye.
   Tell your Ma it wasn't I,
   Cry-baby, cry!

Extras

1 Give everyone a copy of the poem by Allan Ahlberg in Box 111. After you have explained any unknown vocabulary, students read the poem.

BOX 111

Please Mrs Butler
This boy Derek Drew
Keeps copying my work, Miss.
What shall I do?
    Go and sit in the hall, dear.
    Go and sit in the sink.
    Take your books on the roof, my lamb.
    Do whatever you think.

Please Mrs Butler
This boy Derek Drew
Keeps taking my rubber, Miss.
What shall I do?
    Keep it in your hand, dear.
    Hide it up your vest.
    Swallow it if you like, my love.
    Do what you think best.

Please Mrs Butler
This boy Derek Drew
Keeps calling me rude names, Miss.
What shall I do?
    Lock yourself in the cupboard, dear.
    Run away to sea.
    Do whatever you can, my flower.
    But *don't ask me!*

Ask the class:
- Who does the poet ridicule: the telltale, the liar or the cry-baby? (the telltale)
- What is Mrs Butler's attitude to the telltale? (She doesn't like her/him.)
- Were you a telltale when you were a child?
- Do you remember a typical telltale situation? Relate the story.

2 Challenge students to write at least the first four lines of one more verse for Ahlberg's poem. Instead of Mrs Butler, however, they should use your name (line 1), inform on a friend (line 2) and use *Miss* or *Sir* appropriately (line 3).

Acknowledgment

Allan Ahlberg's poem appeared in *The Nation's Favourite Poems*, edited by Jones (BBC).

10.4 **Cheeky, eh?**

Summary:	The jokes below present snappy answers to the teacher's questions and reprimands.
Level:	pre-intermediate – intermediate
Time:	10–15 minutes
Preparation:	Make a copy of Box 112 for each student. For *Extra 3*, make a copy of Box 113 for each student.

Procedure

1 We all know students who never miss a chance to impress the others with their sharp wit. Cheeky remarks go down particularly well. Give everybody a copy of the exchanges in Box 112. Students match the corresponding sentences. Help with any unknown vocabulary if necessary.

BOX 112

Teacher	*Student*
1 Did your father help you with your homework?	☐ a If you didn't talk so much, I could!
2 If you add 561 and 783, and divide the answer by 14, what do you get?	☐ b Big hands!
3 You can't sleep in my class!	☐ c I'm paying as little as I can.
4 If I had 7 oranges in one hand and 8 oranges in the other, what would I have?	☐ d Oral.
5 Bill, I hope I didn't see you looking at Liz's paper.	☐ e The wrong answer.
6 All your responses must be oral. OK? What school did you go to?	☐ f Not really!
7 You missed school yesterday, didn't you?	☐ g No, he did all of it.
8 I wish you'd pay a little attention!	☐ h I hope you didn't either.

© Cambridge University Press 2002

Check the answers with the whole class.
Answers: 1g, 2e, 3a, 4b, 5h, 6d, 7f, 8c.

2 Students in pairs discuss what makes these answers cheeky. Which do they find the cheekiest? In your own school, how would teachers generally react to such cheek?

Extras

1 While Box 112 contains two-liners, this box provides a few three-liners for a change:

> 1 Teacher: George, name two pronouns in English.
>   Student: Who? Me?
>   Teacher: Excellent! Well done.
>
> 2 Student: I eated seven cakes at my birthday party.
>   Teacher: Don't you mean 'ate'?
>   Student: Okay, I eated eight cakes at the party.
>
> 3 Student A: Could you help me with my homework?
>   Student B: Certainly not. It wouldn't be right.
>   Student A: Maybe not, but you could at least try!

Discuss the source of humour in each joke.
Answers:
1 The student is unaware that the two words in the questions happen to be pronouns.
2 This pun is based on the identical pronunciation of *ate* and *eight*.
3 The humour lies in the double meaning of right: 'morally right' versus 'linguistically correct'.

2 The butt of jokes is generally the teacher – except in this one:

> Student: I don't think I deserve zero for this paper.
> Teacher: I agree, but it's the lowest grade I can give you.

3 Everyone looks at this cartoon, reads the three snappy answers, and then makes up a fourth one. Volunteers read their wisecracks to the whole class.

© Cambridge University Press 2002

Acknowledgment

The cartoon is from Jaffee's *More Snappy Answers to Stupid Questions* (New York American Library).

10.5 He's a bit slow

Summary:	Students practise expressing themselves tactfully.
Level:	intermediate – post-intermediate
Time:	10–15 minutes
Preparation:	Make a copy for each student (or a transparency) of Box 114.

Procedure

1 Give everybody a copy of the cartoon in Box 114.

BOX 114

'I often say, Mrs. Dent, I'd rather have your little Christopher in my class than **all** the bright, clever ones!'

Students look at the cartoon, then answer the following questions:
* Who are the two characters?
* What is the teacher's opinion of Christopher?
* If you were a teacher, would you tell a parent to her/his face that her/his child was dumb?
* If you were a parent, how would you react if you were told that your child was slow?

2 The teacher's message in the cartoon is obvious, but she softens it in a clever way. Thus, instead of saying 'Your son's stupid' or 'Christopher's not as clever as the others', she emphasises her affection for the boy. Suppose that Mrs Dent, understanding the covert message, asked anxiously: 'You mean my son's stupid?' Embarrassed, the teacher might say to herself: 'Gosh, what shall I tell her?!' She would have several options for an answer. Put these options on the board:

> Not at all! In fact, he's quite brainy.
> Stupid – that's the right word, I'm afraid.
> He sure could do with more brains, but he's a nice boy all the same.
> I'd rather say he's a bit slow.
> Yes, but very diligent.

Which would be the most appropriate answer in the given situation? Students take their pick. Can anyone suggest a better solution perhaps?

Extra

Tell the class this joke:

> A new teacher went into her class for the first time. One student, jumping on top of his desk, was making animal noises. 'Stop acting like an idiot,' the teacher shouted. 'He's not acting,' said the student at the next desk.

Note that in almost every class there is a clown, ready to fool around at any moment. Is there such a person in this class, too? (Do not ask for names!)

10.6 Student bloopers

Summary:	Students tend to make silly mistakes in all school subjects.
Level:	pre-intermediate – advanced
Time:	15–20 minutes
Preparation:	Make a copy of Box 115a or Box 115b for each student, depending on the level of the class. Make a copy of Box 116 for each student.

Procedure

1 American humourist Richard Lederer is a collector of students' bloopers gleaned from real assignments and tests. (A blooper is an embarrassing mistake made in front of other people.) The sentences in

the boxes below have been borrowed from Lederer's compilation. Distribute copies of either Box 115a or Box 115b.

BOX 115a pre-intermediate – intermediate
1 Blood flows down one leg and up the other.
2 History is a never-ending thing.
3 Sir Isaac Newton invented gravity.
4 Mushrooms always grow in damp places and so they look like umbrellas.
5 An opera is a song of bigly size.
6 I know what a sextet is, but I'd rather not say.
7 Clouds are high flying fogs.
8 Hydrogin is gin and water.

© Cambridge University Press 2002

BOX 115b intermediate – advanced
1 The past does not interest me because we know everything about it.
2 Bar magnets have north and south poles, horseshoe magnets have east and west poles.
3 Parallel lines never meet, unless you bend one or both of them.
4 The Moon is a planet just like the Earth, only it is even deader.
5 Suicide was a way of life for Hemingway.
6 The Dutch people used windmills to keep the plants from sweating.
7 When you breathe, you inspire. When you do not breathe, you expire.
8 A fossil is an extinct animal. The older it is, the more extinct it is.

© Cambridge University Press 2002

As the class are reading the sentences, provide help with any vocabulary if necessary. Afterwards, students discuss the meaning of the bloopers in pairs.
2 My favourite in Lederer's collection is the one about the great composer, Ludwig van Beethoven. Distribute copies of the extract in Box 116.

> **BOX 116**
>
> Beethoven wrote three symphonies: the Third, the Fifth, and the Ninth. He wrote music even though he was deaf. Beethoven was so deaf he wrote loud music. He took long walks in the forest even when everyone was calling him. I guess he could not hear so good. Beethoven expired in 1827 and later died for this. Do you know that if Beethoven were alive today, he would be celebrating the 165th anniversary of his death?

3 Students in pairs single out the most striking contradictions and note them in their notebooks. Afterwards, they share their views with the whole class.

Answers:

The most absurd statements are:

1 If he wrote three symphonies, how come that there is a fifth and a ninth as well?
2 Deafness and loud music are not logically related.
3 If he was deaf, of course he couldn't 'hear so good' and hear the calls in the forest.
4 Nobody can celebrate the anniversary of their death.

Follow-up

As a homework assignment, students create similarly absurd short essays on a famous person of their choice. In class, they read out their compositions.

Acknowledgment

The book I have used as a source is Lederer's *Fractured English* (Pocket Books).

10.7 Teacher bloopers

Summary:	Even the best teachers are fallible human beings – as revealed in this activity.
Level:	pre-intermediate – intermediate
Time:	10–15 minutes
Preparation:	Make a copy for each student (or a transparency) of Box 117. For the *Extra*, make a copy of Box 118 for each student.

Procedure

1 All teachers are prone to say silly things from time to time:

> 1 A physics teacher once, angrily, told his class: 'I've taught you all I know – and now you know nothing!'
> 2 'When you're talking to me, keep your mouth shut.'
> 3 'You will never amount to very much' – said a German teacher to ten-year-old Albert Einstein.

Read out the quotes, then discuss with the class what is wrong with each of these remarks.

Answers:
1 What the teacher meant was that, in spite of all the knowledge he or she had imparted, the students didn't know anything.
2 Obviously, you can't talk with your mouth shut.
3 Einstein, as we all know, was the greatest physicist of the 20th century.

2 Does anyone remember any teacher 'wisecracks'? Students share ideas with one another.

3 Give out the cartoon in Box 117.

BOX 117

En français, Jackson, en français!

Note that *en français* means *in French*. Then ask:
- What lesson is this? (It is a French lesson.)
- What makes the teacher in the cartoon ridiculous? (He is so obsessed with the process of teaching the language that he disregards even such an extraordinary spectacle as a flying saucer.)
- Do you know teachers who become similarly carried away sometimes? Give funny examples.

Follow-up

Students in groups think of a funny teacher, past or present, and collect a few characteristic features of his or hers. Afterwards, they read out their list to the whole class. Which atttributes come up most frequently?

Extra

Give out this cartoon and discuss its sad message.

BOX 118

'That'll teach you. We just wanted the kid
to spell, not want to become a poet.'

© Cambridge University Press 2002

Answers: Poets in many countries have always been poor. In our utilitarian age, this is the last thing parents would want their children to become.

10.8 A big de pottment

Summary:	Students are made sensitive to foreign accents.
Level:	post-intermediate – advanced
Time:	15–20 minutes (in class)
Preparation:	Make a copy of Box 119 and Box 120 for each student.

Procedure

1 Before you give out copies of Box 119, tell the class that the extract is from a series of sketches entitled 'The Education of H*Y*M*A*N K*A*P*L*A*N'. The sketches were written by Leo Rosten in the 1930s, on the basis of his experience of teaching English to adult

immigrants in the US. Hyman Kaplan is a perpetually smiling, plump student in his forties, who is making hopeless attempts to speak 'perfect English'. (Leo Rosten (1908–) is a Polish-born American writer, lecturer and political scientist. His most famous book is *The Joys of Yiddish*.) Distribute the extract. Note that virtually all the sentences Mr Kaplan says are wrong. The text mainly attempts to reproduce his faulty pronunciation, but his knowledge of grammar leaves a lot to be desired too.

2 Students read the text at home, using a dictionary if necessary. Alternatively, you may pre-teach any unknown words.

BOX 119

'Plizz, Mr Pockheel,' asked Mr Kaplan. 'Vat's de minnink fromm –'. It sounded like 'a big department'.

'"A big department", Mr Kaplan?' asked Mr Parkhill, to make sure.

'Yassir! In de stritt, ven I'm valkink, I'm hearink like "I big de pottment".'

It was definitely a pedagogical opportunity.

'Well, class,' Mr Parkhill began. 'I'm sure that you have all –'

He told them that they had all probably done some shopping in the large downtown stores. (Mr Kaplan nodded.) In these large stores, he said, if they wanted to buy a pair of shoes, for example, they went to a special *part* of the store, where only shoes were sold – a *shoe* department. (Mr Kaplan nodded.) If they wanted a table, they went to a different *part* of the store, where *tables* were sold. (Mr Kaplan nodded.) If they wanted to buy, say, a goldfish, they went to still another part of the store, where goldfish ... (Mr Kaplan frowned; it was clear that Mr Kaplan had never bought a goldfish.)

'Well, then,' Mr Parkhill summed up hastily, 'each article is sold in a different *place*. These different and special places are called *departments*.' He printed 'D-E-P-A-R-T-M-E-N-T' on the board in large, clear capitals. 'And a *big* department, Mr Kaplan, is merely such a department which is large – *big*!'

He put the chalk down and wiped his fingers.

'Is that clear now, class?' he asked, with a little smile.

It *was* clear. There were thirty nods of approval. But Mr Kaplan looked uncertain. It was obvious that Mr Kaplan, a man who would not compromise with truth, did *not* find it clear.

'Isn't that clear *now*, Mr Kaplan?' asked Mr Parkhill anxiously.

Mr Kaplan pursed his lips in thought. 'It's a *fine* haxplination, Titcher,' he said generously, 'but I don' unnistand vy I'm hearink de voids de vay I do. Simms to me it's used in annodder minnink.'

'There's really only one meaning for "a big department".' Mr Parkhill was definitely worried by this time. '*If* that's the phrase you mean.'

Mr Kaplan nodded gravely. 'Oh, dat's de phrase – ufcawss! It sonds like dat – or maybe a lettle more like "I big de pottment".'

Mr Parkhill took up the chalk. He repeated the explanation carefully, this time embellishing the illustrations with a shirt department and 'a separate part of the store where, for example, you buy canaries, or other birds'.

Mr Kaplan sat entranced. He followed it all politely, even the part about 'canaries, or other birds'. He smiled throughout with reassurance.

Mr Parkhill was relieved. But when he had finished, Mr Kaplan shook his head once more, this time with a new and superior firmness.

'Is the explanation *still* not clear?' Mr Parkhill was genuinely concerned by this time.

'Is de haxplination clear!' cried Mr Kaplan with enthusiasm. 'Ha! I should live so! Soitinly! Clear like *gold*! So clear! An' netcheral too! But Mr Pockheel –'

'Go on, Mr Kaplan,' said Mr Parkhill, studying the white dust on his fingers. There was, after all, nothing more to be done.

'Vell! I think it's more like "I big depottment".'

'Go on, Mr Kaplan, go on.'

Mr Kaplan rose. His smile was broad.

'I'm hearink it in the stritt. Somtimes I'm stendink in de stritt, talkink to a frand, or mine vife, mine brodder – or maybe only stendink. An' somvun is pessink arond me. An' by hexident he's givink me a bump you know, a *poosh*! Vell, he says, "Axcuse me!" no? But somtimes, an' *dis* is vat I minn, he's sayink "*I big de pottment!*"'

3 In class, give out the task sheet in Box 120. Students in pairs try to fill the gaps with the correct forms.

BOX 120

1 Plizz, Mr Pockheel =
2 Vat's de minnink fromm =
3 Yassir! =
4 In de stritt, ven I'm valkink =
5 I'm hearink =
6 It's a fine haxplination, Titcher =
7 I don' unnistand vy I'm hearink de voids de vay I do =
8 Simms to me it's used in annodder minnink =
9 Oh, dat's de phrase – ufcawss! =
10 It sonds like dat =
11 a lettle more =
12 I should live so! =
13 Soitinly! =
14 Clear like gold! An' netcheral too! =
15 Somtimes I'm stendink in de stritt =
16 talkink to a frand, or mine vife =
17 mine brodder =
18 An' somvun is pessink arond me =
19 by hexident he's givink me a bump =
20 a poosh =
21 Vell, he says, 'Axcuse me!' no? =
22 dis is vat I minn =
23 he's sayink 'I big de pottment!' =

4 Read out the correct solution, with students checking on their task
sheet.

Answers:

1 Please, Mr Parkhill, 2 What's the meaning of, 3 Yes, sir!, 4 In the street, when
I'm walking 5 I'm hearing, 6 It's a fine explanation, Teacher, 7 I don't
understand why I hear the words the way I do, 8 (It) seems to me it's used in
another meaning, 9 Oh, that's the phrase – of course!, 10 It sounds like that,
11 a little more, 12 I should say so, 13 Certainly!, 14 Clear as mud! And natural
too!, 15 Sometimes I'm standing in the street, 16 talking to a friend, or my
wife, 17 my brother, 18 And someone is passing by me, 19 by accident he's
giving me a bump, 20 a push, 21 Well, he says, 'Excuse me!', doesn't he?, 22
this is what I mean, 23 he says 'I beg your pardon!'

Follow-up

In groups of three, students practise reading out the Rosten text, but first
they have to decide who will play which character. The student playing
Hyman Kaplan should pronounce his lines overdoing the accent typical
of learners of English in her/his country.

Laughing Matters

Acknowledgment

This somewhat simplified extract is from Rosten's *The Education of H*Y*M*A*N K*A*P*L*A*N* (Constable Publishers).

10.9 Be more English than the English!

Summary:	A foreign accent is impossible to get rid of – or is it?
Level:	pre-intermediate – intermediate
Time:	10–15 minutes
Preparation:	Have the cassette ready to roll at any short piece of recorded material from the coursebook students are using.

Procedure

1 We all speak with some kind of foreign accent, don't we? For illustration, tell the class this joke:

> A Frenchman and a German meet at a party. They both speak with such thick foreign accents that they can hardly understand each other. Eventually, the Frenchman loses his patience and says (with a strong French accent): 'The trouble is that you speak with a strong American accent and I speak with a strong British accent.'

2 Most students are reluctant to imitate native-like pronunciation too closely, for fear of sounding odd and affected. Why don't we break the barrier by self-irony and exaggeration? Select any taped material from the coursebook the class is already familiar with. Play the tape sentence by sentence. Everyone repeats the sentences by exaggerating native-like pronunciation, that is, they should sound more British than the British (or more American than the Americans).

3 Say a few sentences in the students' mother tongue with a mock English accent, imitating native English speakers when they use the local language. Finish your speech by asking a question. A volunteer answers your question in a similar fashion and adds a few more sentences, but then is interrupted by a fellow student – and so on, until everybody has had a chance to say something in their mother tongue with mock English pronunciation. Ask students to specify what has made their mother-tongue speech thick with accent.

10.10 InNOcent letter$

Summary:	There is an exchange of funny letters between parents and children in this activity.
Level:	pre-intermediate – intermediate
Time:	15–20 minutes
Preparation:	Make a copy of Box 121 and Box 122 for each student. For *Extra 1*, make a copy of Box 123 for each student.

Procedure

1 Give out copies of Box 121. Students read this letter written by a young man to his father.

BOX 121

Dear Dad,

$chool i$ really great. I am making lot$ of friend$, and $tudying very hard. With all my $tuff, I $imply can't think of anything I need. $o you can ju$t $end me a card, a$ I would love to hear from you.

Love,
Your $on

Can students decode the hidden message? By the way, how many times did the son substitute '$' for 's'?
Answer: 12 times.

2 Will Father understand the hidden message? Of course he will! Will he send him money? Of course not! Encourage students to guess what kind of letter the father will send to his son.
3 Now give out Father's reply in Box 122.

Laughing Matters

BOX 122

Dear Son,

It is a real hoNOr for a father to kNOw that his son keeps himself busy with the sciences. AstroNOmy, ecoNOmics, oceaNOgraphy – what a NOble task it is to acquire kNOwledge! I agree: one can never study eNOugh!

I must finish NOw but will write aNOther letter soon.

Love,
Dad

© Cambridge University Press 2002

After students have read it, ask how many times the father said *no*.
Answer: 10 times.

Extra

1 Now give out the letter in the box below for students to read. Explain the meaning of any words they do not know.

BOX 123

Dear Son,

I'm writing this letter slowly because I know you can't read fast. We no longer live where we did when you left. Your dad read in the paper that most accidents happen within 20 miles of home, so we moved. I won't be able to send you the address because the last family that lived here took the house numbers with them so they wouldn't have to change their address.

This place has a washing machine. The first day, I put four shirts in it, pulled down the handle, and haven't seen them since.

The coat you wanted me to send you – Aunt Sue said it would be too heavy to send in the mail with all those big buttons on it. So I cut them off and put them in the pocket.

It rained twice this week, three days the first time and four days the second time.

Your sister had a baby this morning. I don't know if it was a boy or a girl, so I don't know if you are an uncle or an aunt.

I was going to send you some money, but the envelope was already sealed.

Love,
Your mother

P.S. Hope you get this letter. If you don't, let me know.

© Cambridge University Press 2002

252

As opposed to the cunning correspondence between father and son in the main activity, the mother's letter is completely crazy, tearing logic into tatters. In groups, students identify as many of the absurdities as they can. In my estimate, there are nine such contradictions.

Answer:
1 writing/reading, 2 accidents, 3 address/house numbers, 4 washing machine, 5 buttons, 6 rain, 7 uncle or aunt, 8 money, 9 P.S.

The first group to find all nine contradictions hidden in the box can read them out, with the others checking their own answers.

2 At home, students may like to write a reply letter on behalf of Lily in *Extra 1*. In class, let them read out their best ideas to the whole class. If anyone should have no ideas of what to include, provide this sample:

---

1 Her cat died – if it had happened a few minutes later, she might still be alive.
2 Her neighbour warned her not to go into a darkened parking lot unless it was well lit.
3 She went shopping in the nearest shopping centre yesterday after she had learnt that they were launching a new innovative washing powder for the first time.
4 She admitted that she had been trying to be more honest and it looks as if she has at last learnt to fake being honest.

Acknowledgment

Mother's letter was borrowed from *Fractured English* by Lederer (Pocket Books).

10.11 Don't do this! Don't do that!

Summary:	Many parents discipline their children regularly.
Level:	pre-intermediate – intermediate
Time:	10–15 minutes
Preparation:	Make a copy of Box 124 for each student.

Procedure

1 Give out copies of the list in Box 124. Students run through the clichés used by parents, indicating with a tick which of them they heard as children. (If you teach a class of children, use the present tense *hear*.) Students add a few more examples from their own experience.

BOX 124
NEVER = N   SOMETIMES = S   OFTEN = O   ALWAYS = A

		N	S	O	A

  1 I'll tell you when you're older.
  2 Stop picking it, you'll get a hole there.
  3 You treat this house like a hotel.
  4 Wait till your father gets home.
  5 Have you done your homework?
  6 Ask your mother.
  7 Don't spend it all at once.
  8 Don't rock the chair – you'll fall over.
  9 Don't read while you eat.
10 When will you grow up?
11 Don't pick at the food.
12 Santa won't come if you're not asleep.
13 Have you cleaned your teeth?
14 Don't say that; it's not nice.
15 Don't leave it – there are millions
     of starving children in the world.
16 When will you turn off the lights?
17 .....
18 .....
19 .....
20 .....

---

2 In groups, students compare their lists and choose the three most frequent clichés. Subsequently, the scribe from each group puts the 'favourites' on the board. Which ones appear on all the lists?

Extra

Tell students a few things some parents do. Ask which of them they find particularly annoying, embarrassing or rude. Can they add any further items to the list?

Parents:
- criticise you in front of your friends.
- open your mail.
- tell your private secrets to other members of the family.
- ask you to 'perform' for company.
- ask you to be friends with certain kids just because they are friends with the kids' parents.
- hang around when your friends come over.
- enter your room without knocking.

Bibliography

Augarde, T. 1984. *The Oxford Guide to Word Games*. Oxford: Oxford University Press.

Augarde, T. 1995. *A to Z of Word Games*. Oxford: Oxford University Press.

Chiaro, D. 1992. *The Language of Jokes: Analysing Verbal Play*. London: Routledge.

Cook, G. 2000. *Language Play, Language Learning*. Oxford: Oxford University Press.

Cranmer, D. 1996. *Motivating High Level Learners*. Harlow: Longman.

Crystal, D. 1988. *Language Play*. London: Penguin Books.

Davies, P. & M. Rinvolucri. 1990. *The Confidence Book*. Harlow: Pilgrims Longman.

Dörnyei, Z. & S. Thurrell 1992. *Conversation and Dialogues in Action*. New York: Prentice Hall International.

Griffiths, G. & K. Keohane. 2000. *Personalizing Language Learning*. Cambridge: Cambridge University Press.

Jacobson, H. 1997. *Seriously Funny: From the Ridiculous to the Sublime*. Harmondsworth: Penguin.

Klippel, F. 1984. *Keep Talking: Communicative fluency activities for language teaching*. Cambridge: Cambridge University Press.

Kossler, A. 1967. *The Art of Creation*. Laurel.

Lee, W. R. 1979. *Language Teaching Games and Contests*. Oxford: Oxford University Press.

Lindstromberg, S. (ed.) 1997. *The Standby Book: Activities for the language classroom*. Cambridge: Cambridge University Press.

Litovkina, A. T. 2000. *A Proverb a Day Keeps Boredom Away*. Pécs-Szekszárd: IPF-Könyvek.

Malderez, A. & C. Bodóczky. 1999. *Mentor Courses: A resource book for trainer-trainers*. Cambridge: Cambridge University Press.

Maley, A. 1994/1995. *Short and Sweet: Short Texts and How to Use Them. Volumes 1 & 2*. London: Penguin English.

Maley, A. & A. Duff. 1989. *The Inward Ear: Poetry in the language classroom*. Cambridge: Cambridge University Press.

McCallum, G. P. 1980. *101 Word Games*. New York: Oxford University Press.

Medgyes, P. 1999. *The Non-Native Teacher*. Second edition. Ismaning: Hueber Verlag.

Morgan, J. & M. Rinvolucri. 1983. *Once Upon a Time: Using stories in the language classroom*. Cambridge: Cambridge University Press.

Nash, W. 1985. *The Language of Humour*. Harlow: Longman.

Nolasco, R. & P. Medgyes. 1990. *When in Britain*. Oxford: Oxford University Press.

Ross, A. 1998. *The Language of Humour*. London: Routledge.

Sanderson, P. 1999. *Using Newspapers in the Classroom*. Cambridge: Cambridge University Press.

Sisk, J. & J. Saunders. 1972. *Composing Humor: Twain, Thurber and You*. New York: Harcourt, Brace & Jovanovich, Inc.

Taylor, E. K. 2000. *Using Folktales*. Cambridge: Cambridge University Press.

Ur, P. 1988. *Grammar Practice Activities: A practical guide for teachers*. Cambridge: Cambridge University Press.

Ur, P. & A. Wright. 1992. *Five-Minute Activities: A resource book of short activities*. Cambridge: Cambridge University Press.

Wright, A. 1979. *Storytelling with Children*. Oxford: Oxford University Press.

Wright, A., D. Betteridge & M. Buckby. 1984. *Games for Language Learning*. New edition. Cambridge: Cambridge University Press.

Index

CAMBRIDGE HANDBOOKS FOR LANGUAGE TEACHERS

This is a series of practical guides for teachers of English and other languages. Illustrative examples are usually drawn from the field of English as a foreign or second language, but the ideas and techniques described can equally well be used in the teaching of any language.

Recent titles in this series:

Using Folktales *by Eric Taylor*

Teaching English Spelling – A practical guide *by Ruth Shemesh and Sheila Waller*

Personalizing Language Learning – Personalized language learning activities *by Griff Griffiths and Kathryn Keohane*

Teach Business English – A comprehensive introduction to business English *by Sylvie Donna*

Learner Autonomy – A guide to activities which encourage learner responsibility *by Ágota Scharle and Anita Szabó*

The Internet and the Language Classroom – Practical classroom activities *by Gavin Dudeney*

Planning Lessons and Courses – Designing sequences of work for the language classroom *by Tessa Woodward*

Using the Board in the Language Classroom *by Jeannine Dobbs*

Learner English (second edition) *by Michael Swan and Bernard Smith*

Teaching Large Multilevel Classes *by Natalie Hess*

Writing Simple Poems – Pattern poetry for language acquisition *by Vicki L. Holmes and Margaret R. Moulton*